ZULU
WOMAN

ZULU WOMAN

THE LIFE STORY OF CHRISTINA SIBIYA

REBECCA HOURWICH REYHER

HISTORICAL INTRODUCTION BY MARCIA WRIGHT
LITERARY AFTERWORD BY LIZ GUNNER

The Women Writing Africa Series

THE FEMINIST PRESS AT THE CITY UNIVERSITY OF NEW YORK

NEW YORK

Published by The Feminist Press at The City University of New York
City College, Wingate Hall
Convent Avenue at 138th Street, New York, NY 10031
www.feministpress.org

First Feminist Press edition, 1999

Originally published by Columbia University Press, 1948
New American Library, Signet Books edition, 1970

Library of Congress Cataloging-in-Publication Data

Reyher, Rebecca Hourwich, 1897–1987.
    Zulu woman: the life story of Christina Sibiya / Rebecca Hourwich Reyher;
  historical introduction by Marcia Wright; literary afterword by Liz Gunner.
    p.   cm. — (The women writing Africa series)
  Originally published: New York : Columbia University Press, 1948.
  Includes bibliographical references.
  ISBN 1-55861-202-5 (cloth: alk. paper). — ISBN 1-55861-203-3 (pbk.: alk. paper)
    1. Christina Sibiya, 1900–1946. 2. Women, Zulu—Biography. 3. Women,
  Zulu—Social conditions. 4. Solomon kaDinizulu, 1893–1933. 5. Zulu (African
  people)—Kings and rulers. 6. Zululand (South Africa)—History—20th century.
  7. Zululand (South Africa)—Politics and government. I. Sibiya, Christinia,
  1900–1946. II. Wright, Marcia. III. Gunner, Elizabeth. IV. Title. V. Series.
DT1768.Z95S537 1999
968.4'9105'092—dc21
[b]

This publication is made possible, in part, by a grant from The Ford Foundation in support of The Feminist Press's Women Writing Africa project. The Feminist Press is also grateful to Marilyn French, Celia Gilbert, Florence Howe, Joanne Markell, Rubie Saunders, Caroline Urvater, and Genevieve Vaughan for their generosity in support-ing this publication.

Text and cover design by Timothy J. Shaner
Cover Art: Photograph by Hanns Reich. Reprinted from Hanns Reich, *Portrait of Southern Africa* (London: Collins, 1956).

Printed on acid-free paper by RR Donnelley and Sons
Manufactured in the United States of America

04 03 02 01 00 99   5 4 3 2 1

contents

acknowledgements

The editors of this edition extend their thanks to:

The Killie Campbell Africana Library, especially
Joan Simpson for her work with Marcia Wright, and
Dingane Mthethwa, Lisa Stockman, and Janet Twine
for their unstinting and generous help to Liz Gunner;

Michael Cardo of the history department at the
University of Natal, Durban, for research and work
on the Marwick Papers;

Adrian Koopman and Mzwakhe Hlengwa of the Zulu
department at the University of Natal, Pietermaritzburg,
for assisting with the Zulu orthography;

Jerry Brotton and Rachel Holmes for discussions, over supper
one night in Pietermaritzburg, about the emerging afterword,
sex, harems, and the body; and thanks to Elleke Boehmer for
an early reading of the draft of the afterword;

The Schlesinger Library, especially Eva Moseley;

Faith Jackson, for being more than a literary heir;

Many listeners and readers, but especially Bell Chevigny
for her timely criticism of the introduction;

The Feminist Press, especially Florence Howe, publisher
and director, who seized the opportunity to republish
and Sara Cahill, our editor, who saw the point of providing
more than the bare bones.

introduction

Zulu Woman, the brief title of this book as first published in 1948 and then republished in 1970, is misleadingly simple.[1] For this third edition, the formal title has been extended to read *Zulu Woman: The Life Story of Christina Sibiya*. Yet, even with the specification of the subject added, the title cannot fully anticipate the texture of feeling and social relationships that bear upon this unique narrative. In an effort to illuminate these elements, several changes have been made to this edition. While this edition reprints the text of *Zulu Woman*, it also treats the relationship between writer Rebecca Reyher and subject Christina Sibiya, something which raised questions upon the book's first publication.[2] Through the addition of this introduction, a literary afterword, and appendixes that include selections from the transcripts of Christina Sibiya's original testimony, as well as excerpts from testimony later made by Christina Sibiya during an enquiry concerning the succession of the Zulu throne, this edition enables readers to think through questions of agency and the fascinating relationship between subject and writer. It also seeks to strike a balance between Christina Sibiya as narrator and Rebecca Reyher as writer and reteller of the story.

Rebecca Reyher, the writer, met Christina Sibiya in 1934 when she returned to South Africa a decade after her first visit, bent upon reporting about the lives and emotions of Zulu women. At the suggestion of her landlady in Nongoma, a magisterial town in Zululand, Rebecca made contact with Christina, who was locally famous as the rebellious first wife of Solomon kaDinuzulu, the recently deceased uncrowned King of the Zulus. Christina told of her life in a series of eleven lengthy, frequently daylong, sessions spanning the period from 21 August to 13 September 1934, communicating through translator Eric Fynney, who had grown up in Nongoma as the son of Oswald Fynney, a former magistrate. The record of these sessions is contained in five notebooks preserved with the Reyher Papers at the Schlesinger Library, Radcliffe College.[3] In addition, one parallel notebook for the early days was kept by Faith Reyher Jackson, Rebecca Reyher's fifteen-year-old daughter, who in August 1997 also shared her reminiscences.[4]

This account of Christina's life story, then, is collaborative and also mediated—through Rebecca and through translation. Mediated life stories rest uncomfortably between biography and autobiography. Hilda Kuper has drawn attention to life stories as "one of the oldest literary genres," residing "somewhere between history and fiction." Kuper went on to highlight the cultural problems arising when the subject, the writer, and the reader speak different languages. Mediated life stories, she proposes, are not really very different from autobiography as a "portrayal of self, but translated and edited."[5] Some outstanding examples of more recent subject-writer collaboration comparable to *Zulu Woman* are *The Long Journey of Poppie Nongena* by Else Joubert, *The Calling of Katie Makanya* by Margaret McCord, and *Singing Away the Hunger: The Autobiography of an African Woman* by Mpho 'M'Atsepo Nthunya.[6] These recent works have resolved the writer-subject ambiguity in various ways, reflecting changed sensibilities and colonial assumptions. In 1934, the distance between Christina Sibiya and Rebecca Reyher was bridged emotionally, but the racial and social order of the times was manifest in Christina's references to Rebecca as "*Inkosikazi*" (lady of authority) or "Missus" (common title for a white employer). But as Liz Gunner makes clear in the afterword to this edition, the fruit of collaboration, for all the attendant critical problems, enriches and will continue to enrich literature. It would be a mistake to suppose that collaboration should entirely yield to autobiography. Too many voices and experiences stand to be lost by such a narrowing of authorship.

This introduction intends to explore certain facets of the collaboration between Rebecca and Christina, including how these women's different historical and cultural contexts have shaped this collaboration. In exploring this relationship, it will also outline the evolution of the published work from the original narration to the book as it emerges in the context of the 1990s.

CHRISTINA SIBIYA

Christina Sibiya's life may be divided into three parts. The early portion of her life extended from her birth, in 1900, to 1915, when she was a primary school teacher being courted by the young Solomon kaDinuzulu, then recently recognized as the heir to the Zulu kingship.[7] The middle portion of her life, as the wife Solomon first married, extending from 1915 to 1931, forms the core of *Zulu Woman*. In the later portion of her life, after her withdrawal from the royal household in 1931, Christina lived for another fifteen years as an unmarried women in Nongoma and then in Vryheid, a town in northern Natal. Between 1943 and 1945 Christina came to public notice because of the succession dispute in which her son Cyprian successfully advanced his claims as heir to the kingship, challenging his half brother, who was preferred by the regent Mshiyeni and by the inner circle of the royal family.

Christina was one of four children, three girls and one boy, born to Christian parents living in Nhlazatshe on lands managed by the Norwegian Lutheran mission. Her parents' separation when her father took two other wives meant that she remained close to her deeply Christian mother and under the special patronage of the missionary Otto Aadensgaard. For years she lived in the missionaries' house and she was schooled at the mission and finally at the Lutheran boarding school at Mapumulo.

The narrative that flowed from Christina Sibiya on the first days of her work with Rebecca Reyher and Eric Fynney began with Solomon's pursuit. Christina was essentially commandeered into marriage, but with a number of proprieties being observed toward her parents and her missionary patron.[8] As Solomon's biographer Nicholas Cope recognized, Christina epitomized Solomon's determination to modernize the dress and adornment of his wives and to have his kitchen and domestic arrangements managed in the *kholwa* (Christianized) fashion of the Christian Zulu.[9] An "official" Anglican, Solomon episodically called for the group baptism of his newly born children. Christina does not appear, however, to have been a regular churchgoer. For her, Christianity served more as a protective shield than as an active religious faith. Her daughter recalled that she had been successively Anglican, Ethiopian, and (African) Zionist before dying a Catholic.[10]

From the outset, Solomon's modernizing endeavor with his wives was juxtaposed to his necessary respect for his "mothers," the wives of his father Dinuzulu and grandfather Cetshwayo, who remained royal dependents possessed of the moral responsibility and right to maintain order and justice in Solomon's ultimately far-flung and often impoverished residences or royal kraals. A close reader of *Zulu Woman* will appreciate Christina's warm feelings toward the mothers, especially two, okaMtshekula and okaSonkeshana, who had been assigned to look after her during the time before and during the birth of her first child. Christina eventually had four children by Solomon, two daughters and two sons, the elder of whom died young.

In 1931 Christina managed to leave Mahashini, Solomon's impressive homestead where, since 1929, she had been under a form of house arrest for having run away to Durban. She stayed temporarily with a Sibiya relative and then became attached to the Sibiya commander of the Falaza regiment, who lived near Nongoma. Her status as a separated woman was equivocal at best. Christina asked Eric Fynney to explain to the "mothers" at the household where she resided what her business consisted of with Rebecca Reyher and him, "lest she be thought to be 'just running around like a loose woman.'"[11] Her "brother," the head of the household, had challenged Eric Fynney, complaining that she was not preparing his food as expected. Being *loose* meant promiscuity and prostitution, not sexual relations conducted with a single partner. Indeed, Christina had struck up such a relationship with a Vryheid artisan who eventually fathered her two daughters born in 1934 and in 1937 (or 1938). He was a drain rather than a contributor to her economic situation, however. Just as Christina had not

been fully supported by Solomon, so she had to be economically independent from 1931 to her death, supporting herself and providing money for
her children, including those who remained in royal custody. Beer brewing
is mentioned in *Zulu Woman* as one source of income, but it was primarily as a seamstress that Christina made a living in her later years.[12]

In 1945, about the time she gave evidence at the Enquiry Concerning
the Zulu Succession, Christina began to suffer from cancer, which eventually caused her death in December 1946. She underwent a radical mastec-
tomy in Vryheid and sought further treatment in Durban, where she stayed
in the home of the veteran African politician A. W. G. Champion.[13] Neither
the European doctors, traditional healers, nor praying Zionists could halt
the cancer.

Without doubt, our knowledge of Christina Sibiya's later life owes everything to Cyprian's designation as heir to the Zulu throne. This victory did
not improve her income in any direct sense, but it meant that she could get
medical attention, enjoyed the protection of royalists like A. W. G.
Champion, who also opened his home to the young Cyprian, and commanded the attention of the Natal native administrators. Christina's final
statement in the official records, taken by the acting native commissioner,
began: "I have come to report that I am starving. I have no clothes. Ever
since my husband's death I have worked and maintained myself and children. Now I am sick and unable to work."[14]

She could not afford the fare to return to her rented room in Vryheid,
let alone attend a meeting at the royal uSuthu kraal in a matter concerning
Cyprian. Helpless to aid her in life, after her death, Cyprian saw to it that
his mother was buried next to Solomon, which honored his parentage but
added nothing to an appreciation of the individual his mother was.

REBECCA HOURWICH REYHER

Rebecca Hourwich, born in America in 1897, was the child of extremely
well-educated Russian émigrés. Her father, an enfranchised Jewish lawyer,
had been a revolutionary who always hoped to return to Russia to participate in a democratic government. For this reason, Rebecca says, she was
brought up through the age of five speaking only Russian.[15] Her mother,
although also trained as a lawyer, gave up her career to attend to the family. Rebecca in her mid-teens was captured by the feminist movement when
she witnessed the 1913 march on Washington by a radical group that was to
become the National Woman's Party.[16] After several years of undergraduate
studies at Columbia University and the University of Chicago and of the
predictable service in settlement houses undertaken by genteel, socially
conscious young women of her generation, she abandoned her work toward
a degree and joined the staff of the National Woman's Party.[17]

The enfranchisement of women in 1920 was accomplished by the efforts of organizations with many different strategies. The National Woman's Party did not work up from the community or state level as other organizations did, but concentrated on Congress and the president. The party's patrons included wives of the very rich. As an organizer, Rebecca became skilled in making common cause with some of the best-connected women in the country. She was a highly effective administrator, public relations officer, and stump speaker. Even after she had married and given birth to her daughter Faith in 1919, she continued to work for the Woman's Party. Rebecca embraced the party's new agenda, first expressed by the party in 1920, of seeking a constitutional amendment, the Equal Rights Amendment, which would, above all, mandate equal economic conditions for employed women.[18]

Beginning in the early 1920s, Rebecca aspired to a career in writing. Her first major opportunity came when she persuaded the publisher Norman Hapgood to commission a piece about South Africa for *Hearst's International Magazine*. Thus provided with credentials, she ventured forth and in 1924 was received extremely well in South Africa as an American journalist who might draw wanted attention to the young, white-dominated, relatively developed state. C. T. Loram, then one of the three commissioners of native affairs, designed her itinerary and provided many introductions. C. T. Loram's provincial roots in Natal may help account for Rebecca's particularly positive experience there, but he was well connected everywhere. Anticipating her stop in Johannesburg, he wrote to Reinhalt Jones, the race relations specialist, asking him to make arrangements for Rebecca, a "distinguished journalist." He listed as possibilities that "1) she go down a mine, 2) see a Kafir dance, 3) go slumming with the police, 4) meet Phillip and see his work, 5) get in touch with Corner House, 6) meet the communists, etc. etc."[19]

Rebecca's experiences in South Africa during 1924–25 challenged her own points of view. Heretofore, she had considered economic independence and rejection of a sexual double standard to be the hallmarks of feminism. She had reacted strongly to anti-Semitism and other forms of exclusion. When she found categorical exclusion directed against Indians in Natal, she refused to respect it. She formed firm and lasting friendships with Manilal Ghandi, Ghandi's son who remained in Durban, and with other South African Indian activists, drawn both by temperament and a pacifist upbringing to their advocacy of passive resistance. On her 1924–25 visit, she paid a good deal of attention to white women in public life, as well as to white women artists and writers. She seems to have appreciated quickly that white women's demands for the franchise were not progressive, since they would not object if nonwhite Cape male voters were disenfranchised.[20] While she consorted easily with the powerful, she was capable of acute social commentary.

Several of Rebecca Reyher's articles published after the 1924–25 visit appeared in illustrated magazines. These included articles on colonial furniture, American women as educators, Cape Dutch architecture, and cotton-growing in Natal.[21] The only one in any way to anticipate *Zulu Woman,* "Three Black Women," appeared in the progressive weekly *The Nation* in 1926. There she portrayed an unmarried Christian Zulu princess (Christina Zulu) who refused to have her marriage arranged; Mrs. D. D. T. Jabavu, the wife of the noted educator; and Sanni, a woman Christian prayer leader in a Ciskei village.[22] At the time Rebecca believed the feminist cause would only be advanced through the adoption of Christianity, which would liberate African women from what Rebecca saw as oppressive custom.

In 1934, Rebecca, who throughout her marriage had kept her maiden name, returned to South Africa as Rebecca Hourwich Reyher—newly divorced and newly renamed, paradoxically retaining for the rest of her life the name of her ex-husband. The reason, she states, was to identify with her daughter Faith, who bore her father's surname and accompanied Rebecca on the trip. Acting upon her determination to discover the conditions and feelings of Zulu women, Rebecca started by consulting the Fynneys, then retired, with whom she had stayed when she was in Nongoma in 1924. They may have recommended that she take accommodation with a certain Mrs. Ward, the owner of the abattoir in Nongoma, whose large house and garden were buffered from the main road and town by the large cattle pen. In this secluded place Christina Sibiya, Rebecca Reyher, and Eric Fynney spent their days together. Every day, Eric used Rebecca's hired car to fetch and return Christina to her kin's compound, seven miles away.

Rebecca believed that she had found in Christina a soul mate, as well as a source of material "saleable" to publishers. One passage of the narration she underscored vehemently was where Christina demanded that she be released from her marriage: "Because I want[ed to] change myself and appear a different person."[23] Rebecca identified with this resolve and saw it as the kind of counterhegemonic action required for a woman's liberation. The remark suggested to Rebecca that Rebecca had truly discovered the recesses of "primary emotions" she deemed to be universal.[24] It is no exaggeration to suggest that Christina's story continued to be for Rebecca a life work; in the opening paragraph of the first full draft, she wrote: "I have tried to write Christina's story as she told it to me, but her story is mine also."[25]

Zulu Woman may be placed within a transition in Rebecca's vision of the feminist cause and her role in campaigning for it. In 1924 her attention had rested on the acculturated *kholwa* and Cape Christian women.[26] Negative references to sinister barbarism, dirt and disease in impoverished villages, and the iniquities of polygamy were increasingly deployed in *Zulu Woman* to valorize modernity and the estimable aspirations of Christian (*kholwa*) women.[27] She tended thereafter to stress the consequences of "backward" tradition, above all what she perceived as the abusiveness resulting from men's right to plural wives. Following World War II, Rebecca undertook a major campaign against polygamy, faulting the United Nations Commission on Women for evading the issue. She conducted her own investigation at the court of an African ruler in Cameroon and later studied polyandry in Ceylon.[28]

Rebecca Reyher benefited from the rise in Cyprian's political fortunes in particular, and from the greater international attention to South Africa in general. When she returned in 1951 to gather more information about Christina and her children, the published *Zulu Woman* had preceded her. It had been widely read and gave her access to officials and others interested in the Zulu succession. Some were hostile. Eileen Krige, whose career as an anthropologist engaged her with the Zulu, worked parallel to Rebecca Reyher, but with very different assumptions. When they met in 1951, Eileen Krige took the proprietary and, by contemporary standards, rather rigid view that only a trained anthropologist who could evaluate custom should have written the account.[29] The regent, Chief Mshiyeni, was concerned not with the writer's credentials but with the source. Reyher noted, "Msheyni [sic] very excited about the book—felt that Christina divulged secrets—had committed crimes yet she told on others."[30] Most reviewers acknowledged that the candor of Christina Sibiya's story was persuasive. Christina herself admitted how effectively Rebecca had drawn her out: "The readers of your book, they will say, 'She has held back nothing.'"[31] Of course she had secrets, foremost among them a letter written to her in 1930, but apparently delivered after her separation, in which Solomon declared Cyprian to be his chosen heir. This document proved to be decisive in the 1945 Enquiry Concerning the Zulu Succession.[32] Many contemporary readers have found that Christina's objectivity in her narration, her compassion for the other wives of Solomon, and her own determination not to be trapped in hypocrisy are revealing in positive ways.

TOWARD A PUBLICATION HISTORY

The core of the book and its greatest strength, as Rebecca Reyher acknowledged in responding to criticism by a reader of the draft, rests in Christina Sibiya's testimony. The writer's other sources of information, left vague in the published work, can be reconstructed with the aid of the notebooks. These reveal a strong concentration upon wives and daughters of the inner royal family, and virtually no conversations with commoners.[33] Rebecca did attend court cases where adultery was charged, was allowed to look at court records bearing upon matrimonial disputes, and visited a prison to see incarcerated women. Oswald Fynney shared his accumulated wisdom from years of hearing cases.[34] Rebecca was particularly fascinated by magic,

including love philters and "witchcraft." Although she sought out healers of
various orders, had a diviner cast bones for her, and attended an *isangoma*'s
(diviner) performance, her grasp of Zulu belief, therapy, and healing practices remained weak by late-twentieth-century standards.[35]

Other experts for her purposes were the missionaries, men and women,
who shared their knowledge and opinions. Rebecca extracted the proffered
profiles of African women's lives and circumstances, to be absorbed as her
own if they squared with her line of thinking and observation. She faithfully took down but did not fully incorporate the reminiscences of officers who
had fought against and admired the Zulu, and the policy prescriptions of
Member of Parliament for Zululand George Heaton Nichols.[36] Altogether,
Rebecca believed that she was scrupulous as a feature writer, carefully
preparing to go into distant places to report, and checking her findings.

Zulu Woman existed in draft in 1937, was refined again and again, suffered numerous rejections by publishers, and finally won acceptance by the
Columbia University Press, thanks in part to a legitimating preface by Ruth
Benedict and heightening popular curiosity about other nations after 1945.
Columbia published a limited run. A much wider audience was reached
through the digest that was published in *Life* magazine on 25 October 1948
and through a French version, pirated and serialized in *France Soir,* and
later published as a book.[37]

It is uncertain exactly what Reyher intended to result from her follow-
up in Natal and Zululand in 1951. To the playwright Maxwell Anderson, she
proposed a drama that would treat Christina's entire life and might be a
vehicle for the actor Ethel Waters. In the end she settled for the publication,
in paperback in 1970, of a second edition of *Zulu Woman,* nearly identical
to the first. Reyher acknowledged the passage of time and her substantial-
ly increased knowledge by adding a single footnote explaining that, were
she writing in 1970, she would replace the term *native* with *African* and by
adding the brief epilogue that mainly chastises Cyprian (d. 1968) for following in his father's footsteps by neglecting and punishing his wives. Signet
paperbacks aimed to sell in the millions. Rebecca Reyher regretted that this
edition sold only 131,000 copies.[38]

ZULU WOMAN AND CHRISTINA SIBIYA IN THE 1990S

Hilda Kuper's wise remarks about the untidy boundaries between fiction
and nonfiction will continue to caution us, and different judgments will continue to exist. For example, when Rebecca Reyher sought in 1969 to involve
the Zulu scholar Absolom Vilakazi[39] in her projects, he refused, writing that
"I do not think you need my approval in material like this. It seems to me
fictional and highly romanticized." Reyher replied, "None of the material is
'fictionalized.' It is factual, as the subjects, or others told it to me. It is
romanticized in the sense that I was moved by the stories, identified with

them, and did not maintain a coldly objective distance." [40] As Liz Gunner's afterword points out, one of the enduring values of this work is its sympathy, which offers a means to overcome silences on matters of crucial importance to women and society.

This edition omits an appendix on love philters and the very brief preface by Ruth Benedict. The orthography has been silently modernized and certain glaring mistakes in Zulu terminology corrected.[41] Nevertheless, the original English text has been left intact, with all the period and colonial features attributable to Rebecca Reyher. To stimulate further thinking about voice and authorship, we have not only provided this introduction and the afterword but also included short selections from two sources. A few excerpts from the interview notebooks convey a sense of the details that were omitted or elaborated in the published work. They highlight critical moments in Christina's relationship to Solomon and the royal household. Of particular interest in these passages is the recurrent role of the two most significant "mothers," widows of Solomon's father Dinuzulu. OkaSonkeshana (daughter of Sonkeshana) was the "foster mother" to Solomon and his brothers and sisters by the same mother. OkaMtshekula, perhaps the most senior surviving wife of Dinuzulu and of the Sibiya clan, became Christina's special protector, referred to as "my relative" and "Aunt" in the original narration.

The other source for the appendix is the transcript of the public enquiry of 1945 from which Cyprian emerged as the recognized successor to Solomon. Christina, identified as okaMatatela, there testified about her status as the first wife of the late king as a preliminary to producing the letter in which Solomon wrote that despite his disappointments over her desertion, he wished her son to be his heir.

The story of Christina Sibiya may certainly be approached from many angles, especially given the newly identified evidence that will be available to those who wish to carry further the study of her life and times. *Zulu Woman* has its shortcomings. Yet, as few other works, it conveys the humanity of women in an extraordinarily tempestuous and insecure environment. Women caught in a maelstrom of the modernizing, neotraditionalist, colonized Zulu monarchy were more than pawns in a game of political consolidation. Readers will find many of Christina's co-wives to be striking characters in their own right. The richness of the account finally pays tribute to both women, Christina Sibiya and Rebecca Reyher.

Marcia Wright
New York
August 1998

NOTES

A note on the treatment of proper names in this introduction. The treatment of proper names in *Žulu Woman* poses difficulties. For example, Christina Sibiya was Christina to Rebecca Reyher, Sibiya within the circle of co-wives, and okaMatatela, or daughter of Matatela (Hezekiah), to distinguish her from other wives from the Sibiya clan. Rebecca Reyher was Rebecca Hourwich when she was a feminist party activist and began to publish in the 1920s and Becky to her intimates. While Rebecca Reyher referred to her informant as Christina, Christina Sibiya always addressed Rebecca Reyher with a title expressing deference. To help redress these power imbalances, full names are used in this introduction and then, on occasion, first names.

1. See *Zulu Woman* (New York: Columbia University Press, 1948), and *Zulu Woman*, 2d ed., (New York: Signet, New American Library, 1970). Reviewers responded to this brief and somewhat abstract titles by adding their own "subtitles." An example of an extended "subtitle" can be found in the 5 June 1948 *Saturday Review*, which cited the book as *Zulu Woman. The Story of a Modern Woman's Rebellion against Polygamy.*

2. In 1948 the cataloger for the Library of Congress attributed authorship to Christina Sibiya. The New York Public Library catalogued the work as follows: "Sibiya, Christina, 1900–, *Zulu Woman* [Her autobiography, related] by Rebecca Reyher." Many libraries, such as Boston University, consequently list Christina Sibiya as author and Rebecca Reyher as alternative author.

3. The sources for a study of this nature are supplied by the Rebecca Hourwich Reyher Papers, 87-M75 (hereafter cited as Reyher Papers), Schlesinger Library, Radcliffe College, containing notebooks, correspondence, writings in draft, and published and related materials. There is also an oral history of Rebecca Reyher's activism in the women's suffrage movement. See Rebecca Hourwich Reyher, "Search and Struggle for Equality and Independence," interview by Amelia R. Fry and Fern Ingersoll (Berkeley: Regional Oral History Office, Bancroft Library, University of California, 1977). Christina Sibiya is on record as one of the key figures to testify and be cross-examined in the Enquiry Concerning the Zulu Succession of 1945, which resulted in the recognition of her son Cyprian; see pp. 83–87 KCM 2761a, File 50, Marwick Papers, Killie Campbell Africana Library, Durban (hereafter cited as Marwick Papers), and also appendix 2. In 1989, without the benefit of these unpublished archival sources, I treated *Zulu Woman* as a product of Christina Sibiya's own agenda in my "Personal Narratives, Dynasties and Women's Campaigns: Two Cases from Africa," in *Interpreting Women's Lives: Feminist Theory and Personal Narratives,* ed. Personal Narratives Group (Bloomington: Indiana University Press, 1989).

4. Faith Reyher Jackson's memories illuminate the setting in which the narration was taken down (interview by author, Damarascotta, Maine, 20 August 1997). I am also grateful for access to Faith's own diary of the first days of the interview, a document that she still holds privately.

5. Hilda Kuper, "Biography as Interpretation," Hans Wolff Memorial Lecture, Indiana University, April 1980, p. 25, 28.

6. Elsa Joubert, *The Long Journey of Poppie Nongena* (Johannesburg: Jonathan Ball, 1980), Margaret McCord, *The Calling of Katie Makanya* (Cape Town: David Philip and New York: John Wiley, 1995), and Mpho 'M'Atsepo Nthunya, *Singing Away the Hunger: The Autobiography of an African Woman,* ed. K. Limakatso Kendall (Pietermaritzburg: University of Natal Press, 1996 and Indianapolis: University of Indiana Press, 1997).

7. Shula Marks provided the earliest and most succinct discussion of Solomon's efforts to reunite the Zulu. See "The Drunken King and the Nature of State," *The Ambiguities of Dependence* (Baltimore: Johns Hopkins University Press, 1986). The fullest treatment is to be found in Nicholas Cope, *To Bind the Nation: Solomon kaDinuzulu and Zulu Nationalism, 1913–1933* (Pietermaritzburg: University of Natal Press, 1993).

8. For some reason, Rebecca Reyher referred to Otto Aadensgaard as Eckenbren (Reyher Papers, Zululand 1934, Notebook I, Carton 38).

9. Cope, *To Bind the Nation,* 122ff.

10. Interviews with A. W. G. Champion, daughters Greta and Agnes, and Father Ignatius Jatz [June 1951], Reyher Papers, Zululand 1951, Notebooks IX, XIII, and XIV, Carton 40.

11. Reyher Papers, Zululand 1934, Notebook I, Carton 38.

12. Reyher Papers, Zululand 1934, Notebook I, Carton 38; and 8 June 1951 testimony of Agnes, the daughter born in 1934, Zululand 1951, Notebook XIII, Carton 40.

13. Reyher Papers, Zululand 1951, Notebook IX, Carton 40. For Champion, see Marks, "George Champion and the Ambiguities of Class and Class Consciousness," *The Ambiguities of Dependence.*

14. Statement taken at Durban by J. J. D. Nel, 8 January 1946, NTS 78/53 (2), State Archives, Pretoria.

15. Reyher, "Search and Struggle," p. 13.

16. For the National Woman's Party, see Nancy Cott, *The Grounding of Modern Feminism* (New Haven: Yale University Press, 1987), 65ff.

17. Reyher, "Search and Struggle," ch. 3.

18. Susan Becker, *The Origins of the Equal Rights Amendment: American Feminism Between the Wars* (Westport: Greenwood Press, 1981).

19. Reyher Papers, C. T. Loram to Reinalt Jones [1924], Carton 64. Phillips was Ray Phillips, the American Board missionary who had begun industrial welfare work and established the Bantu Men's Center. Corner House was a major holding company for the gold mines. The communists were a recognized, nonracial party in the 1920s.

20. Rebecca's file, "South African Women, 1924–25," contains various materials on white women in politics, including a position paper (1924) by the Women's Enfranchisement Association of the Union of South Africa (Reyher Papers, Carton 14). On white women's suffrage in South Africa, see Cherryl Walker, "The Women's Suffrage Movement: The Politics of Gender, Race and Class," in *Women and Gender in Southern Africa to 1945,* ed. Cherryl Walker (London: J. Currey, 1990).

21. "South African Antique Furniture," *Good Housekeeping* (London), October 1926; "The New England Conscience in South Africa," *The Woman's Viewpoint,* November 1925, sec. III, p. 6; "The Land of the Gable," *Country Life,* April 1926; and "Zululand of Cotton," *Country Gentleman,* March 1926.

22. Rebecca Hourwich Reyher, "Three Black Women," *The Nation,* 17 November 1926, pp. 505–07. This periodical was a voice of the Left in New York at that time and later. Rebecca Reyher kept up with Mrs. D. D. T. Jabavu, and on publishing her obituary in the *Cape Times,* was proud that it was the first time an African woman had been thus honored in the paper (Reyher, "Search and Struggle," p. 135).

23. Reyher Papers, Zululand 1934, Notebook IV, Carton 38.

24. Rebecca Reyher's approach in celebrating subjectivity has an intellectual pedigree. She described W. I. Thomas, her teacher at the University of Chicago, as a pioneer of feminist theory who equipped her to write *Zulu Woman* ("Search and

Struggle," p. 20). She mentions in particular his *Sex and Society.* This book indeed is remarkable for its transcultural views. See *Sex and Society: Studies in the Social Psychology of Sex,* 7th ed., (Boston: Gorham Press, 1907). On W. I. Thomas, see Rosalind Rosenberg, *Beyond Separate Spheres: The Intellectual Roots of Modern Feminism* (New Haven: Yale University Press, 1982).

25. Manuscript draft, September 1937, first paragraph of the introduction (Reyher Papers, Cartons 43 and 45). This paragraph persisted until the final editing in 1947.

26. Reyher, "Three Black Women," p. 505. Rebecca Reyher recalled this article as seminal in her work (Reyher, "Search and Struggle," pp. 135–36).

27. Life stories were sometimes mediated by anthropologists in the 1930s. One of the most poignant and revealing of change is "The Story of Nosente, The Mother of Compassion of the Xhosa Tribe, South Africa," recorded by Monica Hunter [Wilson], in *Ten Africans,* ed. Margery Perham (London: Faber and Faber, 1936). Nosente's life after becoming a Christian hardly conformed with Rebecca's supposition about kholwa improvement. Hilda Kuper sought alternative ways to handle the experience of women, finding that the canons of ethnography denied the validity of personal experience and consciousness. One outcome was a play, *A Witch in My Heart* (London: International Africa Institute, 1980), exploring the consciousness of a childless first wife in a polygynous Swazi household in the 1930s.

28. See Rebecca Hourwich Reyher, *The Fon and His Hundred Wives* (Garden City: Doubleday, 1952). The manuscript on polyandry remains unpublished.

29. See Reyher Papers, entry for 12 May 1951, 1951, Notebook IX, Carton 40. Eileen Krige's *Social System of the Zulus,* first published by Longmans in 1936, described Zulu institutions in a traditionalist and static way. The second edition (Pietermaritzburg: Shuter and Shooter, 1950) was effectively a reprint. Recent historical scholarship shows that Zulu institutions and "tradition" were far less consistent and far more subject to restatement than either anthropologists or officials of the interwar years appreciated. The literature is large, but led by Jeff Guy. See, for example, "Gender Oppression in Southern Africa's Precapitalist Societies," in *Women and Gender,* ed. Cherryl Walker.

30. Mshiyeni, certainly the opponent of Christina's son Cyprian, drew upon false rumors of illegitimate children supposedly born to her before Solomon's death. These rumors circulated in 1934. See Reyher Papers, Zululand 1934, Notebook I, Carton 38 and, for Mshiyeni's allegations, Reyher Papers, 1951, Notebook XIII, Carton 40.

31. Reyher Papers, Zululand 1934, Notebook IV, Carton 38.

32. For details, see Zulu/Usutu Heirship Dispute file, NTS 78/52, State Archives, Pretoria. See also Proceedings of the Enquiry Concerning the Zulu Succession (1945), Marwick Papers, and for excerpts from Christina's testimony, see appendix 2.

33. Mshiyeni's wife Elsie was interviewed several times and served as the interpreter in a conversation with Princess Christina (okaCetshwayo). Reyher Papers, Zululand 1934, Notebook V, Carton 38.

34. Reyher Papers, Zululand 1934, Notebooks I and VI, Carton 38. See also Cope, *To Bind the Nation,* passim, for references to Oswald Fynney in Zululand.

35. Much attention has been given since 1970 to the various orders of healers. See, for example, Harriet Ngubane, *Body and Mind in Zulu Medicine: An Ethnography of Health and Disease in Nyuswa-Zulu Thought and Practice* (New York: Academic Press, 1977).

36. See Reyher Papers, Zululand 1934, Notebook V, Carton 38. For George Heaton Nichols, see Shula Marks, "Natal, the Zulu Royal Family and the Ideology of Segregation," *Journal of Southern African Studies* 4, 2 (1978).

37. Reyher Papers, Jean Guichard (the translator) to Rebecca Reyher, 20 January 1953, Carton 45. See *France Soir,* 4, 15, 17 November 1952. The book appeared as *Chronique maritale d'une reine Zoulou* (Paris: Les Presses Denoel d'aujourd'hui, 1952).

38. Reyher, "Search and Struggle," p. 149.

39. In 1969 Absolom Vilikazi was at the American University, Washington, D.C. He had recently published *Zulu Transformations: A Study of the Dynamics of Social Change* (Pietermaritzburg: University of Natal Press, 1965).

40. Reyher Papers, Absolom Vilakazi to Rebecca Reyher, 4 May 1969, and Rebecca Reyher to Absolom Vilakazi, 6 May 1969, with special reference to "Three Black Women" of which Reyher thought he would approve (Carton 45, File 3).

41. For example, in the text of the first two editions, *Cyprian* is referred to as *Seaprince.* With the assistance of Faith Reyher Jackson's notebook, it has become apparent that Christina pronounced his name in a way that Faith wrote as *Siprius* and Rebecca heard as *Seaprince.* For this edition, we have used *Cyprian* throughout, with the exception of pp. 141 and 193 (footnote).

textual note

For this edition of *Zulu Woman,* the orthography has been silently modernized and certain glaring mistakes in Zulu terminology corrected. The original English text has been left intact.

With the exception of proper names and a few widely used and well-known words that now circulate in English in South Africa, all Zulu words appear in italic. Certain derivative words, including "lobola" for "bridewealth" (for the Zulu *ilobolo*), "induna" and "indunas" for "councillor" or "head" (for the Zulu *izinduna*), as well as "stoep" for "verandah" (from the Afrikaans), remain in roman type.

Rebecca Rehyer referred to certain royal wives and mothers by their father's name instead of *oka* (daughter of). We have added this marker to the text.

In our spelling of Zulu words, we have followed the orthographical rules as approved by the Zulu Language Board in September 1989. Capitalizing in Zulu continues to be full of pitfalls: we have followed accepted usage in the names of rivers such as Umngeni; for members of the Zulu royal the term "prince" or "princess" appears regularly as *uMntwana*; the term for a minister is capitalized as *uMfundisi*; in other cases we have followed the general rule, which is to capitalize the stem of a noun, hence, amaNdebele.

ZULU
WOMAN

Rendering of Christina Sibiya by Richard Barthé. This etching,
based on a photograph, appeared as the frontispiece to
the 1948 Columbia University Press edition.

for Norman Hapgood, Judge Hugo Pam

and Walter Frank

who believed in my African trips
and helped me to realize them

T*he trait in the Zulu character of which it is most difficult to approve is the absence of sympathy for the feelings of the female sex. A man is almost as willing to marry a woman who hates as one who loves him.*

From *The Story of the Zulus* by J. Y. Gibson
(late magistrate in Zululand)

preface

It seemed perfectly natural to me in the spring of 1924 to be walking pleasantly with my daughter's headmistress in the school grounds at Greenwich, Connecticut, paying small attention to the subject in hand— my inattendance at parent-teachers' meetings—while my mind fastened on the irrelevancy that, among other busily engaged parents who managed to come, was a father whose shipping lines had just made a survey of South Africa.

Instantly I was carried away on a trail that commenced with the thought that here was a country I had never even mentioned as a possibility to the editor who had bought four well-paid articles from me and added a substantial expense account, but who now neatly brushed aside all my efforts to travel abroad at his expense, by announcing that every country I proposed was either adequately covered or had a waiting list of more deserving and trained writers.

Three months later that stray thought had hatched a completely organized trip to South Africa, where I spent nearly eight of the most valuable and stimulating months of my life, traveling thousands of miles and seeing hundreds of people.

Most of all I cherished my days in Zululand, first as a guest outside of Eshowe, the capital, at the home of the late Sir Charles Saunders, former Governor General of Zululand under Queen Victoria, and Lady Saunders, and later at the home of the then Chief Magistrate, Oswald Fynney, and Mrs. Fynney at Nongoma.

From them I heard stories that moved me by their simple humanity, and proved that for me the most fascinating search in a foreign land would always be for sameness, rather than difference, and that these Zulus, despite their gleaming black nakedness, were not different from my New York and Maine friends, only a lot more interesting.

My trip had to produce immediately salable material, and I could not linger to listen to stories that might be fun to hear, and write, but might never sell. I knew of no market for stories about Mr. and Mrs. Zulu. But secretly I resolved that if ever another chance came to do that which I most wanted to do, I would head straight for Zululand and just settle down and hear Zulu gossip of everyday life.

In the spring of 1934 I was in Reno for the usual reason, indulging in the usual Reno pastime of introspection and personal stocktaking. The distant hills on which I looked broodingly had been stared at by many such as I, and offered none of us a hint of solace or guidance. One casual day I realized how much the Reno hills looked like those of Zululand, and how much nicer it would be there, where there were no problems of divorce, no civilized memories that legal decisions could not dissemble.

What did Zulu women do? How did they manage lifelong marriage? Were they happy? Was polygamy, as my sophisticated friends assured me, a natural state of man? Was it possible to love with one's body freely and easily, capturing the spirit and taming it to its primary needs? Didn't Zulu women get notions, too? Were the heart and soul of a primitive woman different from mine, or those of the women I knew?

Suddenly it seemed urgent to get the answers to these questions of what Zulu women felt, and did, and talked about. Again this presumably stray thought that Reno hills were not unlike those of Zululand eventually hatched into a trip that brought my fifteen-year-old daughter Faith and me right to Nongoma.

The steps by which we came there are not important to anyone except me. We received generous help and advice without which nothing could have been accomplished. Specifically, I continue to be grateful to Mr. Oswald Fynney, retired, who made all arrangements for me, including "lending" me the services of his son Eric, the son and grandson of Zulu Magistrates, as friendly interpreter and guide.

We stayed on a farm in Nongoma, and drove about seeing the natives* that the Fynneys suggested would have a story to tell. They talked freely to me because of their faith in and affection for the Fynneys.

It did not surprise me, therefore, to find Christina at our gate one day. She had come to tell about the King's courtship of her, a story the Zulus never tired of hearing, and one she thought might interest the *inkosikazi*—wife of a chief—from across the water. Christina was a natural, gifted storyteller, but she was also a woman with a pent-up heart, and from the first minutes with her, I knew her full story would give me many things I wanted to know about primary emotions.

We established a working procedure. Christina came and talked, slowly, sentence by sentence, while Eric translated. Occasionally we interrupted her to ask a question, but seldom. At first, she was awkward, overdressed, self-conscious. Then she began to come in everyday clothes, at seven in the morning, and stay until way past her bedtime, and the words flowed from

---

* This book was written when Africans were generally called "natives." I did not think of it as derogatory, but as indicative of their being indigenous to their territory. Today I know better, I use African, and I offer this explanation as an apology.—RR

her. By the end of the day, with time out only for meals, Christina was tired and drowsy, Eric was an automaton, and I was cramped, with my shoulder and arm stiff and aching from taking notes.

Cold rainy days we sat by a coal fire, Christina on a mat at our feet; but when the sun shone we sat under a tree in a thick overgrowth, while cows brushed by us, and I sometimes wished that Christina's story would last a lifetime and keep me there imprisoned in its spell. At the end of a month her story was done, and I have recorded it as she told it.

Christina cried when I was due to go, and begged me to take her with me, as I would have liked to do, for I had grown to be sincerely attached to her. If her story fails to move others, it is my fault in the telling.

I owe gratitude, too, to the late Dr. Charles D. Loram, of Yale University, one-time Native Affairs Commissioner of South Africa, who planned my first trip for me; Mrs. Douglas Mackeurtan, of Durban, who sent me to Sir Charles Saunders; the South African Embassy at Washington for their courtesies; the South African Railways and Publicity Bureaus for their constant helpful aid; our own Embassies and Consulates in South Africa and Portuguese East Africa, which were always friendly outposts; Colonel Denys Reitz, formerly Minister of Native Affairs and High Commissioner to London, and other distinguished and leading members of the government for their valuable time and the interest, the kind hosts and hostesses who entertained us, and helped me understand their country in briefer glimpses; the many natives who told me their stories out of sheer desire to please; and Dr. Hortense Powdermaker, the good friend who believed in the book and urged me to keep at it.

R. H. R.

Robinhood, Maine

June, 1947

one

There are about a million Zulus in Zululand. No one really knows quite how many, because, though the government levies a head tax on every adult male, with an additional few shillings for each wife, it is considered bad luck by the Zulus to count their children, and their number can only be approximated. Then, too, malaria, fever, and venereal diseases sweep over native villages with the ferocity of an age-old curse.

Zululand is restricted native territory in the province of Natal in South Africa, most of which is held in trust for the Zulus. It is an area about the size of Belgium, partly along the Indian Ocean, bordered by the Transvaal, Swaziland, and Portuguese East Africa, its central and more northern section remaining almost unchanged for centuries. Toward the south, gushing waterfalls cascade down the hillsides, land and foliage are verdant and the forests thick. Brilliant red hibiscus, tangled bougainvillea, bright pink oleanders, and other lush tropical flowers embellish the landscape, where sporadic European settlements are featured for tourists.

Most of the country, however, is barren hills, long since useless from overcultivation. Dotting these hills like mushrooms after rain, are clusters of native huts. Each man's group is a kraal, the several kraals of a petty chief constituting a village. At the larger and more important villages there are apt to be one or more trading stores, one or several missions, a magistracy, and a school. The few white people, representing government, education, religion, and trade, live apart in garden-bordered houses of whitewashed stucco or corrugated iron, depending on their economic status, with what meager comforts the primitive country permits.

Europeans and Zulus live together, and yet separately, in a world of their own. They pass each other on the roads without a word of greeting, but get mail in the same post office; buy in the same store but at different counters, and of different wares; have their own schools, churches, languages, and customs, their points of contact being for the most part shadowy and unreal.

The South African Government represents ultimate authority through its representatives and magistrates, who confer with the tribal chiefs, the direct rulers of the Zulus. Tribal customs continue to be enforced by these chiefs. But the delineation of European-Zulu authority and fine points of state are remote from the concerns of the average Zulu.

Europeans reach into the Zulu community for workers, as domestics for their homes, as the mainstay of manpower for the mines, and for every type of unskilled labor. Few Europeans, however, either know or care what native working and living conditions are.

The mission station, strategically located in every native neighborhood is apt to be the only friendly bridge between the two races. Missionaries tend the native sick, educate them, try to improve their immediate circumstances, and mostly preach Christianity only on Sunday. The rest of the week they try to practice it.

Christina Sibiya, a Christian Zulu, born in the first year of the twentieth century, cannot remember much that happened before 1908, but that year burned in her memory. In the spring, despite having married according to Christian rites which entitled him to only one wife, her father, Hezekiah Sibiya, took two other wives. Hezekiah should have been prosecuted for adultery, for it is carefully explained to all natives when marrying that they have a choice of native custom which permits of an unlimited number of wives, provided they are properly paid for, or by Christian rites which permit of only one, and thereafter any other wife taken is not only a sin against the church but a crime against the state.

When under the spell of the church, natives pledge faithfully to uphold its tenets and creed; they listen with respect when told that marriage is a holy sacrament. But as time goes on, the call of the flesh may intrude in the person of a desired maiden, or a determined maiden of heathen estate anxious to annex a particular husband, and then it becomes absurd to a native to deny himself that which for time without count has been the custom of his people.

Elizabeth Sibiya was too gentle to protest against a visitation of the Lord. The Lord giveth, and the Lord taketh away, and so she believed it had been with the pleasures of married life. Hezekiah was still her husband and she should suffer his sins against her with patience and prayer. Docile Christian conduct came easily to her, as good Zulu women had always patterned themselves on it, except that the obedience exacted and given was to an earthly father.

Elizabeth poured all the pent-up jealousy of the generations of women behind her upon the adulteresses who now called themselves Hezekiah's wives, and at all times thanked the Christian faith that granted her this righteous indulgence of deadly antagonism. She knew that one should love one's neighbors, but she hugged to herself the greater knowledge that the Lord frowned upon adulteresses, and that in hating them she was merely doing His bidding.

Hezekiah moved off the mission lands, taking with him his fowl, goats, and cattle, leaving the cattle kraal to stand empty and grow dry. Elizabeth seemed stubborn and willful in refusing to follow him, for he felt toward her as of always; but he let her keep the children. Though he did not dwell on it, for abstract thought to no purpose is only tiring, he remembered that the church could have him prosecuted, and he tried to keep this parting as smooth as possible.

The missionaries warned Hezekiah never to come back, but for Elizabeth they had only pity, and there on mission land in the village of Nhlazatshe she and her children remained. The minister and his wife with the help of Christian natives, clothed them and saw to their basic needs.

Elizabeth had a garden of potatoes to start with, and later tobacco, which she hoed, planted, and harvested herself. Unlike other native women she had no man to plow, furrow, or hoe the garden, to prepare it for her to seed and tend. She would sell her crops, little by little, and get money in bit by bit. It was hard work, but never did she look with longing or hope at another man, or plan to divorce Hezekiah and take another husband.

A devoted convert of the church, she was ambitious to see her children firmly established in its ways. She sewed tirelessly, for herself and her four children. Clothes were important, not only as modest covering but as a mark of self-esteem, a banner for all to see of rise above the heathen state.

Weekdays Elizabeth and the Sibiya children wore dark blue calico prints, sturdy and serviceable, hung from the shoulders in the simplest style; but on Sundays, Abiot, the son, donned a crisp white shirt; and the girls full-starched white skirts in summer, and fresh white blouses for their blue jumpers in winter. Summer and winter Elizabeth did not vary her Sunday costume of heavy black skirt and white freshly laundered blouse.

As a little girl, Christina would see the children of other *kholwas*—Christians—running about naked. Not once, but many times, she asked, "Mother did we go about like this?" Always Elizabeth answered, self-righteous, shocked, "No!"

The next question would be solemn, even fearful. "Mother, have we got the cross of baptism on us?" When to this would come a firm and heartening "Yes!" Christina would sigh contentedly.

The Sibiyas were clean, healthy, decent Christian natives. Their square two-roomed sod house, with thatched roof, was immaculate; it was furnished with beds and mattresses of sacking and fresh grasses, a plank table, rude chairs, and some unpainted shelves for essential dishes. All about them other natives lived in huts of mud and thatch, dark and close, with a small hole to crawl through. The Sibiyas' home had windows, and a doorway to walk through with head held high, so that all of them, mother and children, were proud of their superior and advanced ways.

Hezekiah, when he first moved away, had neither the time nor the money to build another sod house. With the help of other men he built himself simple huts of thatch that looked as if a stray wind might carry them away, but that was a deception of the eye: underneath the thatch was a skeleton fabric of tightly wound wattles.

Hezekiah's two new wives were proud to have acquired a husband who for so long had been holding himself aloof from other women. They cut fresh grass all day in return for the dried grass that had been lent them, and they worked together and helped each other in every way. They thatched each other's huts until both were finished, and once done, their hearts were so full at having at last become adult women, with a husband, a hut, and a coming child, that in a frenzy of joy they trampled their floors until they gleamed and glistened as a proper native housewife's floor should. Each pile of ant-heap sand and cow dung was carted over for the floor foundation without even a passing thought for its heavy burden. Ever faster the bare feet trod until the floor was ready for the river stone and ox fat. As they rubbed and patted with brisk round strokes, they could see their shadows appear on the hard, glassy, wine red surface, and then they knew their efforts were rewarded, and theirs would truly be an abundant and great house.

Hezekiah was thrifty and hard working, and his wives were plump and satisfied, and properly adoring. So pleasantly did the days and nights go by, that often at evening as he looked toward the setting sun dipping below the distant mountain tops, he would rise upon his toes and stretch wide his arms, and exult in the onrush of new strength. Then mentally he would count his cattle, and subtract the cattle still due in payment for his wives, and the thought that if all went well this time next year he could take still another two wives would make him secretly smile and glow with a yet greater exultancy.

While the joys of earthly living were inspiring Hezekiah's household, religion sustained Elizabeth. Never did she miss a service at the mission church, and hers was the loudest and most fervent voice in prayer and song.

It is doubtful if Elizabeth fully understood the implications of her behavior toward her husband. Once a week she called her children to her and sent them with gifts of food to their father. While it was summer they went regularly, for the mealies were plentiful and beer was ever on the brew.

At eight Christina walked in the assuredness that comes with practiced skill, balancing the black earthenware pot upon her head, a thick layer of leaves covering its surface and peeping over the rim, so the beer would not spill when jolted. She would stand perfectly still while her mother set upon her head the hollow ring of plaited straw that nestled down and held the pot fast and steady. From babyhood she had watched women kneel to place their burdens upon their heads, plant their feet firmly upon the ground, the balls and toes first, then rise slowly, sway from side to side as though a rhythm guided their bodies, swinging them along onward, without catch, jerk, or tremor.

White people would have called the distance between Hezekiah's kraal and Elizabeth's home about five miles, but the Sibiya children figured that it was the distance that took them from the first early rays of the sun to its full blossoming.

The four children—Abiot, Christina, Daisy, and Beauty—followed the custom of their elders when they walked. Abiot, the man of the house, led the way carrying a walking stick shoulder high to protect his sisters from snakes, stray dogs, or other perils; a few steps behind him came the sister carrying the beer, and then in single file, a few steps between each, followed the other girls. Once arrived, they slackened their pace, stood still, and waited at a distance to be called.

The first time their father shouted angrily: "What brings you here?"

Abiot answered for them: "Our mother sent us with gifts."

"What gifts do you bring?" Hezekiah demanded suspiciously.

"Beer," the boy replied with stoic dignity, at which the children came forward and knelt in greeting and respect.

Christina set the pot to her lips and drank first by courtesy, and then silently extended the pot to her father. But Hezekiah had started shaking with rage, and screamed: "She wants to poison me; she wants to poison me!" and tried to push the pot away. Deliberately each of the children took a sip and when Hezekiah saw it was apparently harmless he reached for the beer, seemingly reluctantly, but drank long of it, for his throat was dry with excitement and shrieking, and after many years Elizabeth's beer had come to have a peculiarly refreshing taste.

The two wives spoke kindly to the children, and sent respectful greetings to Elizabeth, but the children were heartsick at their father's demonstration. "Please don't send us to our father again," they coaxed. But faithfully Elizabeth persisted, though Hezekiah sent neither thanks nor gifts in return, sullenly drinking in silence when the beer was proffered. The children disliked their father for the shame he had brought upon them, and would argue with their mother, "If he has cast us aside, why should we bring him presents?"

Usually she paid no attention to their protests, but occasionally she would quietly explain, "Your father has left us, but that does not make him any the less my husband. Once he believed I was like a mother to him, and now that he has behaved badly, it behooves me all the more to treat him as a mother would and send him a token of good-will."

Green hills turned crisply brown, summer wore away slowly through the intensity of its own heat, and then the harvest was upon them. Elizabeth remembered the food that Hezekiah loved best, and prepared for him a fragrant dish of *isijingi*, pumpkin stewed with mealie meal. This was a delicacy to vary plain mealie meal porridge, which the children seldom had, and their mouths watered as they watched their mother throughout each stage of its preparation. Each one of them was allowed a taste before the dish was packed for Hezekiah.

Though it was Beauty's turn, the first *isijingi* of the season was held too dear to be risked with her and Christina carried it. Hezekiah dashed the coveted dish to the ground, screaming that Elizabeth had found another way to poison him. The children turned and left him; once out of sight, their tears streamed down in memory of the food which they had barely sampled, now destroyed, good for no one.

Elizabeth made no comment when told, but she, too, regretted the needless waste of food which would have been enjoyed by her children. Food grown by her own efforts was much too precious to be so treated. When the next Saturday came around she said, "There is nothing to take to your father." Two Saturdays passed, and on the third Hezekiah appeared outside their house. Elizabeth came to the door, and on seeing him dropped her eyes as all respectful women did. Hezekiah sternly asked: "Why do you no longer send me food?"

"Because you say it is poisoned and throw it away, and waste it," she summed up.

"Now I know it is not poisoned, and I want it." A softer note crept into his voice as he added, "Send the children with it, and I will eat with thanks."

Before she could answer, he walked swiftly away. From then on, except when the wind blew hard or the rain came down in torrents, the Sibiya children unfailingly carried gifts of special dishes from their mother to their father.

Gradually, Hezekiah softened toward his wife's messengers. When the sweet potato crop was at its height he gave them of that, and as time went on whenever he killed a beast he saved a portion for them. Never was mention made that Elizabeth was to share in these gifts, but the children sensed it, for they brought whatever was given them directly to her. So, never seeing each other, yet maintaining an unceasing rhythm of association through their regular exchange of gifts, the situation afforded Hezekiah and Elizabeth a sense of peace and quiet understanding.

In the earlier years of running these errands, the Sibiya children suffered agonies of shame and resentment. They alone, of all the native children they knew, had no father. It was bad enough for the sisters, but it was worse for Abiot. Old enough to tend cattle, he had none. It was a source of doubtful consolation to him that fortunately he was a Christian and when his time to marry came, he would not need cattle to purchase a bride; the missionaries would help him arrange it, for what they called love.

two

While her legs still had an infantile shortness, Christina started trudging to the missionary school each morning. Home again, her mother sent her to weed the garden. Finished with her other household tasks, she would huddle in a corner and pore over her books.

When the day's work was done, the evening meal eaten, the dishes washed and put away, and the morning firewood heaped by the doorway, the Sibiya children would draw up to the fire burning in the middle of the hard earthen floor. A shiver of suppressed excitement would pass over them as their old Granny and their mother took on new shapes and sizes in the firelight, and their voices became a humming, breathless monotone, telling endless stories of the battles of Nodwengu and Ondini—the white people called it Ulundi—those famous and difficult days when Zulu women smuggled food to their menfolk who were serving the King.

Eventually the missionaries arranged to give two of the Sibiya children further schooling and a chance to earn a little money for their clothes and books. After school Daisy worked in the mission kitchen and Christina helped with the children.

Routine of any sort captivated Daisy, giving her day substance and plan and a sense of accomplishment with each task done. It would be almost impossible to interpret adequately for modern women fleeing the kitchen's drudgery, the thrill of joy this kitchen work produced in Daisy. Living in a home devoid of anything but primitive necessities, where a mother cherished but one hope, to raise her children above the barbarous state of her friends and neighbors, Daisy had had inbred in her an almost holy respect for the daily round of cooking and dishwashing. The mission kitchen, large and rambling in its higgledy-piggledy country fashion, full of sunlight which lit up and got tangled in an assortment of brass bowls and trays, filled Daisy with a fervor and rapture that was not unlike religion.

What did it matter that heavy pails of water had to be dragged to fill the kettles? The missionary's wife complained occasionally of the difficulties of a short water supply, but Daisy had never seen running water, and it seemed natural to her that clothes were washed at the river's bank, and that those things which could not be carried to the river should have the river brought to them.

Christina, not yet ten years old and already a day pupil and a student aid with the smaller children, was chosen as special nursemaid for the missionary's new baby. She moved her few belongings over to the mission school and became an indefatigable little slavey, giving to her new home, her lessons, her tasks, to everyone and everything around her, the same unquestioning devotion.

Neither in summer nor winter did her schedule vary from its daily round. By six or half past, she was up and attending to the other children. Classes began at eight. During mid-morning recess she ran back to the house and changed or fed the baby, and again after school she was with it until its sleeping time.

Supper over, and the baby asleep, Christina read or sewed, or learned to crochet and embroider under the sharp eye of the missionary's wife. While knitting needles whizzed, one of the older girls or a European teacher read aloud, but Christina seldom listened. There was no life, no color or action; they were a lot of moralisms flimsily strung together and hypocritically labeled a story.

The Sibiya childhood drifted by. Days melted into weeks, months, years. Seasons passed from dry heat into months of cold and drenching rain. Roads were washed out into impassable, shapeless gulleys, and then sketchily built up again. Scanty harvests succeeded casual plantings. Occasionally the arid lands, aided by a spurt of industry, produced tall and waving golden mealies; this was followed by prolonged dancing through the cycle of the moon, for rich, tender mealies made fine heady beer.

Sometimes famine, sometimes plenty, sometimes sorrow hanging like a thick fog over all the village kraals; more often endless routine, aimless tasks half-heartedly done, then calm, thoughtless drifting through sunny moments multiplied into concrete slabs of time.

The Bambatha Rebellion had stirred up all the Zulus. Dinuzulu, head of the Zulu nation, had been sentenced to four years' imprisonment for his share in the revolt. Dinuzulu died; the Union of South Africa had been formed; World War I had been declared in Europe and had penetrated into African colonies, almost one could hear the boom of the guns. Of all this the Sibiya children sensed and felt nothing. Their routine varied only with the weather.

Christina had reached adolescence, but much that other girls learn from each other at this period was denied her by her virtual isolation with the mission baby. Vaguely she was aware of whisperings, giggles, and the dawning excitement of even the carefully guarded mission girls, but she attended to her duties and refused to listen to tales of courting.

From her mother she learned nothing of the tribal secrets of sex.

Elizabeth, as a converted Christian, looked with distrust upon fleshly pleasures. Once her whole being had attuned in passion to her husband, but the
very vigor of her previous joy now convinced her of its evil. Neither con-
sciously nor unconsciously did she permit herself to dwell upon her lustful
memories, packed carefully away in a psychic storehouse labeled "un-
Christian," and so sure was she of her moral position that she suffered no
conflict and lost nothing in nervous dissipation.

For hundreds of years Zulu children and adolescents had toyed with
each other and their elders in a manner calculated to avoid social consequences, a technique reputed to have been adopted by adherents of the
early Christian church in an effort to compromise pagan yearning with
Christian virtue. Christina had heard of this custom, *ukuhlobonga*, but she
had never participated in it, as all the others did, and its full significance
was lost upon her. At fifteen she was as innocent of the essential mores
about her as if she had been a member of a different race. Docile, good-
tempered, she was a Christian Puritan in a pagan land, a stranger among
her own people.

Christina was the logical choice to head the newly established branch
school for converted natives and their children, twenty miles distant. If it
was a great honor, it was also a new responsibility, and her unimaginative,
untrained, childish spirit shrank from the unknown. In all her prayers she
asked that she might have strength to rise above her sadness in parting
from the mission and her family to go so far away.

Outwardly the school invested Christina with adulthood, but actually, so
strong was the habit of reliance on an adult mentor, she had hardly arrived
to take up her duties when she became the spiritual charge and child of the
local evangelist, with whom she made her home.

Haltingly, Christina taught reading and writing in Zulu, in a one-room
rondavel schoolhouse, a well-built white-washed round hut. Good-hearted,
but not very proficient, she was able to give the children an eagerness to
learn and a feeling that somewhere hidden in their books was the key to an
outer world that led to mysterious opportunities for prestige, greater ease,
and comfort.

The pupils were chiefly girls, since boys were needed as shepherds.
Girls were fairly useless and might as well be kept out of mischief. The
learning would not harm them and might even be handy in bargaining for
an extra head of cattle in lobola—the dowry payment every Zulu husband
must make for his wife in cattle.

School started early in the morning and lasted most of the day. Natives
do not have a midday meal, so they did not take time out for eating. But
Christina, gifted with that Zulu instinct of what was good for the race, suddenly bubbling over with the vitality and kindliness stored up within her,
would abruptly stop all lessons and race with the children to the brook,

where they waded, jumped on rocks, and picked berries and herbs.

The pay was one pound fifteen a month, raised to two pounds fifteen the second year. Regularly Christina sent her earnings home to her mother, except what she allowed herself for soap and small trifles that might captivate her fancy at the village store. As an independent woman earning her own living, she would be expected to buy beads, a Sunday kerchief, handkerchiefs, perhaps a bangle, some perfume, but never to spend more than a shilling a month on these luxuries.

"Buy some goats," she would write to her mother. Being of thrifty mind and habit she would invest her money in goats, which would breed and bring forth others and give her a greater return on her investment as the years went on. Goats cost but ten shillings, were turned loose to graze, thriving on the grasses and roots of this fertile valley. Christina began to dream of a large herd that would some day assure, her mother and her, security and position in their community.

The fathers and mothers of the pupils speculated about the teacher, and wondered if too much learning was not bad for a girl unless checked in time, for this young teacher never looked invitingly at the boys and men who began to appear and reappear in her path. No one had ever seen her eyes light up at a male's approach; she always cast them down in proper modesty, manifesting not the slightest sign of coyness or even proper female awareness. Zulu men and women know no greater pastime than that which combines the pleasures of the hunt with love, and here was a full-grown girl refusing to join in the sport.

Nor had anyone yet caught her making beadwork tokens, necklaces, and bracelets for an unknown lover. Her own pupils, much younger girls, were always at work upon these for a favored one to wear as a pledge of affection.

Nevertheless, as the year progressed the men and boys of the tribe began to think of Christina as a likely young wife, good, faithful, respectful, and sturdy, and her very lack of worldliness made a special appeal. They began to be curious about this unawakened, frigid maiden, a novelty among her hot-blooded neighbors, and as such she created a legend of excitement entirely her own.

That legend passed beyond the village and aroused the interest of the most powerful young man of the land, Solomon, heir to the throne of the Zulus, who had never yet failed to win favor where he wished.

three

Solomon was descended of Shaka, Dingana, Mpande, Cetshwayo, and Dinuzulu, through an unbroken dynasty of many generations. These forebears had never known either personal or national peace. There were always rival claimants to the throne, and the loyalty of the Zulus was divided among them. Solomon's grandfather, Cetshwayo, was a powerful figure, recognized abroad as well as at home, but he had never won united and consistent support. He lived in constant dread of poisoning, so that even on his famous visit to Queen Victoria, when out of courtesy the royal cup was passed to him first, he pushed it roughly aside, and told his interpreters he neither would nor could be so easily trapped.

In his time the British divided Zululand into thirteen independent kingdoms, officially dubbed "kinglets," each with a ruling chief. Cetshwayo owned a tract of land for which no chief had been named. His rival Zibhebu, descending upon it, destroyed it completely, burning his kraal at Ulundi to ashes, piling disaster wherever he roamed.

Cetshwayo fled to the Nkandla forest. Many Zulus were anxious to acknowledge him as king of all the kinglets, but others were bitterly opposed. While the British Government was debating the policy to adopt, Cetshwayo suddenly died. He was pronounced dead of fatty disease of the heart, but many believed he was poisoned. There were Zulus who said: "The house of Shaka is a thing of the past, like water that is spilt."

Dinuzulu succeeded his father, but within five years he was banished to St. Helena for conspiracy against the government. In 1897, when Zululand was attached to the province of Natal by the British, he was recalled from exile and repatriated. By 1908 his subversive activities had again come to the attention of the ruling British, and he was tried for aid and conspiracy in the Zulu Rebellion, and for sheltering the leader Bambatha's family. After a seventy-day memorable trial, he was sentenced to twelve months in prison, and fined one hundred pounds. Four years additional imprisonment was imposed for sheltering the other rebels, but he served only several months of his term. He was released in 1910 and allowed to live with a few of his wives in the Transvaal, under close supervision and in government custody. There he died in 1913.

Rumors persisted that Dinuzulu, too, had been poisoned, that he had recovered and had escaped to be a free man in Portuguese East Africa, and that some day he "would come back with the Germans." In the first World War some Zulus refused to fight for fear they would be fighting against him.

The last rites for Dinuzulu had been performed, and the cleansing ceremony, which follows about a year after burial, had taken place. David, Solomon's brother, had been designated the royal heir, but due to political machinations, tribal influence and intrigue, he had been turned aside in favor of his brother. The heir to the throne was not yet officially appointed, but Solomon was generally and popularly accepted as the new king, though in European law he was not actually king but chief of the uSuthu people.

Solomon was startlingly virile even among a primitively strong race; power, vitality, and animal joy electrified the atmosphere wherever he appeared. He loved to hunt and shoot and to ride fast horses. He swung in and out of a saddle easily, never walked if he could ride, never trotted if he could gallop. His keen pleasure in sensation was yet to become a slave to appetite.

He had an acute sense of humor, a ready infectious laugh, and a gay, bantering manner, except with officialdom, when his dignity and quiet poise were faultless. When the Duke of Windsor visited Zululand in the twenties he was said to be charmed with him. But Solomon lacked Christina's natural distinction, and in later years his face and body had the unmistakable stamp of dissolute mediocrity.

Every girl smiled upon him, and while the elders of the tribe deliberated on matters of state, his was the crowning glory of kingship—the choice of any girl in Zululand. A king had to choose wisely, and select his wives from well-placed factions of the tribe to build up his own house, but the elders, on his behalf, kept an eye out for the comely girls of these tribes.

Solomon was engaged to six girls officially. Paradoxically, after a betrothal feast at each kraal with several days of dancing and merrymaking, he was already beginning to sense that the time might come when the horrors of satiety would loom larger than the pleasures of fulfillment.

As an aftermath of a feverish siege of courtships it was refreshing to listen to tales of the aloof Christina. Solomon's curiosity was fully aroused. When next in the neighborhood of Babanango, across the White Umfolozi River, he hid in the bushes to watch her unobserved. As Christina passed by, he took careful note of her pointed, perfectly shaped face and sharply peaked eyes, her long tapering fingers, the pink nails tipping her dark hand, her high firm bosom and gently swaying hips, the proud way she carried her head, the swift energetic way she walked. Instantly he was captivated by her beauty, her air of clean strength, and serene virginity.

An objective observer would have noted that Christina's bone structure was of the very finest, her body spare and lean, her cheek bones high and the flesh stretched thin and taut across them, and that her wrists, and ankles too, were delicately refined. Even in later years when she grew heavy and stout, the molding of her face remained sharp and clear, and her ankles noticeably slender. By any standards Christina was beautiful.

Chaotic and unformed as his dreams of Zulu empire were, he was determined that the women whom he would bring to his kraal to be the mothers of his ever-expanding family, would be Christians, above simple savagery, mud-caked and lice-ridden

When Dinuzulu had been banished to St. Helena he had taken several of his favorite wives with him. Solomon himself was born and baptized during his father's exile at St. Helena. There and later in Zululand, in mission schools, and under the guidance of the late Bishop Colenso, a noted Zulu scholar, and his daughters, he had been trained to a life rooted in white man's ways.

He had that sharp sensitivity to his physical surroundings that makes a man both an aesthete and a sensualist. He wore underwear, shoes, military uniforms, and cocked hats; his riding breeches and boots were made to order. He preferred the soft outlines of a chair, to rest on a mattress, sit at a table for his meals, have light cast upon him after nightfall; to cover himself with ample blankets rather than skins, and lie between clean sheets; to use warm water, and soft towels to dry with; and the feel of a sponge after riding. All those rudiments of living that men of the white world had garnered through the years, he had to pick up for himself, item by item, and he had resolved never to give them up.

Impressed by Christina's reputation and education he believed that in her he had found a girl fit to be the mother of his children, to be his first wife, possibly even his Great Wife!

The woods in the region of the White Umfolozi River are not very leafy or dense. A king, accustomed to take the highway, could not skulk in the bush without creating some stir and comment. The kraals about Babanango were soon whispering that the King had been secretly pursuing Christina and no doubt would shortly command her to appear before him. But as the days went by and he apparently made no such move, general gossip died down, but not before Christina had heard, with fear in her heart, that the King was considering her for one of his girls.

Matters of state began to require the King's frequent visits to the Babanango region. Christina heard of these visits with increasing terror, for now she knew that he was determined to have her. Childlike, she began to dress in borrowed ragged shabbiness, hoping that she would be less attractive. For two successive months, whenever Christina heard that the King was tarrying in the neighborhood, she walked in the woods rather than in the open pathways, and she took the children off into the woods, or huddled in someone's hut, holding school there until she was sure the King had gone.

She was only a young girl, but she knew that the wife of a king must share her life with other women. Though Solomon was considered a Christian, as king he would have to choose many wives, and Christina's religion forbade polygamy. She knew, too, that he was already engaged to six other girls, and she believed that, although at the moment he was fascinated by her, he would soon pass on to other girls, for that was the way of kings.

She had never indulged in undue romantic fancies but she expected that some day she would marry a good Christian man who would take her, and her alone, for his wife. At the end of a few months her vigilance relaxed. She thought that at last the King realized she wanted nothing of him, and had given up his pursuit of her.

In northern Zululand there are few modern sounds. The roads are bad, and there is but an occasional distant automobile and only one daily cross-country bus. Underground tremors of heavy traffic are unknown. Before World War II the Imperial Airways used another African route, and there were no planes overhead. More than sixty miles from Nongoma, seat of the magistracy, a train pulls in and out three times a week. Property requires and receives few improvements; there is seldom need for new building, and there is scarcely ever the sound of hammering.

Within the homes of the few governing Europeans, radios are held down to conversational refinements of voice. Telephones are seldom stridently insistent, for African officials are careful of long distance calls, and there is little necessity to call one another. Servants move about barefoot, practically unnoticed.

Native homes are even quieter. They cannot afford radios, or faucets with running water, or even clocks whose ticktock punctuates the silence. The sun tells the time.

The children move slowly, keeping their voices down to chuckles and quickly passing gurgles of laughter. Simple twanging melodies, from fingers teasing a wire string in a low accompaniment or from treasured imported mouth organs emerge gently with the darkness. Deeply satisfying quiet hovers like a blessing, broken only by the riffle of leaves, the buzz of bees, the call of a distant bird, or the full-bellied moo of a cow.

It was the spring of 1915 in the Umfolozi valley, the first spring of the Great War. On a lovely morning fifteen-year-old Christina sat alone and untroubled in her schoolroom, quietly preparing the morning prayer the Christian missionaries had taught her to use each day. No longer afraid, she had gone back to the neat uniform the missionaries had prescribed as the outward sign of a dutiful Christian.

Suddenly the quiet was shattered by the clatter of hoofs. As Christina rose to see who it might be, there in the doorway, face to face with her, stood the King! She had never spoken to him, but she knew his reason for coming. The sudden knowledge overwhelmed her. She grew dizzy, swayed, and collapsed on the floor.

Solomon looked down upon the barely conscious girl. His voice was gentle, but his words had an ominous ring.

"Today I found you! You have avoided me for a long time. Today I have come to fetch you!"

As from a distance she heard him plying her with questions.

"Are you engaged to anyone? Have you reciprocated any man's affection? Have you given yourself in love to anyone?"

A lie might save her. "Yes, Ndabezitha," she barely whispered. Only her lips moved. She was too paralyzed with shyness to get up.

Her lying did not help her. "Even if you have given someone to understand you love him," he warned with flashing eyes, "I am going to take you in spite of it!"

They could hear the children approaching the school. Reminded of her responsibilities, Christina rose quickly to her feet, and leaned against the blackboard for support. Her heart was pounding so hard it seemed to deafen her, her throat was so dry she could scarcely swallow.

The King had made no effort to help her. He looked searchingly at the downcast face and was satisfied that her fright was genuine.

"I'll see you another day," he said abruptly. "When I send messengers to you I want you to reply courteously to them." He then added the word of formal good-bye, "*Ngiyavalelisa*," and with neither word nor glance from Christina, he rode away. Less than five minutes had ticked by on the schoolroom clock since he had come and gone.

Over and over again Christina reenacted what had happened. She had started for the door out of respect to her King. She had wanted to walk erect, proud, and dignified, because he had come to see her in *her* domain. Instead, she had fainted at his feet. Yet the King did not glare at her; rather he seemed so gentle in his greeting. She lingered over the fact that he had spoken to her with the greatest respect. He had neither abused nor insulted her, he had been pursuing, she had been evading, yet he did not hold it against her.

Next day Solomon sent messengers to Christina with a letter written by himself. Christina treasured that letter until she married, when she burned it, for according to native custom tokens sent each other during courtship are destroyed at betrothal.

The three pages began in English, formally, as a missionary school would have prescribed: "Dear Miss Sibiya." The rest was in Zulu, signed by Solomon with his full name, "Yours respectfully, Solomon kaDinuzulu."

There was also a postscript. The words in Zulu, literally translated would be: "To me reply with soft or gentle words, also with respect."

Between the formal salutation and the postscript were vows of eternal love and the flat statement that he was planning to take her to live with him at his Embatheni kraal.

Perhaps because it pleased her vanity Christina never doubted that the King loved her, but she could not understand how a man of such high estate would want to marry anyone so lowly as she. Her family had nothing political or material to offer either the King or the chiefs of the tribe.

As soon as she read that he was in love with her, Christina felt that she was really in love with him too, that her love had developed from the very moment she had seen him at the schoolhouse door. Never before had she visualized God, but had anyone asked her now what God looked like, she would have described Solomon as he rode up before her on his white horse.

At the end of the day, when school was over, Christina wrote her reply. She, too, started with a formal English salutation, and went on in Zulu, but the formal tone prevailed, faintly reminiscent of the business form recommended in Zulu readers.

"I have received your letter and read it, and realize what you are proposing, but I cannot understand its true meaning, because you are a man of high office."

On the second day an answer came from him.

"It matters not at all that I am King, and that you are only a lowly girl, so long as I, the King, desire to court and wed you. I love you, and want you to come and stay with me at the Embatheni kraal. I am a very lonely man— I want you to marry me."

For two weeks never seeing each other though they were but a short distance apart, they sent letters every second day, using practically the same phrases and the same words.

Finally Christina wrote: "I am completely overcome. I consent. I surrender." The Zulu way of saying, "I love you."

Solomon answered, merely noting the fact and thanking her. To the usual I am thanking you—*ngiyabonga*—he added *kakhula*—in plenty.

Solomon rode into the kraal where Christina was living followed by a cavalcade of six men on horseback. It was Sunday, and the Christian natives, dressed in their Sunday clothes, were idling about. The women all looked alike, in tight-fitting pink or white silk blouses and heavy black skirts, black kerchiefs bound closely around their heads, and the men, too, appeared all the same in ill-fitting store suits. Both men and women were barefoot. Shoes were put on once a week, at the road bend nearest the church, and painfully endured only through the service.

Christina, seeing the King approaching, fled. While Solomon was welcomed by the men, two of his attendants went in search of her. They found her a huddled against the wall of a rondavel, and thrust a parcel at her:

Automatically she laid it on a table near by, greeted them respectfully, and secretly prayed that they would leave.

"Why don't you open your parcel?" they inquired kindly.

"Is it *mine*?" she asked.

Smiling at her childish naïveté, they commanded, "Open it!"

Obediently she undid her parcel, pausing first to wind up the string. The men did not take their eyes off her, so that later they could faithfully report each detail to the King, who took great delight in hearing of the pleasure his gifts had brought. There were combs, a brooch, and a gay silk kerchief of white with all-over floral pattern. The brooch was made of tiny stones that shone with a brilliance that caught her eye at once; the combs gave off more of this strange light. But with no outward sign of pleasure Christina folded up the parcel and put it back upon the table. Their duty done, the men bowed themselves out.

Solomon came in and now Christina and he were alone.

"Hallo! I see you, little girl," he gaily greeted her.

The sea was swallowing her up, the wind was blowing her helplessly about, thunder was beating in her head. Outdoors there were fragments of familiar voices, but here in this room nothing was normal. Silence closed in upon them as the two of them stood, he continuing to look searchingly at her, she not able to breathe properly.

He spoke again, trying to break her silence, "I thank you, Christina, for reciprocating my love."

Still she stood numb. Helpless before any strain or awkwardness, he strode to the door and shouted for his attendants. They rushed in, and at a signal from him they chorused, "The King wished us to thank you on his behalf, daughter of Sibiya, for giving your love to him." But Christina remained spellbound, her eyes cast down, her head bent.

Solomon sat down as if for strength, the attendants gathered around him on mats, and she, too, sat down when motioned to a chair. Everyone was waiting for something to happen, for the King to give the cue.

"If Christina had not been a Christian, I would not have arrived with so few men," he began abruptly, hoping to banish what he sensed was a paralyzing shyness. "I would have come to make a huge display. Out of respect to her, however, I did not want my arrival to take on any of the air of a heathen ceremony."

News had spread that the King had arrived. As men crowded into the hut, Christina quietly slipped out. Trembling and frightened, she forgot she had ever been excited by Solomon's love or dashing appearance.

Solomon craved diversion from the tension and strain. He ordered the men out and sent for the girls of the kraal. Hurriedly the girls tidied themselves, put on clean *amabayi*—a scanty blanket shawl suspended from the shoulder and leaving one breast exposed—and, seminaked, streamed toward the King.

Christina remained in hiding. Solomon noted her absence and sent for her, and humbly she followed his messenger into his presence. It was like an encore pantomime—Solomon again motioned to a chair beside him, and again she sat where indicated. Something protective and unaccustomed stirred within him at her obvious distress. Once again he tried to cover up her shyness by a rush of words.

"Christina, here, has accepted me," he told the assembled girls. "Now that she is going to marry me she will give up teaching. I shall take her to my kraal to care for me."

All the girls were excited, eager, friendly—all except Christina. This was beginning to be too much for Solomon. He thought happily of beer, and the relief it would bring. After a long draught of this never failing bracer, Christina's coolness was still puzzling, but more pleasantly so.

Solomon rose, in full command of himself and his people. "Bring to me the head of this kraal," he ordered, and the evangelist was summoned. "I want you to go to the head of your mission and tell the white *uMfundisi* that Christina is about to marry the King," said Solomon, speaking as to an equal, but with an undertone of authority. "I want nothing to worry Christina, now that she has accepted me and is going to be my wife."

The evangelist was the male, next of kin, in whose authority Christina had been placed, and he now basked in the same radiance that her relatives might have, upon being told that one of their women had been honored by a proposal of marriage from the King.

"I gladly give my consent with great pride to our noble King," the evangelist orated, in the rising sing-song cadence he used on Sundays. "My people and Christina's will try to deserve this honor that has come to our kraal. The King will find he has done well in his choice of this, our worthy pupil. My only regret is that I will lose a valuable teacher for my flock—"

Solomon cut short the efforts at oratory. His errand was accomplished, not without effort, and he wanted to be on his way.

There were only a few minutes left for the King and his future wife to be alone. It never occurred to him to take advantage of their first moments of intimacy, to come closer to her, to touch her, or even to breathe upon her as he spoke to her, as men of another race might have done. Nevertheless, Christina was acutely aware of their aloneness and terrified by it, but she felt compelled to make matters clear to him, and opened her nervously twitching mouth to speak for the first time since his arrival.

"Forgive me," she whispered hoarsely. "But grant me time, grant me sufficient time, and permission to go myself to the *uMfundisi* and explain what has happened. He will not understand, he will be angry unless I am the one to tell him. Even so, he may never understand."

"Do not worry, Christina. Do not be anxious," he tried to reassure her. "I myself will write a letter to the *uMfundisi* and dispatch it by messenger."

The urgency of the situation gave her a surprising boldness. "Let me be the first one to tell him," she pleaded. "I would much rather you wrote to him, my King, after I had seen and talked with him myself." Gravely he agreed.

"Come a little way with me," he suggested. She darted ahead hiding behind some trees until he caught up with her. Though prompted by shyness, this was, nevertheless, her first budding of coquetry. Then, unlike a native man and a native girl, accustomed to the man's walking a few paces ahead, they fell into step side by side with each other as lovers and comrades of the white race do.

There was a smile in his voice as he said: "Why did you run so far? What are you afraid of?"

Her voice was freer of tension, and somewhat belied her words, "I am afraid of you."

"Why? Am I a wild animal?" he teased. "You must cease being afraid of me as you were the day I saw you at the school."

They continued walking, perhaps half a mile, when Solomon spoke again: "Three days will pass, and on the fourth I will send an escort to fetch you. I will send a horse for you to ride as well."

Christina was prompted by an inner urge of practicality. "I am frightened to ride a horse, a frisky horse like yours," she said.

"I will send you a quiet horse," he reassured her, tenderly and laughingly.

The afternoon light was beginning to fade beyond the trees, when Christina stopped. "I have gone far enough; I must go back to the kraal," she said, calm and apparently no longer afraid of him.

Formally, and without a word, they shook hands as they had seen missionaries do on important occasions. This was the first time they had ever touched each other. Before she turned away, he dug into his pocket, and still without a word, handed her a gold sovereign.

four

Early morning sunlight was streaking the sky when the evangelist and Christina rode out from the kraal, but the midday sun was blazing on them when they came in sight of her home mission.

A tight-lipped, pale-faced Scandinavian missionary met them. "What brings you here, Christina, on this day and at this strange hour?" he queried in great astonishment. "And, you too, my son, what brings you?"

Disregarding the *uMfundisi*'s curiosity, the evangelist began the routine greeting prescribed by good missionary manners.

"Thank you, I be well, and I hope you and Mrs. Eckenbren be well, too—"

But the *uMfundisi*, determined to know what had happened at once, interrupted him. "What brings you here, Christina?" he insisted.

"The King wishes to marry me!" Christina blurted out, since she instinctively obeyed orders, and knew nothing of the subtleties of persuasion or finesse in the presentation of a cause. "I have come for your permission, *Mfundisi.*"

There was a second of tense silence, ripped through by furious anger.

"How dare you even think of such a thing?" stormed the *uMfundisi.* "Never will I give my consent to your marriage into heathen polygamy!"

"You are to blame for this!" he shouted, turning upon the evangelist. "I put Christina, a young girl, into your charge, and you saw in her a means of advancing your position. You betrayed my trust in you, you put your petty political ambition before the teachings of God!"

Christina and the evangelist stood with bowed heads. They had not been invited in nor were they going to be, until the missionary had relieved his feelings.

"Christina," he thundered, "you had better come back to the mission and live here again like my child until you get over this madness. You know that the King will have to take unto himself several wives. Eventually, he will forget all about you, and you, heart-broken and neglected, will continue to live in sin. Better forget him before he has dragged you down to this degradation."

The wily Zulus and the directors of his church had taught him to temper anger with persuasion and kindliness.

"You see, Christina, I brought you up," he spoke more gently. "I paid for your education, because I saw you were a bright sweet child, and you have accomplished the end for which I have educated you. I am proud of you, and so is Mrs. Eckenbren. But what have you done up to now to repay us, either in money, in services, or in thoughtfulness, for the worry and the care that we have expended on you? You want to marry Solomon. You want to be taken by the chief of your tribe to go into service for him. You want to give to him that which belongs to us. You are even prepared to throw away your Christianity, because the King is not Christian. I, as a man of God, His teacher for you, cannot permit you to thrust aside the faith we have struggled so long to implant within you. Your family, too, are good Christians. They would not want this to happen."

He gestured more in sadness than anger, but went on more determinedly, "I feel I must call upon all your relatives, the *abazali*, those you are born to, and the *amalunga*, the native elders of the church, and tell them about this. They will help me make you see the path of righteousness, and wean you away from this folly. Now go and see Mrs. Eckenbren, and she will assign your duties to you for the day, and tomorrow I'll speak to you again."

Christina found the courage to answer a superior, "I am going home, back from where I came."

"What does this mean?" The *uMfundisi* gaped at Christina in genuine amazement.

"Please, *Mfundisi*, I have a borrowed horse," she tried to explain. "He belongs to the King. I cannot leave him unattended all day, with no way of stabling him, or even enclosing him."

"I will attend to the horse," curtly replied Mr. Eckenbren. With that she agreed to remain over until the next day.

Just after midday there was a cloud of dust and the sound of galloping hoofs as Solomon, with three attendants, rode into sight.

The King was already there, talking, when Christina came into the study. The *uMfundisi* politely interrupted to order her to sit down, but Solomon did not greet her.

"I am taking Christina with me, *Mfundisi*," he was saying, matter of factly. "I want her for my wife."

"Christina told me of this only a short while ago, and I am exceedingly sorry," replied the *uMfundisi*, carefully emptying his pipe and keeping his eyes upon it.

"Why?" Solomon bluntly asked.

"Because she is like my own child," the *uMfundisi* spoke guardedly. "She has returned nothing to either my wife or me, for the pain and trouble we took in educating her." Perhaps he was not above hinting for some compensation or donation from the reputedly wealthy king. But Solomon looked stolidly ahead, and made no comment.

The *uMfundisi* turned to Christina. "My child, do you love Solomon?"

"Yes, *Mfundisi*," she barely whispered.

"And you, Solomon, will you cherish and care for Christina, forever?" he asked, with a piercing look.

Solomon, too, merely murmured: "Yes, *Mfundisi*."

As tea was brought in, the *uMfundisi* saw the day was slipping by, and tried to arrive at a compromise. "I had intended to put this matter to the elders and to Christina's relatives," he said, looking out upon his garden, "but now that you have arrived to fetch her, there is no time."

Solomon ignored the delicate hint for delay. Unworldly as she was, Christina realized that the *uMfundisi* respected the King's rank and position, and made allowances for it. They rose to go. Christina was close to sobbing at the parting. "Good-bye, my child. I shall hope to see you again," the *uMfundisi* told her kindly.

A girl, who had come to the mission school as a barefoot charge, who as a special privilege had been allowed to act as nursemaid to the missionary's child, was back again at the mission gate, this time riding away by the side of the King.

It was dusk when the King and Christina pulled up at the Embatheni kraal. A group of natives were waiting with cattle and goats, as they had seen the King passing earlier that morning and understood that he was returning that night. As was becoming to a modest woman, Christina went directly into the girls' hut, while Solomon remained outside to greet his people.

Later Solomon and Christina squatted on the floor upon the same mat. From a small pot of beer placed in front of them, they drank jointly—official recognition of their betrothal.

The King began swapping loud tales of Zulu heroism. Everyone sensed it was but a prelude to the story he was about to tell of his own exploits. Downing another pot of beer, he shouted: "I was afraid that had I not gone to fetch Christina in person, she would never have returned from the white *uMfundisi*."

"Yah—yah," the men shouted back, their bodies swaying responsively.

"The *uMfundisi* and his wife were upset at her leaving them," roared the King, and once more the men chanted, "Yah—yah," and for further emphasis, "were upset—were upset."

In contrast to the rise of drunken hilarity around her, Christina steadily saddened. Ringing through her head was a thought she could not banish: "Kings do not cherish their women. They do not know how."

The fumes from the beer in the warm hut were making her drowsy and uncomfortable, but dizzily her mind kept remembering admonitions about the plight of a Christian girl married to a king.

Everyone was drooping from the liquor when Solomon rose in a signal for all to leave. An attendant staggered in with sleeping mats, dozens of them.

Outside the hut natives were shouting the King's salute: "*Ngonyama! Ngonyama!*—Lion! Lion!

Christina was aware that unused blankets and mats were being brought in and that there was an air of solemnity and expectation about the place.

Scarcely had the mats been laid, when Solomon shouted: "Meat! Meat! Bring me meat from the goats that have been killed."

Maphelu repeated the orders to men standing at attention as if they had not heard. Maphelu was the King's chief attendant, a bodyguard who never left him, diplomat, secretary, a man of recognized influence and power, since he had the King's ear at all times.

Someone tapped Christina on the shoulder, and led her away to eat at another hut; she was not accustomed to eat in a King's presence, and they knew it would embarrass her. Thoughtfully Solomon sent her a bowl filled with chunks cut from his own portion. In her overexcited and nervous state, the meat stuck in her throat, but she ate every piece, because she was ravenously hungry.

When she returned to the hut only Solomon was there.

Timidly she came toward him, and now fear rose within her, clouding her vision, and making her body tremble. In the presence of her heathen husband she prayed to the Christian God for protection. But from nowhere in that dark hut came light to direct her.

"God, God in whom we place our trust, I know the King is to be my husband—and I am to be his wife—and that he loves me very much. But I'm *afraid* of him. Oh, God, what shall I do?"

Solomon could not hear that prayer, nor was he even aware that she was making it, but deep in his male consciousness he realized that the woman he had chosen, and whom he believed he wanted above all others, was afraid of him.

"Christina, Little One," he coaxed. "Do not be afraid of me. Come to me. Come nearer, come closer."

She stood rooted in horror. "I cannot marry you! I am too young!"

Solomon continued to be kind. "This is all right. I will bring you up as a father. You will be my child. I will send word to your relatives that you are now my daughter, and that you are to be my wife."

"Thank you, Nkosi."

"Don't call me Nkosi. Men must call me that; it is their duty. You are to call me Zulu."

She tried to murmur the word: "Zulu . . ."

As her lips tried to make the sounds the upper lip had somehow become misplaced and bobbed up and down, completely out of control. With her lips behaving so strangely, and her body shaking, Christina felt a stranger to herself, and that she could no longer bear. She fell on the mat, a crumpled heap of sobs.

When Solomon rose from the side of the girl, who, though sleeping, still shuddered fitfully and in sobbing breaths, he went to the door and looked out at the hills as if to get guidance from them.

"Maphelu," he called "bring beer. And then the King has a special service he wishes you to perform."

For a long time the King and Maphelu murmured in low voices, while the King looked abstractedly at the light of morning coming over the distant hills. "Maphelu, you must tell her that the customs and the laws of my house must be carried out," he said finally. "Tell her what is expected of her in her position. Tell her whatever it is that she ought to know, that those Christian women who have brought her up have forgotten to tell her."

Suddenly a disturbed note, almost pleading, crept into his voice: "Be an uncle to her, Maphelu, be one of her brothers, she's only a child. Tell this child not to be afraid of me."

Maphelu entered the hut and stood over the sleeping girl. As she lay there with her breath coming quickly, she did indeed look like a child, and his fatherhood was touched. Startled, she awoke, and tears came to her eyes.

Maphelu was much older than Solomon, but for several years he had been accustomed to do as Solomon bade him, and sometimes, as he faced the men of his tribe, the orders were difficult and he had moments of unpleasant hesitation.

"So this is what I, a Zulu warrior, have been reduced to doing for my King. Woman's work! Why did not a 'qhikiza, whose duty it is to prepare young girls for their woman's responsibilities, tell her? I'm just an auntie, an old lady!"

Something in Christina's shaking shoulders brought an automatic response and prompted him to kindness and wisdom.

"Christina, you are a child, but you are also a grown woman," he began, gently and sensibly. "You should be proud that the King has chosen you to be his wife. You must not be afraid of him. He is a noble warrior, a great and powerful man. You must listen to him. You must do anything he asks you to do, because he is not only your King, but your husband."

"Maphelu," she said, as she rubbed her toes back and forth across the mat in a routine semicircle that seemed to ease her body of its strain, "Maphelu, it is all a darkness. It all seems wicked to me. I am a Christian girl. I cannot do the things that the King wants me to do."

Something was instantly required of him. Somehow those Christians had given this girl ideas that were weaning her away from nature. It was preposterous, horrible.

"My child, Christian women and women of the *abantu*, all women, do as their husbands tell them," Maphelu declared emphatically. "After a while it makes them happy and they have children. You must remember you are a daughter of the Zulus. They always had courage and pride of service. You have the greatest pride of all. You are personally to serve your King!"

"Maphelu, I know what you are trying to tell me . . ." Christina haltingly replied. "I had never heard . . . I did not know . . . the King tried to tell me something, but it was terrible! I could not listen. Every time he tried to touch me, I began to cry."

Maphelu stood up and heaved a sigh of relief. He had done his duty. The crying would last for a while, but he knew it was only a matter of time before she, too, would look upon her fears as silly. As he turned away, Christina called softly after him: "Thank you, Maphelu."

And Maphelu answered, as he left her: "I am your friend, Christina," a pledge of friendship he never forgot, and one she grew to rely on heavily.

Solomon came in, and since Christina never looked at him directly, her downcast glance, instead of emphasizing the awkwardness between them, helped pass it off. "Did you understand Maphelu, Christina?" he asked kindly.

She nodded.

"Answer me, Christina."

The voice was still kind, but there was an edge of authority in it.

"Yes, Zulu."

"Then I shall expect you to obey me in all things hereafter."

A man of another race might have tried to soothe her, to win her by the promise of peace in his arms, but he did neither.

"I shall take you home, now. For three days I shall be at Nongoma. On my return I shall come to fetch you to be with me, *impela*"; *impela*—in truth—the Zulu word implying finality, the Zulu way of expressing Forever and forever, Amen.

five

A native store in lower Africa has little visible arrangement, the eye and nose being simultaneously taken with a medley of gay fabrics, sticky candy, loose cookies, and strongly smelling boots. Whether or not it is large and prosperous enough to command a cleaner and tidier European section, there exists a tacit understanding that it is primarily for native trade, and that rightfully natives meet and idle here. This is the real native center, usually also the recruiting station for the mines at Johannesburg. No one knows better than the storekeeper when a native's credit is exhausted.

It is said that in the early days in South Africa the missionary and the storekeeper each pitched his tent in the wilderness simultaneously, the missionary recruiting for souls, the storekeeper for cash customers. Since cash was almost unknown in a remote rural area, the natives ran up debts and came into the storekeeper's power; they were forced to go to the mines for which he was recruiting and to pay an exorbitant interest rate on the debt contracted. Invariably the missionary objected.

That is largely of the past. Neither the storekeeper nor the missionary was responsible for the modern native. The diamond and gold rush of the seventies and eighties swept the country, uprooting white and native peoples alike. The missionaries helped temper that tidal wave of early madness and greed with knowledge, schools, education, and trained leadership. The mining industry, after many bitter lessons, organized labor recruiting under government supervision into a system that aims to prevent petty exploitation of individual natives, and the storekeeper became a small agent of a tremendous machine.

Mrs. Dalton—the storekeeper is always a European—came forward eagerly to assist her best customer.

"Will you please show me some things suitable for this girl?" Solomon asked her most politely in Zulu. Instantly watchful natives crushed each other in efforts not to miss any detail of this royal shopping.

"What would you like, Christina?" offered Solomon generously.

Confused by so overwhelming an occasion, with new experiences crowding in upon her in such rapid succession, Christina was tongue-tied. Mrs. Dalton waited with that blend of patience and irritation peculiar to her profession.

Solomon made the selections—a voluminous clumsy gray coat; a brown felt hat that covered all the hair, sat midway over the eyes, and rested practically full upon the nose; some sturdy and coarse calico with gay stripes that zig-zagged across it; and some soft delicate dress material that was caressing to the touch and reminded one of love.

"Is there anyone who could make up these dresses quickly?" Solomon inquired, fondling the fabric.

Mrs. Dalton looked at Christina with an appraising eye, pulled out a tape measure, and in quick practiced movements held it taut around Christina's hips, bust, and waist.

"The wardrobe will be hurried," she brusquely promised.

Solomon produced a wallet from inside his belt, paid three crumpled pounds, ignored the curious natives, and followed by Christina, rejoined the horsemen.

Solomon was escorting Christina back to the mission school, until the time when he was to take her formally from her father's home. Among Zulus who are not Christians, a marriage ceremony does not necessarily precede conjugal relations.

At the school, Christina prepared for her departure. There were some clothes to wash, and some trinkets, a primer, a notebook, and a Zulu hymnal to pack in her suitcase. If they could afford it, mission children used, when traveling, a rudely constructed wooden box sold by the village store, to show their rise above the heathens who carried a traditional bundle. Christina had advanced further; she had a flimsy paper suitcase.

Christina was not unconscious of the new, almost cringing respect she now received from the community, which had previously shown her simple affection and good will, but it was merely sweet to her pride to realize that wherever she went she walked in the dignity of the King's choice.

Hezekiah was delighted that fate had taken such a turn in his favor, that a daughter of his had been chosen by the highest of the land! He and his wives welcomed Christina effusively, and kept running back and forth in fruitless abstraction.

If her marriage were to have proper sanction and ceremony the King would have to fetch Christina from her father's home, but as a special tribute the messengers were instructed to take her to her mother also, and officially notify her, too, that her daughter was about to be married.

Christina tried to tell her mother about her love for Solomon, but Elizabeth would have none of it.

"You are only a child. The church is your only protection. God watches over all of us, if we will only do His bidding. If you live with this man in sin," her voice took on a note of deep bitterness, "I don't care if this man is King or not, like all the others who do not have a God—who have never seen His Image—who have never followed His teachings—he will cast you aside. You will give up your God. You will put all your trust in the King, and then after a short while, because he is rich, he will take first one wife, then another. You, a God-fearing, Christian girl, will help him make a mockery of the teachings of Christ, so that he can go his way, seeking pleasure!"

"Your father was a good Christian," she drew a long sigh, and continued in the first tirade of malevolence her daughter had ever heard from her. "He knew better. The missionaries taught him that a good man has but one wife. I served him faithfully. Never once did I fail in my duty to him. God was good to him. We had children, we had plenty to eat. But when that girl from the Nkonjeni kraal came along and smiled at him, he forgot me, forgot the teachings of the church.

"You know he left me here, hungry, alone, with no home, and took all his cattle away from us. You, who were his children, he threw aside.

"The missionaries helped me bring you up in the Faith, to educate you, to make you good children. And now, Christina, you are ready to throw your lot in with a heathen. Just as if this had never happened in our family before! You are making ready to go and of your own choice bring disaster upon yourself, as if you had not been warned by people who have far better knowledge of the world than you have.

"If your heart is filled with love you must turn that love to a good end. You must love God. You must love the missionaries who helped you, who helped me. You owe all of us gratitude, which is the flower of love.

"If you leave us and go to that man to live in sin with him, God our Father will bring punishment to our house; to me who failed in holding you to Him, and to you, who so willfully turned away from him."

Christina wept, but even as she was torn between loyalty to her mother and to her lover, and as the fear of a half-tutored mind presented an angry God avenging himself upon her, she knew that, sinful or not, she would follow her love and not her God.

Meanwhile, at her father's home preparations were being made for the betrothal ceremony. As it takes four or five days for native beer to be prepared, all the girls and women of the kraal were promptly set to work grinding mealies, fetching wood and water, and setting aside the thick liquid to ferment and rise. Some allowance could be made for *iminjonjo*—the special beer which would be brought for the more dashing men by their favored girls.

When Solomon arrived a week later the entire countryside was ready for him. Five head of cattle had been killed. Hezekiah selected an especially fine beast to present to the King, and Elizabeth prepared her own brew of beer for him. Christina's heart became lighter, for she knew that whatever her mother felt, the tendering of her beer was the outward symbol of good will. Beer is not merely something to drink, it is part of native ritual, a symbol of hospitality, of tribute to authority, the occasion for the gathering and giving of news.

Great numbers of natives came forward and cheered the King. But there was not a girl among them. It had been decided in family council that no Christian girls were to come into Solomon's presence. For so strong a feeling did they have about their church, they feared the King would break its hold upon the kraal if he influenced any other girls away from it. And so, on Christina's betrothal day, all her mother's friends and kin guarded closely lest even then her successor be chosen from their midst. Later, out of necessity, a few heathen girls came carrying their fathers' offering of beer.

Wherever the King went, his own meat and food went with him, unless he were sure that somewhere in that kraal was a woman already attached to him, who would zealously watch over its preparation and protect him from poisoning. The King's retinue always set up a temporary kitchen and prepared all his meals. Not even at his betrothal could he risk eating the meat that would be killed for him by the friends and relatives of his bride.

Solomon had suspected the kraal would not be wholly friendly. He paced back and forth, hand in hand with Christina, as if on parade. He also brought lavish and handsome gifts; a large cashmere shawl, some dress materials, and a silk kerchief for "her, who had borne Christina."

Natives stood by and smiled their approval, and undoubtedly Elizabeth was pleased, but she was also saddened, for though she was poor and these were fabulous gifts, she held her daughter's happiness much too precious to trade her eternal salvation for them.

When the feasting was past its peak Solomon called Hezekiah and Elizabeth before him. This was the first time Christina's parents had faced each other in many years. In the very rigidity with which they refused to acknowledge each other's presence was evident the tragedy of Elizabeth's long denial of him.

An expectant hush fell on everyone. Even the leaves in the trees seemed to have stopped fluttering.

"I am taking Christina for my wife. I will send my representatives to complete the transaction of lobola," the King briefly stated for all to hear.

Hezekiah nodded in agreement, and replied, "I am honored, Ndabezitha! I am satisfied." Had it not been the King to whom he was giving his daughter in marriage, he would have insisted on more definite discussion and something on account to bind the transaction. This casual handling of Christina's lobola was to have repercussions in all their lives.

Whereas among many other nations the people progress from barter of goods to gold, and then currency, the Zulus have reversed the process. Three generations ago the Zulus did not use cattle for lobola, but a crude currency of copper, gold, and silver metal cylindrical bars, cut into large and small rings shaped, some hold, into a phallic symbol. The large rings represented cows, the small, calves; and a woman fetched, in price, a specified combination of the large and small ones. Men were always in battle, or on the move. They had no time to corral cattle, but they could always manage to have a handy metal bar or two around when needed.

Fifteen head of cattle is traditional lobola, though as tribal conventions have been weakened by European disaffections, six head of cattle among humbler ranks is frequently regarded as quite satisfactory, even generous.

The fire had died down, and the feasting was long since over, when Christina tried to say good-bye to her mother. But Elizabeth crumpled up in weeping, and they wept together. Only then did pity and sympathy surge through Christina, for she realized that if indeed she were not to return she might never see her mother again. They clung to each other, then word-lessly fell apart.

Hezekiah shook hands with Christina, and said unctuously, "Thank you for choosing my daughter to go with you." Christina parted from her father with not one qualm of regret.

As the party made ready to ride forward, and the King had already mounted his horse, he noted Christina was afoot. "Get off that horse and give it to this girl!" he commanded one of his riders. "You walk and carry her suitcase!"

All over those hills and roads ordinarily one saw a man astride a horse, while one, two, or more wives and girl children struggled behind, bearing atop their heads the family mats, beer, and other lumpy packages. More than one passerby looked at this unusual scene of a woman, young and strong, mounted on a horse with a man following on foot behind her. Surely Christina must be forgiven if she was filled with an onrush of pride and joy in her new position.

six

Christina liked the Zibindini kraal on sight, with its huge, dominant hut and finely built reed stockade, its grounds swept clean, its air of deliberate tidiness. Loose stones, dry skins, recently used pots and pans, the usual slovenly front-yard paraphernalia were magically absent. At regularly spaced intervals were the women's quarters, a row of smaller huts thatched with meticulous precision.

The central, royal hut had a floor that shone like a pool of water in bright sunlight. She could almost see her reflection in it. That floor captured her warming heart and won her completely to her new home. Her aesthetic pleasure was heightened by other features foreign to native huts, the brass bed, with its hand-embroidered spread, some chairs, an open cupboard with brightly patterned china, and a table covered with gleaming patterned oilcloth.

Christina would have liked to linger to finger each article lovingly, to touch wonderingly and to see at her own pace, but Solomon's sisters swarmed in upon her. The mothers stayed away because they were still in mourning for Dinuzulu, their husband, and during a period of mourning married women are not permitted to enter a chief's hut.

There were giggles and shoving, and the excitement that hovers over all brides. "Come out," one of the bolder girls wheedled. "We want to see what you look like, Sibiya."

Christina would be known as Sibiya, the name of her family and her tribe. Only her intimates would refer to her as Christina. There might be ten Sibiyas, and yet they would all be called by that family name except if it were necessary to distinguish between them. Christina would then be referred to as the "daughter of Hezekiah."

Young and old women swayed gracefully in single file from all directions with black, bubbling pots upon their heads. As each woman approached the presence of the King she raised her arms above her head, placed her hands upon the pot, and automatically brought her knees to the ground in curtsy and salute, holding the pot before her as an offering. It might have been the formalized movement of an ultra modern dance. At a barely perceptible gesture from the King, she brought the pot to her lips and tasted. The beer was good, wholesome, and safe; she, having guaranteed it with her own life, passed the bowl to the King.

Sometimes he took a sip, bringing his face close to the bowl as it was held before him; sometimes he himself held it, his head thrown far back as he took a long, cooling draught, and then passed it back to the kneeling woman; occasionally he waved the pot aside to the man next in rank. A sip here, a long draught there soon made for a surfeit and drunken jollity.

With the approach of drunkenness, men and women gave way with abandon, banter and love-making increased, and the awe in which the King was held vanished. They drew around the hut fire, and the King told them every detail of what had happened while he was away.

Like most natives Solomon had a true dramatic instinct, acting out every part of his story, unconsciously mimicking the tones and manners of the people with whom he had been dealing. When he came to the European minister, who was angry at Christina because she chose Solomon rather than her duty to him, he burlesqued him mercilessly.

This time Christina was delighted with his tales about her, for he did not treat it as solely his adventure, but as something which concerned all his relatives, and it gave her her first consciousness of belonging to him, of being a part of this large family.

*Solomon thought of all his father's wives as mothers to him, as well as his blood mother—the mother who bore him. Anyone of them was free to correct him, and all had the relationship of mother-in-law to Christina.

Several old women squatted upon mats in solemn conclave. They were in mourning, in faded black Mother Hubbards, with black kerchiefs bound taut about their heads. Their feet were bare, and their ears, wrists, ankles and neck were free of any of the trinkets and adornment usually worn by Zulu women.

One calls a Zulu woman old when wrinkles, the decay of tissue, and all the debility of age are there, though in years the woman may not yet be forty. No wonder these women jealously guard their prerogatives, for hope has long since died in their hearts, and only barren authority is left.

The mothers stared long at Christina, who stood motionless before them. At a nudge from her neighbors one of the mothers spoke. They called her *Mngoma*, the wise woman. More often they honored her by referring to her as the female elephant, *Indlovukazi*, powerfully strong, never forgiving of an injustice.

"Do you realize that in coming here to live with Solomon, our son, you have come also to live with us?" she said, her eyes cold and probing.

Christina's head bobbed automatically in the affirmative.

"We shall expect you to show us respect at all times," the mother's voice grew menacingly deliberate, "and to listen to whatever we tell you, not to just what he, whom you love, says."

Solomon appeared in the doorway. "We have only just seen her," the

---

* Compare here through p. 43 with the record of original interview, appendix 1A.—Eds.

mothers protested. "We have barely had a chance to tell her anything."

"Never mind," he laughed gaily, leading her away. "You will see her on plenty of other days."

As he looked upon her he was filled with pride and joy.

"Order up the regiments," he bellowed loudly to his induna—sub-chief —carried away by his mood of the moment. "I want my wife to see them!"

It was shortly after Dinuzulu's cleansing ceremony, and the regiments called up to take part in it had not yet disbanded.

Christina could hardly breathe as she sat on a mat beside her husband. No other woman was in sight, but she knew they were peeping at her from hut doors, envying her and yet preparing to worship her exalted position.

The Mbokodebomvu—Dinuzulu's crack regiment—sang their song. The Felaphakathi called the King's praises, the Hayilwengwenya—mouth of the alligator—gave their salute. Every one of the twelve most noted regiments performed. The air resounded with the beat of drums, dancing feet, eerie shrieks, and mass songs. Men were leaping, rushing, seemingly in a confused mass, but actually every movement was weaving an intricate pattern, and the massed movements, despite their seemingly insane abandon, were building up to a crescendo of meaning.

Historically and traditionally the regimental dances go through the sexual cycle. Solomon and Christina sat there, vicarious participants in the stirring panorama before them, withdrawn into each other, everything heightening their intimacy, pointing up their aloneness, drawing them into a mutual passion and delight they could hardly restrain.

At a gesture from the King the regiments broke ranks and vanished. Solomon nodded toward the hut, and Christina followed him there.

Now when he drew her to him, there was something in his bearing that charmed and thrilled her, and filled her trembling body with hot strength that flamed and raged within her. Fear was a strange thing of the past.

Next morning as she busied herself about the hut, performing small personal services for him, Christina reviewed the brief days she had spent with Solomon and knew that she could never be afraid of him again. Every nerve cell in her body throbbed with the knowledge that this great man, this King, her Zulu, loved her so passionately. Her whole life, from then on, was dedicated to the fulfillment of her love, to the service of the man she loved.

"Tomorrow we will kill a beast to honor Christina's initiation into our kraal, and she will take up her duties under you," Solomon announced pleasantly to the mothers. "I hope you teach her to be a good and faithful servitor, and that she will be grateful to you."

He led her to a round enclosure, fenced in by crude, irregular branches.

"There, Christina, is the beast for you!" he pointed out.

From then on, that particular head of cattle belonged to her; she could sell it, give it away, or kill it for a feast day. By specifying a beast in her honor, Solomon had committed himself to an essential form of the native ritual of official and recognized marriage. Christina was a wife with a definite place in the kraal.

She fetched and carried wood, cooked, tended fires, washed clothes at the bank of the stream, ironed, polished boots, swept the hut, and performed not only personal service but all the housewifely duties of the royal hut. She was busy from dawn to dusk, but she had never been idle, and now every task was glorified with love and the privilege of service to the King.

Christina and Solomon continued to live alone, their intimacy close, passionate, and friendly, with never a moment of discord.

Yet Solomon was seeking other women. The implications were perfectly clear to Christina but she had been trained to believe that even a flicker of jealousy was disloyal to her King. And, if she was jealous, even she was unaware of it.

"I am going to fetch one of my girls," Solomon said one day. "Men will go for her and bring her to me. She is Nqothi's daughter, of the Mambatheni people."

Upon her return from the river bank, Christina found the girl in the hut. She was just an ordinary *'bayi*, wearing a shawl clasped over one shoulder, one breast pendant, exposed. The two women shook hands, and no one could have detected anything but cordiality in their manner.

Christina busied herself about her normal routine, the preparation of food. A strange numbness had come over her, her tasks seemingly doing themselves. The young man who usually carried the food from the cooking to the royal hut went forward with it. For the first time in two months Christina did not join Solomon, but waited to be called.

When Solomon had eaten he sent for her.

"I want you to prepare the mats," he said abruptly. "You are to sleep upon the bed, and Nqothi and I will sleep on the floor."

Two months of idyllic happiness and then this! Yet she moved expertly, unemotionally, making the hut ready for the night. She unrolled the mats and unmade the bed, tenderly folding the spread so dear to her. Solomon remained waiting outside. Nqothi crouched upon the floor in a dark corner, scowling, neither offering to help nor speaking. Christina ignored her.

Solomon stripped himself naked, while Christina picked up his clothes and neatly folded them upon the chair. It was as if Nqothi were not there. The light of the candles cast shadows in the hut, which flickered and died suddenly when Solomon snuffed them out.

"Here, girl!" He did not even use her name! "Come here and lie beside me. We are ready for the night. Christina is going to remain with us."

From the floor in the darkness came little cries of passion. Nqothi was an experienced girl. There was no fear there, just animal excitement and pleasure.

Long Christina lay there reminding herself: "Maphelu told me this. Maphelu said he would bring other girls to his hut; that was the King's privilege. He, himself, told me he would have other girls. No, I am not jealous, I am the King's wife. I am sleeping upon the bed, and that girl is upon the floor. He has not shut me out, even from this. He will not separate himself from me. He will let me stay with him at all times. He will do nothing in concealment. I will always know about him and his girls."

Hardly had these thoughts run through her mind, hardly had she composed herself to enforced sleep, when she felt the blanket stir beside her and Solomon's hands groping for her, and though he had already slaked his passion and she had envisaged every detail of it, it was as though it had not happened, for he was crushing her to him as he had done every night these two months past. Nqothi no longer mattered. The King was finding peace and surcease with the woman he loved.

As time went on Solomon brought more girls to the hut. Regardless of whom he took he always wanted to come back to her, uppermost in his mind and heart was Christina.

Sometimes the girl at his side would experience an uncontrollable frenzy that would fill her with resentment and anger. Sensing that her hostility was directed principally against Christina, if he were not yet overcome by the fumes of beer, he would sternly reprove her: "There you are, a girl jealous already." He would fling her aside and go to Christina.

All this feminine rivalry pleased and excited him. A lurking vanity had begun to magnify within him. But he enjoyed a new and deeper intimacy with Christina, which seemed to wall them in more closely if another woman were present.

He appreciated the tangle of emotion, the complexity of feeling he was arousing. He knew full well he was going contrary to native custom in insisting that a woman give herself to him in the presence of another. Ordinarily a native wife had her own hut where her husband visited her, or the husband sent for his wives in turn to come to his hut.

Concubinage was different from marriage, and every Zulu man recognized the fine distinction between the two. Just where Zulu etiquette prescribes formal engagement preparatory to marriage, as against concubinage pure and simple, it would be difficult to say.

When a simple native courted a girl, he gave all his time and attention to her, even though shortly thereafter he might concentrate upon another. A Zulu man may be engaged to as many girls as he can get, but a Zulu girl may be engaged to only one man at a time. Nevertheless, a girl was flattered by the attentions of the King, though she knew she was to be deprived of the exclusive devotion due her in courtship.

Solomon honored a house by taking a girl from it, for at any time he might raise the status to marriage and bind himself to that house in political alliance. Some of the girls were ambitious, inheriting the political sagacity and shrewdness of their men. They were willing to gamble on the chance they might be mother to a king, and they deliberately set out to captivate the King, in hope that he would marry them.

All through these first months of their married life Solomon kept getting engaged, until finally it seemed to Christina that the kraal was overrun with girls. In all truth she could not keep track of them, could not remember their faces or their names. She did not realize she did not want to.

Sometimes the girls were neither experienced nor ambitious, but simple-minded, unaffected, and reminiscent of Christina when she first met Solomon, young and frightened as she had been. The night Solomon brought the little girl from Babanango, Christina lay upon her bed rigid with cold terror.

Suddenly she remembered her God. Not for months had she prayed to Him, but now she lay there in the dark and appealed to Him: "If only You will tell her, God, that soon it will be right; that she will come to love him. God, I cannot get off this bed and go to her, but even though she is a *'bayi* girl and knows nothing of You, come to her in this moment when she needs you."

Christina fell asleep to the rhythm of heaving sobs. Next morning she spoke to the girl with maternal tenderness, though she herself was not yet sixteen.

"Believe in the King. He is kind and good and will love you. You must do as he tells you, and then peace will come to your heart, and a great happiness will come to your body."

Not many nights later, another fresh, untouched girl lay beside Solomon. They were engaged in a fierce battle, for though she was young, she was strong and a match for him. She bit, scratched, kicked, and fought him off, until he became enraged and slapped her thighs sharply. The girl screamed and fell down sobbing beside him.

Christina was no longer troubled. For the first time, she, who had been kind, listened with delight to the girl's sobbing surrender. This girl had said cutting things about her that had made the other girls laugh.

Had her mother been watching over her that night, it would have been to note with dismay and pity that the poison she feared had begun to work its slow corrosion.

seven

"**N**ot only am I marrying this girl, but so are you," Solomon was telling Christina, as he nodded at the strange girl who stood beside him. "*We* are making her our wife. You and she will be brothers, and will divide between you the work of looking after me."

Members of a tribe, or relatives, are referred to as *abafowabo*—brothers. Girls attached to the King are, therefore, called brothers, too.

"I want you and Mbatha to be good friends, as my wives should be," Solomon admonished paternally. "I do not want you to quarrel. If you do I shall punish you. This kraal is full of wickedness and intrigue. The others are all jealous of my affection for you, Christina, and your loyalty to me. They will try to set you two against each other because Mbatha is from a strange land, and they are always afraid of strangers. She does not know anyone here, and she will feel as homesick and awkward as you did. I want you to make her feel at all times that she is welcome."

For one long moment the two wives took each other's measure. As the senior wife, Christina spoke first.

"Mbatha, you are coming to be the King's and my wife," she parroted, but added independently, "I shall try to treat you kindly. But if you do not treat me as you should, I'll ignore you and carry on with my work of tending my husband. If you give me the respect that is due me, an older wife of longer standing, I shall remember it and you will have nothing to fear from me."

"The King has already told me about you, that you live with him in his hut, that you are not a quarrelsome person, nor jealous, nor unkind, that if I make a friend of you I will not be sorry. I shall try to do your bidding in every way," Mbatha replied without hesitation.

Mbatha joined Christina and Solomon in their hut. Some nights Solomon would sleep with her on the floor, other nights with Christina upon the bed. Then again he remained with Mbatha the whole night through, and on these nights Christina would repeat to herself: "No, I am not jealous; I am not afraid of his showing favor to anyone else, for after all he always keeps me with him. I am better in his affection than anyone."

Eight months after she came to the kraal Christina became pregnant. As she grew heavy with child she found it difficult to do the many things expected of her. She was becoming short of breath and slower in her movements, when Solomon called her to his side.

"I am going to have a special hut built for you, to which you will go when the time is ripe for you to have your child. I will see that you are properly looked after," he assured her tenderly, as his caressing hands roved over her. "Meanwhile, it would be well if you were to teach Mbatha what all my needs are, and what will be expected of her when she remains alone with me."

A shudder of apprehension passed through her, but it was only momentary, and she did not show it.

Women busied themselves thatching Christina's hut, for she was no longer well enough to be of any material assistance. What pleased her most was that her hut was prepared as carefully as Solomon's had been, and the floor, on orders from him, was as highly polished as his.

What she did not know was that with each motion of the greased stone, as the women polished slowly and surely across that floor, they tried to weave in a curse upon her hut. Other women had prepared their own floors, and they saw no reason why this girl should be pampered in such a silly way.

Solomon had purchased European and native medicines for Christina to ease the birth of her child. As she began to feel occasional shooting pains, and was racked with recurrent nausea, he hastened to the doctor to get her still other ones, for it was strange that she should be so ill at this time. She would cry out with pain at night, and having learned to listen for these interruptions in her breathing, he would drop the other girl, even if he were in the midst of an exciting moment, and rush to her.

If Mbatha resented this, she never showed it, never called him to return to her, never spoke of it to Christina. Nor was Christina deliberately trying to attract her husband by a new technique; she was genuinely sick.

"The pain will go. Do not be afraid," he would whisper lovingly as he held her close. Natives are accustomed to childbirth as incidental to married life and the needs of the race, but he sensed the foreboding and fear in her, and tried to comfort her. Neither of them realized that his solicitude was in any way unusual.

Christina sat while she gave Mbatha her final instructions; it made her dizzy to stand.

"Here are the keys for everything," she enumerated, "for the cooking hut, the supplies, the clothes closet, the cupboard. Never leave the King's cupboard or his cooking hut unlocked. Someone might get in and poison the food or dishes."

Overwhelmed with her responsibility for the safety of the King, Mbatha merely nodded.

"Here is the money which the King gives me to buy his food. He will need eggs, sugar, tea, rice and flour," she listed methodically, despite the pain. "If the King wants anything else he will tell you. He will expect you to remember very carefully how you have spent his money, and if he thinks that you are not watching your spending, he will never trust you again."

"Remember, also, that the King must never be left alone," she cautioned, to reemphasize the dangers ever surrounding him. "You and Zazeni between you are expected to guard the King. Zazeni always stands by outside, but whenever you leave the hut make sure that he is there. Otherwise, he will report that it was you who left the hut exposed to the King's enemies."

Zazeni's father had been a reputable and trustworthy body servant to Dinuzulu, and it was generally agreed that Solomon had chosen wisely to place the son in the same position in relation to himself.

"You will enjoy your new responsibility." A note of wistfulness crept in, "It is a great honor for you, and I hope that you live up to it. I shall expect you to look well after the King, even as I would have done."

Her last words to Mbatha were: "Go tell Solomon's mothers that I am on the point of giving birth." Then slowly she walked toward her hut.

In the average life of a native woman the words, "Her time is coming," have a prophetic significance. All the sadistic and cruel tendencies, the pent-up hatred and enmity of the older women break out when one of the younger brides is about to have a child. The women crowd around her, pin her taut upon the ground, bruising her arms and legs in their stranglehold, until the laboring mother becomes suffocated, and the child passes through her rigid body in a final agony.

No further proof of Solomon's love for Christina was needed than his concern about her confinement. Due to his specific insistence she was spared this violence of female revenge.

Just before dawn, just before her strength gave out, Christina gave birth to Solomon's first child, a daughter. It is hard to believe that despite the detailed preparations for her own hut, the knowledge that she was going to leave Solomon, the sight and feel of her own growing body, the child itself growing heavy and active within her, Christina was unable to grasp that all this really meant she was to have a child. Vaguely she was aware of physical changes taking place within her, but in no way did she translate them into what was to be their culmination. She knew as an isolated fact that she would have a baby, but it was impersonal, lacking in conviction and identification.

Not until she had bitten her lips and chewed her hands, rolled and tossed upon her mats in unattended travail, and the child came tearing through her, did she suddenly realize, in a spasm of fright, that there before her was the fact of childbirth, the consequential fact of her marriage.

The baby was born as Christina was half-kneeling, half running away.* Three old crones were watching, but did not dare touch her by order of the King. OkaSonkeshana, whom the King had appointed as special adviser, laid

---

* Compare here through p. 50 with the record of original interview, appendix 1B.—Eds.

Christina back upon the mats, anointed her with hot fat, bathed her stomach, and crooned little whispering admonitions of courage to her. She took the *uMntwana*—the baby—and laid it on the mattress beside Christina and assured her this was *her* child, and sent them both off together into a deep and contented slumber.

The mothers could be heard muttering amongst themselves and giving thanks, and though it was still night, Mbatha came hurrying over with Solomon's gifts, a packet of matches, candles, a small box of scented soap and some white flannel, which he wanted Christina to have the very instant she was able to use them.

They washed the baby with the soap, and wrapped it in the flannel. Then all three mothers, okaMtshekula, okaMthunza, and okaSonkeshana, left to notify the indunas formally that a daughter had been born to the King, and that they had witnessed that it was truly Christina's child and his.

At daybreak, only a few hours later, Christina got up and walked out of the hut. Mbatha followed her with water she had boiled, to wash away the blood upon her body. Meanwhile, the mothers hurriedly picked up the stained mats from the floor and removed them to be torn up and thrown into a hole and buried. A mattress was brought in that Solomon had sent, and when she reentered the hut Christina lay upon it.

The mothers had prepared coffee which they gave her to drink to regain her strength. For the first time Christina thought she saw kindliness upon the faces of these older women.

She awoke toward midday. She had slept soundly, as the natives say, "as a person who is dead."

Solomon, who had been away on tribal business, arrived unexpectedly a few days later. Some children playing saw him approaching the kraal and shouted: "Sibiya is nursing a child, holding a child to her."

Direct to his mothers' hut rode Solomon and demanded full details.

"Where are you going?" they called after him, as he ran from them.

"Straight away to see the child in the hut," he called back.

"No!" they shrieked indignantly. "It is not yet time. You must see it another day."

According to custom among royalty, a chief does not approach a hut where there has been a recent birth.

Angry, as always when crossed, he retorted: "This is my child, not yours. I do not need to wait for a day of your choice in order to see it."

Perched uncomfortably on a box just outside Christina's door, he coaxed: "Mama, bring the child to the door, that I may see it."

"And you, Christina, where are you?" he whispered. The mothers motioned to her not to speak. "Christina, are you there?" he insisted. "Christina, is this the child that you gave birth to? Is this your child?"

She was too weak to answer, but he persisted.

"But you said you were only a child. And being a child could not have a child. What is this?" By now his voice was a teasing roar of laughter.

"Give the child to Christina, and let me see her hold it in her arms," he begged one of the mothers.

Christina recognized the urgency in his voice, and no power or custom could stop her. Tenderness illuminated his face as he saw her with her baby cuddled against her. "I am so very thankful that you have come through so well," he murmured, sighing with relief. "I had not expected so successful a birth."

Atingle with the knowledge of his protective love for her, she contentedly drowsed off again.

Solomon sent Mbatha running over with a small flask of whiskey. It was Christina's first whiskey, the first hard liquor she had ever drunk. The King himself had been introduced to "White Man's Liquor" only a short while before.

As befitted this special occasion, Solomon proffered beer and waved okaSonkeshana, okaMtshekula, and okaMthunza to seats about him. In turn, he asked each one to report meticulously what had taken place from the time Christina had entered her hut. Satisfied the child was indeed hers, and that his wife had in no way been harmed by the malice or overzealous attention of his mothers, he relaxed as if a burden had been removed from him.

"You had best kill a beast in her honor, for according to our people, a beast should be killed on the birth of the first child," one of them suggested.

"I have already attended to that," he interrupted impatiently.

He had more original ideas to report. "I have decided on the name of my child; it shall be 'Velangokubonga.'"

A Zulu child's name has a distinct significance. The Zulus began calling Solomon, Ndabezitha, "the salute," in colloquial usage comparable to our "Sir." The child was born at the peak of his importance, and so Solomon named it Velangokubonga, "the child arrives with salutes!"

He wrote this name on a piece of paper, and sent it to Christina, informing her this was what he had named *his* child. She replied by note thanking him for naming *her* child.

When it was quite dark, and the mothers gone, Solomon knocked upon Christina's door. She was alone, and it startled her. Custom forbade his entering but he sat at the threshold.

"Tell me, is there anything you need, or would like to have?" he urged. "The first thing in the morning when I get up, I'll send to the store for it. I'll send you some paper to make a list of whatever you would like, or whatever is required. If you do not put down everything, I, myself, will add whatever I can think of. It would be so much easier if you would save me the trouble of having to worry my head."

Her list included towels and soap for the child, rice, flour, coffee, candles, and soap for herself. To this, Solomon added two shawls for the child, a blanket rug for her, potatoes, curry, beans, mealies, baking powder, sugar, and a packet of chocolate.

Despite their disapproval, the mothers did not openly object when Solomon came to take his child. It was futile to oppose him and demand that he wait the customary ten days. "Look here, what I've got!" he shouted to the men who accompanied him wherever he went. "Look and see me with my child in my arms!"

He was the hero. He, Solomon, the King, with his firstborn in his arms! Excitement, laughter, and joy mounted in him. But sentiment, too, flowed warmly through him as he asked, "May I kiss it?"

The mothers sternly forbade him, but it was obvious they were only teasing.

"The mother kisses it. Why shouldn't I, the father, kiss it?" he demanded in mock petulance.

Gently he placed a kiss upon what little of the baby's cheek emerged from the flannel swaddling. The supplies he had ordered were brought in, and he opened the packages himself, undid the small shawl, and wrapped the child in it. Still snuggling it closely against him, he asked Christina: "Would you prefer beef to the goat that was killed for you?"

"No, I have not yet felt any desire for beef."

In these few words, there was a depth of meaning. Everyone understood that Solomon had asked Christina if there was anything more his love could do for her. Her answer had been that her cup was full, that there was nothing she wanted.

"If Christina should want beer, give it to her. If she wants anything else, give it to her. I want her to have anything she wants."

So did he give public proof of his confidence in her, and his certainty that she would not abuse it.

eight

"**S**ibiya's mother is coming to the kraal!" the children shouted.

There is a native custom that a person who has been traveling a great distance must not enter the hut of a newborn child, lest the foreign air hovering over people passed on the journey may affect the child harmfully. After a two hours' wait, it was considered safe for Elizabeth and her daughter Beauty to approach Christina.

While Elizabeth was still mumbling prayers of thanks over Christina, hugging and kissing her, and crying intermittently, the King appeared in the doorway.

"We see you, Mother," he greeted.

"Yes, Ndabezitha," she replied with respect.

"Now that you see the child Christina is nursing, are you still displeased and unhappy?"

"No! Ndabezitha, I am full of gratitude," she honestly admitted. "All the worry I had about the agony Christina would have in giving birth, seeing that she herself is only a child, has vanished."

The King ordered beer for them, and Christina and her mother were left alone.

"Give the child to me, and let me look at it," commanded Elizabeth. It was not well for a woman to remember her pain at childbirth, and she did not mention it again.

Caressing the child, she looked fondly at her daughter. "I now forgive everything," she said. "I am happy for you, and for me. Give me your hand in both of mine, and in my handclasp you feel that all my soreness of heart has vanished."

OkaSonkeshana was inquiring politely of Elizabeth about her journey when Solomon again stood in the doorway. "Christina, come outside to me!" he demanded.

OkaSonkeshana interrupted indignantly. "Christina, I forbid you to go to him. It is not right for you to go outside as yet."

Both Elizabeth and Christina accepted the fact that it was to okaSonkeshana she now owed obedience.

"If your mother refuses to let you go, have your sister come out," countered Solomon.

Beauty dutifully joined Solomon and his attendant, the cattle killer, who took her with them to the cattle kraal and pointed out a beast for her and her mother. A mother may not eat at her daughter's kraal before a beast is killed in her honor. Solomon was so prompt and considerate about this that all the women spoke of it.

Elizabeth brought Christina two mats that she, herself, had made, and Beauty, the little sister, laid on the bed a woolen bonnet, socks, and three small dresses. These she had bartered for her services to the missionary's wife who made them.

The child was now eleven days old, and Christina was getting stronger, was even able to go down to the river and bathe, but she was still considered not quite well enough to be left alone in her hut at night. While Elizabeth was there, the other mothers moved out.

Elizabeth stayed for four days. She and Christina chatted ceaselessly about the baby, Christina's hope that some day it would be wondrous to look upon like its father, of the joy she had in serving her loving husband, of the comfort Elizabeth now had in knowing her daughter was fulfilling her destiny in marriage to a good, kind man.

Solomon sent for Hezekiah to pay the cattle due him on Christina. Hezekiah arrived, accompanied by Christina's brother Abiot, and Solomon showed them the six head of good breed that were to be theirs. Three were heifers, and three young bulls. Hezekiah, out of respect and appreciation of an alliance with the royal house, did not want to bargain but Abiot demanded that the King pay fifteen head, the traditional lobola.

Solomon agreed, but only gave the six on account, and promised that at a future date the others would be presented. They never were! Years later this point of incomplete lobola was to have a far-reaching significance. The Zulus would have said they were "beasts paid by mouth," and not "beasts paid on their feet," the distinction between a credit and cash transaction.

The cattle given to Hezekiah and his son were out of Solomon's father's estate, which was indication that Christina was a wife of the first rank, that her issue were eligible to the succession. Had Solomon purchased her with cattle belonging to his own estate, not inherited cattle, she would have belonged to a lesser, or auxiliary house, and her sons could never have been eligible for either kingship or high tribal rank.

After Elizabeth had gone, okaSonkeshana, and another mother rejoined Christina to help look after the child. Gradually Christina's vitality returned and she again took up her duties at the King's hut. Three months after the birth of her child the King began to visit Christina in her own hut, always after dark, when she was alone.

Almost invariably, from now on, Solomon received girls in pairs, perhaps because he feared to be left alone with one of them, but possibly because he could only create the excitement that had become so necessary to him by pitting one against the other in jealousy and anger.

Two girls served as a protection against each other. Never was the King free from fear of poisoning. Zulu poisons are concocted in secret and administered in treachery and for murder. Undoubtedly he also feared the innumerable potions and love philters with which each woman might try to bewitch him.

Since competition in love is keen, and wives guard against each other, and the husband strives to protect himself against them all, when a young woman is about to marry, her father sends her to the *inyanga*—the witch doctor—to get perfumes, essences, fats, and other beauty accessories. The *inyanga* also provides her with love philters, secret potions and devices by which she can hold her husband's love. Unmarried women bootleg these love philters.

Some love philters are eaten, some rubbed into the body. Some are taken for personal effect, others secretly fed to the loved one. The general practice is the same, but each *inyanga* claims special and favorite essences. Men or women are the venerated practitioners, each of whom has served an apprenticeship under older and more established ones. Successors are chosen with great care, grudgingly or under pressure, or because their known ability and interest in this specialized field is recognized.

Girls' names were on everybody's tongue. No matter how rapidly Solomon acquired new connections, or satisfied passing fancies, the members of his kraal kept abreast of them. The day would come when this would irritate him almost to a frenzy, but so far he recognized he was their hero, and as such, all their stories and dreams had to be woven around him.

Solomon seldom saw Christina alone, except at night, and then they were preoccupied with fulfillment rather than analysis of emotion. She sensed that he was sorry for her, and that he wanted to reassure her that he was still devoted. With three women in his hut in steady attendance upon him it was only rarely, and but for a few minutes, that he could get away. No longer was he able to spend the night holding her to him.

"Do you ever long for me, when you are alone?" he would ask her.

"No, I do not long for you, now that I have another I love so well," Christina would say.

Was he afraid of losing his hold upon her? Was he jealous of his own daughter? Repeatedly he would ply her with the same questions implying that she must be lonely, and always she would insist: "No, I am not lonely now; not very much, because I have my child. I am so fond of her."

Never did she show undue emotion, or let him suspect she was not perfectly satisfied. "I seem even happier in advance for what may happen to me than I was before," she said once. "Now that I have the child I am made happy by the two of you."

Mbatha and two other girls shared the King's hut with him. Christina was head of this working squad, but she also tended him personally, set his food before him, directed the other girls at their work, and again handled the money and the keys to the cupboard. She worked inside the hut, the others outside, and whatever intimacy they each had with Solomon was fragmentary and at his express bidding.

Solomon began to call Christina to spend half the night with him at his own hut. Her motherhood had matured her, and she would turn her face away from the other girls as he held her in violent embrace. With the eyes of other women riveted upon her, she grew rigid with self-consciousness. Ever sensitive to all her reactions, he was aware of her tension and sometimes he would curtly order the others to leave. They could not show their resentment, but once out of sight, they would give vent to their feelings. Next morning Christina would find herself a target of taunts and insults.

"I am now two months with child," Mbatha blurted out one day.

With her pregnancy Mbatha abruptly changed to moods of constant irritation and hatred. "He does this for you, and that for you, and what does he do for me?" There was not a day that she did not complain to Christina. "He does not care for me or my child that is to come. He thinks only of you."

The other wives would egg Mbatha on. Solomon's hut, which had been a haven of love and harmony, became a place in which Christina moved with lips tightly set, and ears pretending not to hear. Mbatha reiterated bitterly that the preparations for her confinement were not the same as for Christina's, and used this general premise to point up every slight and imagined grievance. Each time she complained Christina would mutter: "I will ask the King why he made this difference."

But when the King and she were alone she hesitated to mention it for she had not yet learned to discuss petty matters with him. However, the nagging of the women became intolerable. "This person who has to cut her own grass, is she to be worrying me and making me tired?" she finally asked him. "She wants to know why I did not have to cut my grass as she has to."

The King saw neither treachery nor meanness in her face. He had noted the sullen faces of the others, and he was aware that all was not well between his wives, but he thought it was some passing trivia that would adjust itself.

"I have told Mbatha to cut her own grass because there is a scarcity of labor at the kraal," he explained. "You will remember at the time when your hut had to be thatched it was not so very long after the cleansing ceremony, and many people had remained behind, who were drafted into my service."

"The mothers sent a lot of women out into the fields to cut grass, which was put away for future huts. Those natives were proud to clean the kraal and leave behind them their mark of respect for me. There is no more grass left, and if this girl is to have her own hut, she must cut her own grass and thatch her own hut, as women always do.

"I cannot understand all this nonsense. You know I have nothing to do with the building of your huts. That is my mothers' department. It was they who spoke to the indunas of the regiment about your needing a hut.

"I will send for Mbatha and have this out with her at once."

Solomon was furiously angry when Mbatha faced him.

"What have you been saying about Christina, about your hut and her hut?" he demanded.

Impassive, silent, her nervousness expressed itself in the small arc her toes kept marking.

"Why did you not come and ask me, instead of going to Christina and talking about it to the whole kraal?" he insisted.

Never again might she get another chance to present her grievance to the King. "When you built a hut for Christina, she did not have to do a single thing, but I have to go and cut my own grass," Mbatha burst forth.

"Suppose you do, why do you bother her," he sternly reproved. "If you have any complaints to make about how I act, you make them to me! If you have any questions to ask, you ask them of me." His voice was rising in ever increasing anger. "If you do not understand why I am behaving in a certain way, you come and ask me to tell you. Do you hear?"

It was with difficulty that Mbatha, who knew an answer was expected of her, managed to say: "I am afraid of you!"

If she expected any sympathy she was disappointed.

"Is Christina your shield behind which you plan to hide?" He paused a minute to let his words sink in, to give her a chance to answer him. But she was past replying.

"Do not think I am bringing you to trial about this," he continued, "I am having this out with your because I do not wish my wives to quarrel over me.

"I have already told you about Christina, and how I took her, a child, wholly ignorant of the ways of grown-up people. She had been brought up by the missionaries. She did not know how to cut grass, nor how to build a hut. You know how natives live; you are accustomed to work.

"This is the first hurt Christina has ever brought to me. I told you when you came here that you would have to respect and obey her. She has never said anything harmful of you to me nor to anyone in the kraal. Yet I know that you have been gossiping and stirring up trouble for her.

"I will not have that! I have explained everything to you and I shall expect you hereafter to live in peace with Christina, and do nothing that may offend or hurt her.

"You will go from here and tell her what I have had to say. As long as you behave yourself you will find in me a friend, but if I hear anything further about this, you will be sorry for it!"

Mbatha's vanity had been fully satisfied by so much special attention from the King, even if it were a scolding, for he had taken pains to explain his conduct to her, a humble handmaiden of his kraal. What if it were prompted by a desire to make Christina's life more peaceful and harmonious.

Her apology was sincere and brief: "Forgive me, Christina, for having been so hasty in my thoughts about you."

Mbatha completed her hut and gave birth to her baby there. The birth was an easy one, and word spread about the kraal at midmorning that Solomon was the father of his firstborn son.

When the mothers reported to him the child had come, Solomon sent for candles, soap, and some flannel for Mbatha. It did not pass unnoticed that at the time of Christina's confinement he had kept soap and candles carefully locked away in the cupboard to be at hand when needed, yet for this wife, he had nothing ready.

Ten days later Solomon visited Mbatha and her child. Casually he gave her a pound and told her to buy whatever she needed. He did not arrange for the purchases himself, as he had done with Christina. One of the kraal messengers did her errand, so that jealousy and anger were again rising within her.

Several days later, as Christina and Mbatha appeared before him, Solomon held and fondled each of the babies in turn.

"I have decided on the name for my son. He shall be called uPhikokwaziwayo," he announced.

The name meant the denial of things that are known, or literally, to argue about a thing that is known. *Ukuphika* means "to argue," *oku* "that which," and *aziwayo* "is known." He named his son uPhikokwaziwayo because it rankled within him that some of the tribe favored his brother David, denying the known fact that he, Solomon, was the appointed heir of Dinuzulu. Solomon never forgot those who acknowledged his kingship and came saluting him, the name he gave Christina's child, and those who tried to deny him, the name he gave Mbatha's child. The name given to his second child concerned itself with that which was still uppermost in his heart and mind, the struggle to gain and maintain his position.

As the men gathered over their beer, Solomon informed them of his son's name. The head induna, Buthelezi, casually inquired: "What do these names of yours signify?"

Everyone knew this for defiance. Buthelezi had not favored Solomon, and stirrings of the old intrigue flared between them.

"It would be well for you, Buthelezi, to learn the names of my children and never forget them!" Each word cut through the breathless hush. "'The denial of things that are known,' and 'Arrives with salutations.' When I next see you, I shall ask you to tell me their names, Buthelezi!"

nine

Buthelezi's taunt and show of independence was a sign of the opposition to the uSuthu that had not yet died out. For generations the two main factions of the royal Zulus, the Mandlakazi and the uSuthu, had been embroiled in ceaseless battle.

Zibhebu had been the gallant leader of the finally defeated and routed Mandlakazi. His heir, Bokwe, had little power or influence, but that little was not to be overlooked. If Solomon were to consolidate his position among his own tribe, the uSuthu, and permanently triumph over the Mandlakazi, the strategic place to establish the royal kraal would be near Nongoma in the hills of Northern Zululand, where Zibhebu had lived, where Bokwe now lived, and where the activities of the Mandlakazi naturally centered. This he planned to do, and take Christina with him.

At an average distance of twenty miles, a good day's travel for horses, the King would have a wife and growing family, where he was always sure of a loyal welcome and an established, restful relationship. Though the King could tarry where he wished, command the attention of whom he pleased, he could lay claims only to that land and those womenfolk who rightfully belonged to him by definite agreement, inheritance, barter, or purchase. A wise King made alliances all over the countryside, taking care that he set up his own kraals, not only among his enemies but in the midst of his friendly allies.

In two years Solomon had visited many of the kraals inherited from his father, conferred with innumerable of his head men and chiefs, and cemented a substantial number of friendships.

But he looked back upon a trail of conspiracy, rebellion, and treachery. Two resolutions emerged to which he remained faithful throughout his life, within the limitations of his temperament: to give unqualified support to the white man's government, and to win behind him a united Zulu nation.

The South African government, which reputedly made Solomon an allowance of £600 a year, was backing him as the choice of his people, but many of its leaders privately believed the Zulus had a King unable to live up to the past glory and opportunity of his position. Among many Zulu statesmen Solomon was suspected of a bravado front masking fundamental weakness.

The population of South Africa, of which Zululand is a part, is overwhelmingly native: about 6,500,000 natives, to 2,000,000 Europeans, and but 750,000 colored, and 200,000 Indians.

Manual labor is considered "infradig" for Europeans. Domestic service is largely performed by natives, and so is practically all unskilled labor. Translated into everyday terms it means that a housepainter is white but a native boy goes along to carry his bucket of paint; that a poor white farmer, unable to employ native help, sits on his stoep and watches his crop rot rather than harvest it; that all work is involved in a caste system based on race, and that the white structure of economy depends on a continuity of a native labor supply.

Gold is South Africa's chief source of income and wealth. The gold mines at the Rand in Johannesburg require several hundred thousand men a year, but the urgent need for native labor has not historically coincided with the native's desire to seek work outside his own territory. Natives preferred to remain at home and live as they had for centuries.

Early in the nineteen hundreds the Rand mines imported Chinese labor, of whom about half deserted, though it was a criminal offense. In the neighboring province of Natal, sugar planters had created a problem dating back many more years by importing indentured Indian servants to work in the cane fields. Mohandas Gandhi, a successful lawyer of the Transvaal, became an impassioned leader of the Indian cause in South Africa, and until recently his son remained behind in Natal to carry on his famous father's work.

South Africa came to the belated conclusion it must draw on its own labor supply. The Chamber of Mines, representing the mining industry, developed a recruiting system capable of organizing and handling several hundred thousand men annually. Transportation, tariffs, terms and validity of contracts, rates of pay, housing quarters, medical inspection, sanitation, diet, wages, work schedules, are all subject to government supervision.

Natives usually work underground where native police and indunas assist in the maintenance of discipline, where the very physical atmosphere contributes to the possibility of occasional abuse and assault. Inevitably there is bribery and favoritism. Offenses are punishable by severe fines, deductible from wages. Such deductions are noted by fathers and brothers at home, who pool their earnings, and by the chiefs, who depend on these wages for cash income to maintain the tribal hierarchy. The chiefs institute their own methods of discouraging tribal lapses.

The mines permit their men occasional absences of an evening or a night, not long enough to travel hundreds of miles home, but enough to permit indulgence in drunkenness, prostitution, or homosexuality. Compounds, barracks packed with tens of thousands of men, are womanless, and the period of employment runs for many months. Wherever possible men of neighboring or the same tribes are segregated to live and work together, but simple tribal relationships are not always strong enough to compensate for the loss of normal satisfactions.

Permission to leave is controlled by a pass system. Each man has a paper similar to a passport and is a definite cog in a highly centralized, police-patrolled, working army.

Solomon was a familiar figure to the mining industry. Frequently when unrest was threatened he was sent for to address large gatherings of his people. In his honor, thousands of natives sang and danced, gave an incomparable performance, accompanied by a hundred-piece orchestra of pianos, drums, and wind instruments fashioned from discarded petrol cans. Unbelievably fantastic, truly magnificent, and inspiringly beautiful to the performers and others privileged to see it, this traditional expression of tribal unity served to counteract any seeds of rebellion.

Tribal organization is of profound importance to the whole European economic structure, and the head of the Zulu nation is, therefore, to be assiduously cultivated as a source of stable labor supply, and a symbol of authority. The King is the base of an established status quo in a rapidly changing world. He, like the British monarch, represents to his people, loyalty, tradition, responsibility to the nation, a fixed place for that nation, and for each member of it. With the weakening of the King may come tribal chaos which will be instantly disastrous to the European community. Consequently, Europeans, as well as the Zulus, kept in close touch with Solomon's daily activities, and were to show increasing anxiety at his unprecedented preoccupation with frivolity and pleasure.

Christina overheard the mothers discussing Solomon's plans for her departure to Nongoma with him, and her heart froze within her. Never before had she sought out Solomon, but this time she went directly to him.

"You are taking me with you to Nongoma. You said nothing of this to me," she upbraided him. "I will not leave a child so small!"

"The child will be all right." There was almost pleading in his voice. "It is going to remain with one of my mothers. OkaNdemele will look after it as if it were her own."

She temporized, fear still clutching at her heart, "It would be better if the child were able to walk. But it is too small for me to leave it now." Anything rather than face the flat order of separation.

The intensity of her feeling touched him. "I will think it over," he promised.

That was her dismissal, and mechanically, her eyes unseeing, she hurried away to the mothers, tears pouring down her face, her voice choked with sobs.

"Help me! Oh, help me!" she sobbed. "Do not let the King take me away from my child!"

Whatever the younger women of the kraal gained in protection, comfort, or pleasure, they owed to the united front the mothers made on their behalf. Passion had once been important, but it had been years since any of them had moments of it granted to them. Their only happiness came from their children, and in their friendships with each other.

Custom compelled formal allegiance to their men and to their King, but their hearts were with the women. Some of them had resented Christina; for they invariably allied themselves with the neglected of their sex. But they had agreed she had little in common with other favorites, never indulged in petty tyranny, was simple and kind, and wrapped in a haze of love for her husband. In appealing to them Christina acknowledged her first lack of confidence in her own influence upon her husband.

"Do not despair," okaSonkeshana tried to pacify her. "I will go to the King and speak to him on your behalf. I will take you," gesturing to one of the mothers, "and you," nodding to another, "because the King listens to you. We will tell him that we are taking the part of Christina in this matter."

Three black-shrouded figures stood before the King, their very rigidity an indication that there was trouble among the women of his kraal. "What brings you here, my mothers?" he inquired pleasantly.

"Solomon, our son, we want to know what has upset you?" There was no royal courtesy in okaSonkeshana's voice. "What is it that is worrying you? What is it that Christina has done against you? Why do you see fit to separate her from her child, when the child is yet so young?"

"Ah, so that is it!" flashed through his mind. "They're planning to rebel against my orders, to thwart me. What has set them off?" But he said aloud: "Mothers, I refuse to leave Christina behind. She is the one who knows how to cook for me, wash for me, write for me. She knows all her work thoroughly."

Ask a Zulu who is his favorite wife, and he will deny there is one, but ask him which of his wives is the best cook, and he will name her. Depend on it, she is the favorite. Usually she has sound business acumen, too, and her husband consults her on the sale of cattle.

"You have other girls who are *kholwas*, that can be of use to you, at the uSuthu," okaSonkeshana suggested.

Furiously angry, Solomon stalked out of the hut. Later he sent for Christina. Before she stepped across the threshold he demanded: "Why did you refuse to go with me? Who is going to look after me, attend to me, care for me? Who will serve me when we are apart?" His questions were merely to relieve his rage. "I am leaving tomorrow, and I plan to take you with me!"

Pride is a dominant trait in the Zulu character. It has carried many a Zulu woman through situations that women of other races would have crumpled under. In this moment Christina forgot all the conventions. For the first time she looked straight up into Solomon's face.

"I beg you," she urged with a passion he had never seen in her, "to let me remain until the child is a little older!"

What wisdom prompted her next statement? "I shall not be able to live in peace and gratitude with you, if I am separated from my helpless child."

He was so moved he did not notice the latent threat in her words.

"I feel the same as you about the child," he argued. "It is *my* child as well as *yours*. I shall not forget it. I love it just as you do."

All her forces had been gathered for her plea, and she was losing. The tension snapped; she stood before him racked with uncontrollable sobs. Surely Solomon loved Christina, for though accustomed to unquestioning obedience, his voice came like a caress. "I will not say that I am definitely taking you with me."

Christina spent the next twenty-four hours in a daze, hugging her child to her, crying almost without stopping, and even Mbatha who had hated her was moved to pity. Not until Solomon was almost ready to mount his horse did she know his decision.

"You are remaining here with your child," he told her. "Not for always, nor do I know for how long. I am still going to think it over."

Gratitude overwhelmed her, and she barely heard his next words.

"Here are three pounds for you, which will cover anything that you and the child may require while I am away. Here are one pound, ten, which you will give to Mbatha for her and her child's needs."

If money were evidence, Christina was still leading in the King's affections. When she remembered her manners, she murmured thanks to a receding back.

Warmed by the knowledge that the child was still with her, due to Solomon's kindness, Christina's first doubts about her behavior, her first anxiety about her marital relations which she had taken for granted, began to disturb her. Emotional insecurity was bewildering and unfamiliar to her, and the women of the kraal soon began to whisper among themselves that she looked sick, that something had gone wrong with her.

There was so little to do when the King was away, Christina missed him, more by day than by night. That, too, was a new development of which she was not aware. The days became a dull ache, broken by a letter from him to send some things he had left behind, with the assurance he "respected her feeling for her child and her duty to it while it was so young," and the promise he would not disturb her for three months. He sent his *imikhonzo* —regards—to all his girls.

Toward nightfall some days later, when Solomon returned unexpectedly, he called to him the two girls who had been living in his hut, and deliberately ignored Christina. The next night he called some visiting girls. As the week progressed, the kraal began an orgy of feasting and drinking such as Christina had never before witnessed.

Christina went about her duties as usual. Her dearest wish, to remain with her child, had been granted, yet her heart was heavy. The emptiness of the days before Solomon's arrival, instead of vanishing, had increased.

Always a little drunk nowadays, Solomon probably was a little more so when he boasted to her: "I have taken four more girls for myself at Nongoma and two of them are with child."

"You take so many women in one year," she answered impulsively.

Automatically he tried to comfort her, for she seemed so troubled, "There is no harm in that."

Passion was stirring in her; the physical and psychical release that had come with nursing her child had long since gone. At the peak of longing for her husband, she found him preoccupied with other women. Nevertheless, it seemed to her she resented his unfairness to all of his women as much as to herself.

"So many women in so short a time!" she thought. "My spirit no longer leaps from mountain peak to mountain peak, but it is down in the valley. Where will the taking of all these women lead?

"It would not be so hard if I had two children. But here, all in one year, at the Zibindini kraal, he has had four women. Two of them are with child. And four women, two of them with child, at Nongoma."

According to Zulu custom the right time to start another child is when the older child can run about. The women of the kraal swear at a woman if she has children too often and say, "Oh, she doesn't *khulisa*; she will have too many weeds." No one knows when the Zulu custom of birth control— *ukukhulisa*—first came into existence. All Zulu women practice it, usually by making a packing of the woolly hair from their headdress. To *khulisa* means you wish to give your children a chance to grow strong and healthy, that you do not want one child growing inside of you and one at the breast.

Christina's thoughts refused to be curbed.

"What of these other women? They, too, are ready to be pregnant, but he pays no attention to them. I should have had two children, but I find myself with only one. Yet he spends his time with other women who are already with child.

"He does as he pleases. He does not think or care about us. He is not just. He does not take us in turn. There will be no end to these new women.

"He cannot satisfy the love of a growing number of women," she would cry out to the dark night. "If only he were a man of humbler rank, and had only a few wives, four or five. This large number already, and still more, and more! What will happen to us all?"

She was beginning to formulate a philosophy. "One person cannot love so many people, cannot even carry the same love for two people, each with an equal amount. Each wife never has an equal amount of love. Even when there are only two wives, one has more love than the other. There is always a favorite."

If she suspected, she did not fully admit even to herself that she, who had once been the favorite, was losing ground.

When Solomon was about to leave, and clasped her to him as if he craved the peace which he never failed to find in her, all her doubt and hurt melted away. That night, though alone, she fell asleep as soon as she touched the mat, with the comforting thought: "There is nothing in the law of love that he has broken with me. There is nothing that I can take fright at."

Gradually the anxiety about her child disappeared. The child was weaned, and ran about playing with the small son of Mbatha.

Christina no longer slept with her child. On orders from Solomon she spent her nights in his hut even though he was not there. He had sent to the Nobamba kraal for a daughter of an induna, okaNdemele, to look after Christina's child. Though okaNdemele was one of his mothers, she did not belong to the Zibindini kraal, and the mothers there resented this slight upon them. It was never explained why the King had chosen a mother of another kraal for this purpose. It may be that he feared the jealousy of mothers resident there, and he wished this child specially protected. That fear was prophetic.

OkaNdemele was given two pounds to buy necessities for herself and the child, and their housekeeping was set up independently. Christina missed her child, but she knew the time had come when she must choose between her child and her husband. With the addition of so many women to the King's household, her position of favorite was definitely threatened, and her opportunity to satisfy her passion and retain her hold upon her husband would come only if she were conspicuously available.

Two girls of the uSuthu kraal arrived to give birth to Solomon's children. Christina welcomed them, asking about their health and their journey, and expressing the hope that they would like it there. Solomon had given them a letter, ostensibly because they might come on a day when he was absent, but actually because he wished those of the kraal who knew how to read to see in black and white and pass it along the kraal grapevine, that he had instructed these girls to place themselves under Christina, to do her bidding in his service.

Had anyone seen these newly arrived wives busy at their tasks, they would have presented a picture of complete harmony and cooperation. Actually they were prepared to be enemies of all the wives, and felt kinship only for each other. "You wives here at the kraal do not begin to realize how many women the King already has, and how many he is planning to take," they taunted. "There are so many at the uSuthu, he cannot keep track of them. We know of four that arrived to stay before we left. They are not merely girls that have come for a visit. He has paid full lobola for two of the four, eleven head for one, and fifteen head for the other."

When Christina heard that two strangers had been fully paid for before they were even pregnant, while she, the first wife, had been but partially paid for, even though she had presented the King with a child, she knew the full tortures of insecurity.

Again she took her troubles to one of the mothers.

"I have to spit it out of my mouth," she exclaimed. "My anger and my hurt no longer let me keep it to myself!"

Other wives, and other girls, came often to ask that justice be secured for them. Most of the complaints had been against Christina; that the King took her so frequently, when in fairness it was their turn. The old crone knew a spasm of eager anticipation, but so strong is justice implanted in the heart of the Zulu that almost immediately she was metamorphosed into a dispassionate Goddess of Justice.

"It is the luck of this place, my daughter. Some people have the good fortune to have the full amount of their lobola paid, while others bring misfortune to their fathers because their lobola is not paid. After all it's the father's worry, not yours. Of course, the full amount of your lobola should have been paid, but my son loves you a great deal. It is only matter of cattle, and that is for the men to fight about.

"My son knows that you will not be any different, nor will your father bother him if he waits still another while before he pays it. Do not trouble your head about this," she advised.

As Christina served the King she waited tensely for him to tell her of his new marriages, as he had done the first time. But he waited for her to broach the subject.

Solomon had become more cunning in his ways with women. Whenever he came to the kraal he first pried loose from the mothers all essential information about his wives, a sort of barometer chart of their feeling toward him and each other. He had already heard that Christina was disturbed because he had paid for other wives and not for her, and he still cared enough for her to want to know how she felt at all times. Impatient and curious of her reaction, he finally blurted out: "I have taken two more wives, and paid in full for them to their fathers."

"How is it you paid full lobola for them? Why? Because of what?" came tumbling from her.

His next words were not carefully chosen either: "I am afraid of their fathers. They are ill-tempered."

"Those who are nice, those who are worthy, and those who are bad tempered and do not respect you, which of these get their reward?" she demanded. "They who respect you, are your dogs, and they get nothing!"

Something intangible flared between them. Cloaking himself in the authority of the Kingship, in a freezingly impersonal voice, he ordered curtly: "Fetch two of my mothers immediately!"

"I have brought the two girls of the uSuthu here at this early stage of their pregnancy, so that they can cut grass for themselves and thatch their huts," he addressed the mothers, but his words were meant for Christina. "I have done this so that we can avoid the trouble we had with the girl from Eshowe. It will behoove you to tell the indunas to build the huts, and to set the girls to work at grass-cutting and thatching. Meanwhile these girls will share your hut with you."

"If these girls make any trouble with any idle talk, I shall expect you to stop them. I insist that my wives shall live peacefully with each other."

From then on, although he would stop and casually talk with these girls if he happened to see them as he walked about the kraal, he had nothing further to do with them. Resentment at troublemaking wives had begun to crystallize within him.

Falteringly, as a child counts, Christina found herself figuring: "His love for these two girls from the uSuthu is not equal: his love for the two girls who were here before at the Zibindini is not equal; his love for the woman from Eshowe, who already has a child, is different from his love for the rest of them, but of the whole lot of us, he loves me best."

A discerning spirit might have detected the first signs and wistfulness of defeat.

Her day's work done, Christina would join her child at play but the child would abruptly leave her and run to its granny. The grandmother was looking after the child as well as she would have done, and it seemed only natural to her that the child should give her granny first preference.

On the whole, this was an idyllic period for Christina. Solomon was again paying her a great deal of attention, sleeping with her for part of almost every night, keeping her by his side and in his hut the entire time. It seemed to her that he had kept his pledge to cherish her forever and ever.

The thread of their close union remained unbroken even when he went away, for he always wrote to her whenever he wanted anything, and there was not an induna for miles around that did not know that she might at any time bring orders to him from the King. This increased her prestige with all the men and women of her kraal. All this merely signified to her that her husband needed her above all other women, and that their relation had a special meaning, not only for her but for him. Secure in this new confidence of her hold on him, she was full of a new sympathy for those unfortunate women who would never know the same love and kindness.

The members of the kraal were asleep in their huts when Solomon arrived unexpectedly one night, and woke Christina.

"This time I have come to take you with me to the Nongoma kraal," he abruptly told her with no preamble.

Half-asleep, she clung to the pact he had made with her: "But you said I was to remain here for three months."

"Never mind the three months; the child is now walking."

Christina was glad of the last-minute tasks that crowded the next few days, for she found herself shaken by the knowledge that the time had actually come for her to leave her child and her beloved *isikhundla*—her nest. It was here she had come as a bride; it was here she had had her child; here she had known happiness. The future stretched before her unknown and strange.

ten

For days it had been wet and gray. No longer did dust shroud travelers within its cloak and settle thick and solid upon the tongue. Though the rainy season had not quite set in, already the White Umfolozi River was a roaring torrent.

As long as the people of Nkwanyana lived at the crossing, the Zulus would not need a bridge. No one remembered when this family had first become renowned for helping wayfarers across that vicious rise of water. No one had ever suggested it to them, but the need was there, and they and their sons had filled it.

At a shout from Solomon from the opposite bank, the men of Nkwanyana jumped into the angry river and lay upon it, effortlessly directing their occasional strokes, swimming with the current. While waiting for them, Christina, the only woman in the party, removed all her clothes except her petticoat. Solomon and the other Europeanized natives peeled off everything but their long shirts.

The human substitute for a bridge went into action. A cordon of natives was formed; two Nkwanyana men plunged downstream, and three upstream, separating Christina from Solomon. One man swam at her side, guiding her left arm, another at her right, keeping her afloat, her head and shoulders well above the water. The others were to guard against the King's being washed down the river, or to go to his assistance if necessary.

Solomon swam across, not permitting anyone to touch him. It was a matter of pride to show the natives that although he did not live at the river bank, and had only occasional recourse to swimming, he could do anything as well as any man in the land.

Christina lay breathless on the bank, watching the men swim back and forth, holding aloft the boxes and bundles, not one of which was lost or dropped, or even splashed by a spray of water. The sun glistened on their wet, dark bodies, which made a sound like the rhythmic dip of oars. As the travelers went on, praise and a gift of money were left behind for the Nkwayana.

Night had fallen. The natives at Ndwandwe's kraal, who knew the dangers of the Umfolozi at this time of the year, had begun to be anxious about the King. When he finally arrived, the head of the kraal gave voluble thanks, presented him with a beast and added that a large goat had been reserved for Christina. Solomon smiled engagingly at Ndwandwe's daughter, and suggested she personally escort Christina to a comfortable shelter.

Alone in his hut with his attendants, Solomon was capricious and petulant; not even the long tiring journey could explain it. He would not eat the meat of the beast that had been killed for him, nor did he feel like eating the meat he had brought with him; only a portion of Christina's goat would do.

Hours later, when the goat was cooked and ready to serve, Solomon sent for Christina and the daughter of Ndwandwe. "I overheard the youngsters snickering that your goat was a skinny one," he told Christina. "I ordered it to be killed even though it was late, in order to satisfy myself of this point."

"I thanked them very prettily for that goat," she murmured. Laughter overwhelmed them; her polite answer was understood to mean: "The dirty dogs! They tried to trick me."

The daughter of Ndwandwe looked down, wishing miserably for escape.

"Your father has done something ugly, inexcusable," Solomon bluntly charged. "When he presented Christina with a gift, it was as though it were meant for me. It behooved him to give her one that is suitable."

Ndwandwe had found himself in a dilemma. To avoid ill favor with the King he had to present Christina with a gift, but he bitterly resented her. A fitting compromise appeared to be a gift that carried with it a deliberate slight.

Unless Solomon specified a particular wife to supersede her, to become the Great Wife and the mother of his heir, Christina, as the first wife, ranked higher than any of her successors. So far, Solomon had specified no one, Christina, nor anyone else, nor could he do so without consulting the elders of the tribe; nevertheless, whenever Christina met with a slight, as she frequently did thereafter, Solomon's quick defense of her was accepted by the knowing ones as proof that, when the right time came, she would be established as the Great Wife.

The daughter of Ndwandwe hurried away to prepare the guest hut for fear Solomon would come to see whether, here, too, Christina had been neglected. Her fears were well grounded; he came and counted the mats to see if there were a sufficient number to lie on comfortably, and only when he found there were five was he satisfied. From then on Solomon was alert to any insults to Christina.

"May I go to bed?" Christina pleaded nervously. "I am tired. I have been shaken by the horses and the water."

"Do not feel badly because we are sleeping in separate huts. This is not my kraal," Solomon said, kissing her, and coaxing her good will as any humble lover might have done.

Solomon would spend the night with the daughter of Ndwandwe; it was customary that she, as the chosen daughter of the kraal, would sleep with him.

Men might make tribal laws, and women accept them. The laws of the land might outlaw female jealousy and refuse to recognize it; but the King was aware of his wife's hunger and jealousy, and his love could not ignore it.

"Which would you rather have, beer or the liquor of the white man?" he said, trying to make amends with the best he had at his disposal.

Promptly she said she would like both, and he went to his hut close by, and brought the whiskey himself. A girl was sent to fetch a small pot of beer, as well.

Still suffused with tenderness for her, he made one last gesture of honor and flattery by presumably consulting her as to their plans. "We will rest here tomorrow. Will that be agreeable to you?"

"Very agreeable," she murmured, as she was expected to.

Before he retired into his own hut, he was heard appointing a boy to stand guard by her hut.

Many natives arrived next morning, and Solomon spent most of the day conferring with them. It was afternoon before he had his first food. The intrigue, the crowds, and the freely flowing liquor wore him out. Too tired to push on that day, the party waited until midday of the next, when they rode out of the kraal into a rising wind.

As they crossed the Sikhwebezi River two red bucks were startled into their path. Instantly and automatically, it became a scene in pantomime. Not a sound was made. Solomon waved his arms at the baggage carriers, who, in what seemed like one amazingly efficient movement, set down their loads and sped to head off the bucks. In instinctive cooperation, others ran to take strategic positions to cut off escape. Solomon alone aimed, his shot piercing the tense silence. One buck fell; one escaped.

River and woods resounded with war whoops and shrieks of joy. The men fell upon the buck with their assegais and stabbed it repeatedly to make sure it was dead. Having tied its legs, they slung it triumphantly upon their shoulders, leaving a bloody trail behind them.

Soon the exhausted but exhilarated party came in sight of a large kraal where they planned to celebrate with a barbecue and dance. But when the kraal gathered in greeting to Solomon, everyone waited in silence as one of the mothers nervously cleared her throat. It was evident that she wanted immediate permission to speak and that her words would be of disaster. At Solomon's nod she said hoarsely,

"Our son, there is a sickness spreading in all the kraals. Two of your sisters and one of your mothers are so sick they cannot get up from their mats."

It was the year of the influenza epidemic. Men may write of the isolation of the Dark Continent, of the gap of thousands of years in culture and civilization that separate it from the more advanced centers of Europe and America, but when Europe became embroiled in devastation Africa was made a battlefield too. Whether from the campaigns of German West or German East, or direct from the battlefields of Europe, influenza made its way into the primitive huts of South Africa and completed the international unity that philosophers and political strategists debated.

Solomon feared illness with superstitious dread. He pretended to brush it aside as an incidental unpleasantness that time would right, but as soon as he could, without making it too obvious that he was fleeing from it, he announced that urgent business would call him away from the kraal the next day.

That night the King clung to Christina for solace in this fresh calamity. When morning coffee was brought, to the amazement of the kraal, he told the food bearers to bring another cup, ordered one of the girls to pour the coffee, and handed it to Christina to drink beside him.

Others had been stricken in the night. Two were girls with whom the King had slept only a short time ago. Regardless of what the kraal would think, Solomon dispensed with ceremony, rushed to the cooking hut, and told the servants to hurry with the cleaning of the pots and pack immediately. Everything was done instantly; the usually slow-moving natives were as frightened as he. They, too, were anxious to flee from the illness.

*Christina was captivated with her first glimpse of Mahashini, the royal kraal. The gates were swung open by the armed guard, on duty twenty-four hours a day. Within the kraal there were the usual huts, but they were surrounded by a tall stockade, neatly made of saplings, fronted by a tall green-growing hedge. The only concession to European custom was an enormous shed built of corrugated iron for Solomon's ever-growing stable of horses. Dlamahlahla, Solomon's brick house, had not yet been built. Rolling barren hills stretched in every direction as far as the eye could see. Cool breezes swept across them, and the kraal seemed to promise peace and serenity.

The mothers had urgent news for Solomon. "The sickness is very bad here!" their spokesman announced, without the customary prelude of greeting and exchange of inquiry as to health.

To pacify and reassure them that they had not been specially marked for bad luck, Solomon told them of the illness at the uSuthu kraal, and specified the sick ones there.

"The sickness here," insisted the mother, "is taking old as well as young. Your grandmother, the wife of Cetshwayo is very sick."

Solomon was shocked into greater fear for himself, which he did not trouble to hide. Though he had a cabinet stocked with the medicines provided by the government that Mrs. Fynney, the beloved wife of the Magistrate, had selected for him, and with which he mercilessly dosed the sick, he, himself, never took a drop of them. This fear of medicine, which amounted to a mania, was familiar to them all.

---

* Compare here through p. 74 with the record of original interview, appendix 1C.—Eds.

"I have brought Christina to look after me as she did at Zibindini."
Everyone was relieved when he turned the talk to other things. "I will see
she has a place to live in, a hut of her own. The wives that are here will be
taught by her what to do for me, and how to do it. I want them to respect
her, to pay attention to her as if it were I who were giving orders."

"I have already separated Christina, while young, from her mother, and
again from her child, which is still a baby." A new note of sympathy crept
into his voice. "If she is badly treated now, her heart will be very sore."

Surprisingly his next words were directed at her. "Christina, you have
been parted from your nest at Zibindini. It does not mean that you, yourself, are to change, or that you should lose your common sense," he publicly
emphasized. "Be firm in that, and depend forever on it. Whatever happens,
whether for good or evil, you are to tell me. You have always spoken the
truth. I know that here you have arrived at the source and school of lies. It
is here they are nourished, and it is here they flourish!"

"Christina will never tell you lies, having learned to tell the truth," one
of the mothers replied, ignoring the accusations. "It is meant for her to listen to you always, and fear you."

As his mothers filed out, one by one, Solomon called, "I want the mattress which was purchased for me put in okaMtshekula's hut for Christina
to sleep on." This mark of solicitude was immediately noted by the kraal.

Early next morning a runner arrived from the uSuthu kraal with word
that the sickness was spreading, that two women were dying. Solomon
ordered Christina to pack a medicine kit without delay. "Do not send too
much, because I want some for this kraal," he admonished her frantically. "I
am still waiting for more to arrive from the courthouse."

The runner would be expected to bring back reassurance from the King.
"Tell them at the uSuthu to take these medicines, that they will make them
well," he blustered, adding quickly, "Tell them that I will not be down to see
them, for I, myself, feel that my body is growing listless, that life is ebbing
away. I, too, must be getting the sickness."

The messenger's kit contained a huge packet of pills, castor oil, epsom
salts, and, as comforting delicacies, a package of tea and a two-shilling package of sugar.

Once the messenger was on his way, Solomon turned to Christina. "Now
you go and dose my grandmother!"

Simple as the words were, they presaged a crisis.

"I have never seen your grandmother nor has she ever seen me. How
can I, an unknown person, bring her medicine?" she demanded.

"You are right. She will think you are going to kill her," he admitted with
a chuckle. "We had better go together. She will trust me."

UMntwana, the daughter of a chief, the widow of a great King,
crouched upon the floor, fast asleep.

"Wake up, *Gogo*—granny—it is I, your grandson!" He gently shook her. "How do you feel?" He spoke softly in deference to her age and so as not to startle her.

"I am not well." She made of it a formal greeting, her eyes still blinking with sleep. Pointing to her head and clutching her stomach, she indicated that she was in great pain.

"I have brought you medicine to rid you of your pain," he told her, as to a child.

The old woman was suspicious. "Is the medicine not bitter?"

"It is the medicine of the white man—*wabelungu*," he reassured her.

The old woman wanted to enjoy this visit. "Who is that girl with you?" she asked, abruptly changing the subject.

But the King was not to be diverted, and pressed the medicine on her.

"Far better had I seen what you took it out of, or from where," she said. She looked inside the cup, sniffed, and had a sudden inspiration. "Did Cetshwayo ever drink this medicine, Child of my child?" Zulus do not worship ancestors, but they treat them with superstitious respect. They worship a Supreme Being, a creator of all things, *uNkulunkulu*.

The *uMntwana* took the cup in both of her hands, sat looking at it for a long moment, then glumly intoned, "Now the *abelungu*, the white people, are going to kill me! Now, I, too, am going to die!" But she threw back her head and drained the cup.

As Solomon and Christina left the hut, anxious mothers ran toward them inquiring: "Did the *uMntwana* drink the medicine?"

"She would not have taken it had not Christina been there with me," Solomon replied proudly.

The day proceeded like so many others, but when all the routine tasks were done, Solomon led Christina toward the cattle kraal, and there pointed out a beast for her.

"I am giving this to you in honor of your arrival at Mahashini. I will tell the *izinceku*—the servants who kill cattle—to cure the skin, because it has nice markings, and it can be spread upon the floor of your hut when it is built." The hut which was to be built of good intentions, and existed only in Solomon's conversation.

eleven

Christina was not happy at Mahashini. She could not become accustomed to having no hut of her own. With four other wives she now occupied a mothers' hut; the promised hut still had not been built. There was no close friend of her own age, no one with whom she could gossip about her shared intimacy with the King.

Solomon spoke to Christina with the native courtesy of the Zulu but was brusque with the other wives and girls. Unceasingly the girls chattered about him, and to Christina's dismay, their gossip was almost entirely vindictive. More than one girl said: "He speaks nicely to us only when we are in sleeping attendance upon him." The King called some girls every fortnight, some every three days. Christina noticed that the former were bitterest and loudest in their rancor. The two groups formed into natural cliques, incapable of mutual friendship or task cooperation. Neither group wished to have anything to do with Christina.

The two major cliques were waging warfare, their quarrels growing louder and more insistent. The Zulus say a wild cat never catches a rat by sitting still. Whenever Solomon heard the raised voices, he would leave his hut, and unnoticed, creep about the girls' hut, noting the flying taunts about him.

"I know those girls are always complaining about me," he would say to Christina. "They say you are my favorite, and that I am not fair to the others, that I do not take them in turn. I heard them threaten to beat each other."

Better not to comment; the King was careless, he might repeat her words and it would only increase the animosity against her.

The King would call Christina every third day, sometimes every second day, so that she still had first place in his favor. Besides she again attended to all his wants during the day, and spent much time with him in his hut.

The girls' antagonism would flare out when Christina allocated their duties.

"Why do *you* come to tell us what to do, Sibiya?" they challenged.

"What are *you* doing?" the bolder ones would ask pointedly.

Ignoring irrelevancies, she would tell them exactly who was to wash, iron, help in the kitchen, sweep, do any of the innumerable tasks of the

King's household. When she had assigned the round she would leave.

Sometimes Solomon would personally assign specific tasks. The girls would listen silently, with bowed heads and modest appearance. Back at the hut, one of the fortnighters would turn on one of the three-dayers: "I did not come here to work only. You grind his mealies. It is *you* who see more of him."

As the bickering increased, Solomon would stride toward the girls' hut in a black fury. Standing in their doorway, he would shout at the cowering figures: "Why is it that when I send Christina to you, you quarrel with her? Do you want *me, the King*, to come here every time to tell you what to do?"

Not even he noticed how often he was running across to their hut in anger, nor how his formerly serene days were interrupted by all this unpleasant trivia. There was little he could do. He could not break up the cliques and send the girls home; so many of them were pregnant. It seemed to him that five were, but he was not sure.

Meanwhile, influenza continued to ravage many of the other kraals, each day bringing its quota of bad news. From the Zibindini came word of the death of a child at birth. This was more than bad news of illness, this was an evil omen, pointing to ill luck directed against the fertility of Solomon's house and the good health of his wives.

As the epidemic waned, Christina discovered she was pregnant again. This pregnancy weighed her down with apprehension, for besides the usual morning nausea she had a sharp searing pain in her womb. Contact with Solomon became physical agony.

Though Solomon had been baptized and adhered to many Christian standards, the superstitions of his race had burrowed deep within him. As Christina sickened, "at the very root of her femaleness," Solomon attributed it directly to the curse that was spreading over his kraal, manifested most recently in the death of one of his children.

He feared that some of the women had called in the aid of witch doctors and had now cast a spell upon Christina so that not only would she suffer, but through this evil he and she would be separated, and that he would naturally seek satisfaction elsewhere.

All native husbands fear witchcraft. But Solomon did not consult a witch doctor and have a smelling out ceremony, as most natives would have done, to discover who was responsible for Christina's illness. Instead he decided to dispose of the curse in another way.

"Do not worry, Christina," he tried to comfort her. "Your pain and sickness are only little things to the doctor of the white man. They send away sickness every day, and will do the same for you."

There was a doctor at Middleburg, near the Thengisa kraal built for Dinuzulu when he had been released from prison after the Bambatha Rebellion. Solomon had been summoned by the authorities to discuss this property. For once he was energized into prompt action, and decided to take Christina with him there.

OkaMtshekula, one of his mothers, was not surprised when Solomon appealed to her for help. "Sonkeshana will welcome the journey to chaperone Christina," she assured him. But she took advantage of the opportunity to press another issue. "Seeing you are going to visit the doctor, why not take these two wives of yours who after so long a time have been unable to become pregnant? The white man's doctor knows how to make women fertile."

"Thank you for reminding me," he responded enthusiastically. "Indeed, yes! I shall take them," and added, hopefully, "The white man's doctor will remove this curse which is beginning to creep upon us. One woman's child dying, Christina's womb stricken, and these two women stubbornly remaining sterile!"

Christina and the two sterile wives, who wore *amabayi* and would have to be outfitted for the trip, set out for the village store with Solomon, the women afoot, he on horseback. At the store he gave each an equal sum of money. "Does anyone wish me to make their selection?" he inquired rhetorically. Ntoyintoyi's silence was sullen, but her negative head shake emphatic. Nomapasi was tongue-tied, except for a hoarse, "Yes." Christina said: "There is nothing I cry out for, but on the journey there may be."

Never before had Nomapasi been in a village store to buy more than a tickie's—threepence—worth of beads. Frightened and ignorant, she did not know what to choose. Ntoyintoyi, equally ignorant, was, however, so delighted at having money of her own to spend she had to be sharply reminded when it was time to go.

From the materials they had bought, Christina would be expected to make dresses for herself and the girls, who did not know how to sew on the machine Solomon had given her. Ever since he had seen his first sewing machine at the home of the Magistrate, and others in the stores at Johannesburg and Vryheid, he had determined to have one at his kraal. Christina had served as the excuse. In fairness to him, however, it should be said that he enjoyed giving her a valuable gift and he felt much as a European might in giving his favorite a handsome car that he, too, would enjoy driving.

Christina was cutting a dress without using a pattern (she "sewed out of her head") when the King came in. "When you get tired pushing the machine, I will sew for you," he offered, for he loved to operate the sewing machine. They took a week to do their sewing, she making the dresses, he making the petticoats. Solomon never grew tired of watching the machine's quick movements, and the miracle of seams it produced. He liked taking his turn at unwinding the spool and threading the needle, and no child on a velocipede ever got a greater thrill than he, once he set the machine at its full speed, and pedaled away at a fast rhythm.

The wardrobes were ready. A wagon was borrowed from a Dutch farmer who lived not too far away near the Ngome forest. The four women, okaSonkeshana, Christina, Nomapasi, and Ntoyintoyi, piled on with their bundles and rattled down the road. The wagon creaked and shook under its load as the horse picked his way along winding hills. Christina held her sides, trying not to show how the pain stabbed every time they took a bump.

They made two breaks in the journey. Just outside Vryheid, the wagon drove into the eKubuseni, Solomon's uncle's kraal. Natives arrived, paid their respects to the King, and asked if they might be allowed to see his wives. Zulus lay silver in the palm as they shake hands with a stranger whom they wish to honor, and they greeted these royal wives with fifteen shillings.

Vryheid has its native community—a location where natives live, with compounds for laborers, stores, and a Bioscope which natives may attend provided they have a government pass permitting them to be on the streets after dark.

Solomon quickly got rid of his respectful subjects so he could take Christina to the Bioscope. Not having seen a movie since she was a small mission child, and never with Solomon, she was visibly excited at the prospect. "Why is he taking *her* and not *us*?" Nomapasi and Ntoyintoyi promptly demanded of okaSonkeshana. "*We* want to go, too!"

It was a mother's duty to protect the rights of wives and okaSonkeshana was acting on principle when she asked Solomon: "Why are these wives to be left behind?"

"Because they know nothing of civilized ways," was his curt reply. "They are not accustomed to walking on city streets, and going among a lot of people. I would be shamed by them if they went with me."

The picture had already started when Solomon and Christina came in. The King took liberties denied to anyone else, calling greetings, and interrupting the picture. When he spied his local girl, he nudged Christina and whispered, "There she is!"

Christina had heard about black houris, and every town girl seemed one to her. Kimberley and Johannesburg had been boom towns where gambling and vice had reached their lowest level. Harlem was to coin the term "High yaller," but this gayer species of colored skin knew its first triumphs in the diamond and gold rush. There was no longer a strata of native society that did not have its questionable women. Wherever there were native compounds, concentrating labor for the white man's mines or industries, there was near by a nucleus of itinerant women. The daughters of a race that had met the slightest moral infraction with the death penalty had learned the ways and practices of the meanest prostitute. Already Solomon had begun to form the habit of going without food all day after unduly large doses of white man's liquor. Girls from the town would egg him on, urging him to drink.

That night the Vryheid girl slept with the King. At dawn she slipped out to walk several miles back to town where she was employed as a chambermaid.

When Solomon awoke and called for Christina she was not immediately available. "We have brought girls with us," he asked her exasperatedly, "cannot one of them attend to the kitchen?"

"They can."

Something in her manner aroused his suspicion, and he sent for Ntoyintoyi and Nomapasi. "Why do you just sit and do nothing? Are you my girls? Or are you my wives?" he insisted.

Girls were casual, wives were permanent. Nothing definite was expected of girls, whereas wives paid for their status in daily duties.

"If you are going to be quarrelsome and ugly, you will go no further," he warned them. "I will not have ill-tempered women surrounding me."

Just then a boy came in weighted down with packages, Solomon's purchases of the day before, which Christina was told to open. Given first choice, she took a brown coat with collar and cuffs of black fur. The other girls' coats were gray, also trimmed with fur, one woven in a broken check. There was a shawl for the mother as more becoming to her age.

Ntoyintoyi and Nomapasi thanked Solomon without any show of emotion. "I want to hear what it is you two have to look glum about," he demanded. "If you have anything to complain about, say it in front of me. If you do not like these coats you can go with an escort to the shop at which I bought them, and select your own."

An induna whispered to the King, who followed him out. Christina took this opportunity to say: "The King chose those coats for you because he liked them. If it were I, I would not exchange them."

"Sibiya is right," said the hitherto silent okaSonkeshana. "The King may say that, but he will not forget that you were unwilling to rely on his taste for you. But if you insist on going, I will arrange it for you."

The girls were determined to exchange their coats. Christina told okaSonkeshana when she was alone with her, "I was trying to teach them respect for the King. If he gave me a gift I did not like, I would nevertheless accept it with a show of pleasure. I was trying to help them. One of these girls refused to allow him to buy her clothes before. He is getting tired of this continual crossing of him."

Later Nomapasi was apologetically demonstrating to Solomon, "I exchanged my coat because it was too tight, it did not come together," adding, "and I did not like the markings on the material, like that of a beast. I wanted plain material like Sibiya's."

The King wanted to know of Ntoyintoyi, "Why didn't you exchange yours?" obviously hoping that from her he would get an admission that his selection had been the best. But Ntoyintoyi remarked, "I did not see a nicer coat at *that* shop."

"Would you like me to get you the money instead, so you can go to the other stores and see if you can find a nicer one, anywhere?" he asked with exaggerated patience. That was just what she wanted to do, and he had to stand by his offer.

Hiding his increasing irritation he turned Nomapasi about slowly, examining her coat in great detail. "It is indeed very nice. It is much better than the one I selected." Nomapasi did not recognize sarcasm, and her face broke into smiles at this tribute to her taste.

When Ntoyintoyi returned from her shopping trip, everything was packed, and they were ready to leave. "Put on your coat and let me see you in it," Solomon called to her. "Oh, it is nice, very nice! Turn around, I want to see every bit of it. Oh, my! You do look grand, great and big, my child. I bought a size that was wrong for you. That is because I do not know how to buy for women." His sarcasm was lost on her, too, for she beamed with pleasure at his praise.

This was a dramatic episode of an exciting journey for the girls, but for Solomon it marked the beginning of a dislike that bordered on hatred for these women whom fate had thrust upon him as wives.

Autumn was in the air this May in 1919 when Solomon, Maphelu, the four women, and attendants left Vryheid to board the train for Johannesburg. Practically all of the eKubuseni kraal came to the station with them.

Cars reserved for natives, back of the third-class compartments, are usually loud with demonstrations of affectionate farewell, but, on this day, as the King appeared the shouts were deafening. The women felt the eyes of their world upon them, and a great pride in their status as members of the King's household wiped away memories of the past few days of bickering.

Since Solomon was not an ordinary native, he was permitted to travel second class. The women went with him to his compartment, but Maphelu and the other attendants traveled third.

When they reached the Park Station at Johannesburg, they were hustled into three horse-drawn cabs and driven to a suburb, Sophiatown, to the home of Seme, one of South Africa's leading native barristers, where arrangements had been made for them to stay. But no one was home, even the gates were locked.

The King found other accommodations, with a Cape colored family willing to rent to him. The colored race in South Africa is officially recognized as having an admixture of white blood and is regarded as entitled to a higher political and social status than that of the natives.

This family spoke English, which Christina, being mission bred knew, and could interpret. Solomon could understand a little, but spoke none at all. Whenever European authorities dealt with him about the multiple affairs of his race and position, they spoke Zulu, which men in authority in native affairs invariably know. In rare cases where they do not, they engage a Zulu interpreter.

The King and his party traveled most of the next day and reached Middleburg, their next stop "at the cock's crow." Again the wires had miscarried, for there was no one to meet them and take them beyond the town limits to the Thengisa kraal. Prompt connections are difficult for people who think of time in terms of light and sun.

A taxi driver who had known Dinuzulu recognized Solomon and okaSonkeshana, and offered his help. He was white, but he was proud to be the friend of a king, even though the King was a native.

A meal was prepared, and, while Solomon and his women were eating, a Boer arrived in a carriage to fetch them. This man had bought Dinuzulu's farm "on debt"—the installment plan—and now lived at the Zulu royal homestead.

All of them were exhausted as they finally drove into the Thengisa kraal. Beer was ready and passed about, and a beast was presented to Solomon with proper ceremony and greeting. Then Solomon made an announcement that came like a thunderbolt. "I am sorry, but I must leave this very night to catch a return train for Pretoria and Johannesburg!"

"I have come this long way with you," he tried to explain to his terror-stricken women, "because I wanted personally to make certain that you would be properly looked after, but now that you are settled comfortably I must be off. There are urgent government matters at Pretoria which I must see to, many compounds at Johannesburg I must visit." They watched him go, with none of the confidence he had tried to instill.

As soon as the amaNdebele, the local natives, heard that the women of the household of the King of the Zulus had arrived, they came with gifts— *amabele*, a variety of native corn, mealies, ordinary corn, pumpkin, browned cowpeas, jugo beans, and beer. But the women found themselves in great difficulty, for they could not understand the local language.

For two months Solomon wrote at infrequent intervals. His letters always caused a stir of hope among the women—until they heard them through. Never was there any mention of the date of his return. The wives tried not to show their hurt and disappointment, to keep up a pretense of hope, but when the letters stopped altogether it was impossible to hide their resentment and bitterness.

Christina's pain had grown steadily worse, yet she had not been to see a doctor. The two wives, whose families were waiting to hear they had been tied to the royal family through the children the wives would bear the King, had not even become pregnant. They had all begun to taste that degree of bitterness which masks its pain in laughter. They made a pun of it, "He has sold us out!" *Thengisa*, meaning "to sell," was the name of their kraal; they said he had "*Thengisa*'d" them.

They were drawn together by their common misfortune. No longer did Christina think of the others as "those girls." Of the two, she liked Nomapasi better, for, she thought, "Her head is stronger." Nomapasi was not subject to fits of jealousy. Even for Ntoyintoyi, Christina had nothing but pity, for she realized she was controlled by a wild current of passion, and Solomon gave her only a teasing outlet for it. However mean her tongue might be, there was a defiant honesty about her, which Christina had to respect.

Ntoyintoyi would become so restless with unashamed sexual hunger that Christina wondered if there was some way they could get her to a doctor, even without the King's permission, so if ever she did sleep with the King again she might become pregnant and this fever die within her.

Four months passed in waiting. A native doctor prescribed for Christina but she was never wholly free from pain. Their food had given out; there was neither meat nor tea; only porridge was left. The women went hungry because they were not used to eating porridge morning and evening, with not even tea or beer to drink it down.

Solomon had developed their taste for meat. Most natives have meat only on rare occasions. The King had it constantly, because beasts were presented to him wherever he went, and he never failed to give generously of them to his women. Though the supply of porridge was scanty, they missed the beer most. Beer is the natives' staple diet, and they depend on it not only to heighten their spirits and relieve the monotony of endless drab days, but for the mainspring of their energy. Native beer looks like a heavy brown milkshake and tastes somewhat like a thickened, soured, creamy European beer. It has so much substance natives almost chew it. In addition to beer, ordinary natives drink a good deal of heavy clabber. It was not petulance or pique that prompted Solomon's womenfolk to resent a diet of porridge; the fact was that soured milk and the creamy beer had furnished definite ingredients their organisms had grown dependent on, the lack of which now left them spent and hungry. They were actually in want, but since the people of the kraal did not volunteer to help them, they asked for nothing.

Eventually, a letter came to Christina from Solomon asking her to reply quickly if there were anything they wanted or needed, so that he might bring it with him when he came to the kraal. Christina read the letter aloud. "I am not going to answer him," she announced with tight set mouth. No one argued that she should.

The women were asleep when Solomon opened the hut door. "I am sick! I am sick!" he groaned.

Four pairs of eyes fastened upon him and not even his mother asked what was the matter with him. Tears welled up in Christina's eyes, but they were tears of anger. Simultaneously the other women rose, took their blankets and clothes and filed out to another hut. In a faint voice Solomon asked Christina, "Please get me some water." She handed him the water, then briskly went about her tasks of preparing the hut for him to sleep in. Occasionally she felt his eyes upon her, but she never looked at him.

"Don't you want to stay with your husband?" he coaxed.

"No!" came with unmistakable undertones, tempered somewhat by her lying explanation: "I am sick!"

He could have ordered her to remain with him. He could have drawn her down roughly beside him, but instead he inquired tenderly, "How is your pain?" He was tired, he wanted to sleep, but the sight of her tormented him. "Were you comfortable here?" he continued quietly. "Did you get food and everything you needed?"

"We got everything at first, shortly after you left," she measured her words deliberately, "but afterward, we began to want for everything, especially for beer and for tea." Every word seemed to open a chasm between them. "Call Ntoyintoyi to stay with me," he finally said.

Ntoyintoyi had scarcely left Nomapasi before she returned to their quarters. "Why are you here? What did the King say?" Nomapasi demanded.

"He wanted me to watch over him, to stay with him. I came when bidden then walked out, and here I am!" she almost caroled.

Nomapasi began to laugh with the first lightheartedness she had shown in months.

"Didn't I tell you," persisted Ntoyintoyi triumphantly, "didn't I tell everybody, I would return to Mahashini and my people before I slept with him again?"

"I didn't think you really meant it," explained Nomapasi with awe.

A messenger came from the King for Nomapasi. Cheerfully Nomapasi lied rather than desert the others: "I am not fit to stay with you. I am not well."

The night's experience had begun to wear on Solomon. All his masculinity was deflated, and he was in no mood to ravish one of the untouched girls of the kraal. The problem of who would watch over him still remained but his cunning mind devised a way. "Nomapasi, tell the others to come along with you."

They slept that night in the hut, the King and his three angry wives, with no one at his side.

Solomon woke late. He sent for his mothers and for their benefit reenacted his suffering.

"I have been very sick in Johannesburg. Now I am better. But I have received no welcome here!" he complained. "I came at night and found my wives angry with me. Christina, in truth, had something to be annoyed about. I brought her here sick to see a doctor, and then left her here for months without one. The others are just trying to vent their spite upon me." The mothers mumbled sympathy, but it was not convincing.

Solomon felt trapped in a maze of feminine spleen, yearned for a little warm friendliness, some gesture of affection. How else to make them forget their grievances than to shower them with gifts? He gave each of the two girls two pounds, and waited for the light of love to illuminate their faces. Nothing happened. He gave Christina two bolts of material and two dress lengths, besides. She did not even thank him. He gave his mother, okaSonkeshana, a kerchief for her head, as well as two pounds. Her brief thanks were the first.

Then for Christina he produced a superlative gift—jewelry—a pair of silver earrings! There was not even the gesture of an emotion. He was genuinely hurt, but he pretended she had been overcome with pleasure.

"Are you glad I have given you money?" childishly, he pressed Ntoyintoyi and Nomapasi, without a passing thought for the real suffering he had caused them, who had not yet known a moment of tenderness or affection from him, had met with only neglect and abuse, and knew from their observation of other kraals the years would bring increasing misery.

Since no one spoke, or showed any signs of sharing his friendly mood, he resumed his cloak of authority. "Tomorrow we return to Johannesburg," he announced. "We are expected at Preacher Shwabete's house, in Benoi. We will be taking the daughter of Shwabete home to Mahashini, with us. Before we go home, you, Christina, and Ntoyintoyi and Nomapasi will go to a doctor at Kroonstad.

He did not bother to explain the change of plans, nor why months had been wasted in fruitless delay in seeing a doctor.

This was the beginning of Solomon's curious way of leaving his wives at some point short of a promised destination.

twelve

"**T**his is the daughter of Shwabete." The King was introducing a shy, retiring girl to Christina. "She is a Christian and, like you, has a Christian name, Ethel. We will spend the night at her home. But I do not want people to know where we are sleeping."

The King was aware of the undercurrents of feeling which made for conflict in every community. Often he ignored rivalries. Sometimes he merely dreaded the compulsion to take another girl, when he was already emotionally or sexually preoccupied, for with each new girl acquired, another group invariably began to push their candidate.

They spent the night in the preacher's house, Solomon and Ethel in one bed, Christina opposite in another. For nearly one hundred years, missionaries had invaded Africa to implant Christian standards of morality, but natives made their own adjustments to it.

Next evening, Preacher Shwabete's weekly prayer meeting took place as usual at his home. When the last of the faithful had gone, Solomon again retired with the preacher's daughter, but this time alone. Early in the morning, Ethel fetched Christina back to the King.

"Christina, are you still in great pain?" he asked. "No, I am a little better," she answered. Each understood that Solomon had asked for forgiveness, and she, open-heartedly, had granted it. The Thengisa days were definitely over and forgotten.

Solomon and Christina, accompanied by Maphelu, visited Seme, the native barrister, whose house groaned and creaked under the strain of far too many men and women, two native choirs, a group of dancing girls, and a moveable organ that had been brought for the royal entertainment.

While Solomon walked about greeting different groups, Maphelu took over the ceremonies.

"You, natives, and the household here, are doubly honored by the King tonight," he told them. "You see before you Sibiya whom the King took as a first wife."

Natives closed in upon Christina greeting her with money, almost knocking her down. Daylight was streaking through the window before they went to bed. Tired as she was, Christina tingled anew with her old pride in her position as the King's favorite.

"**I** want you, Christina, to select material proper and fine enough for the baptism of my children," Solomon announced, "for as soon as we get home, I plan to call up all the *abaNtwana*—the children of royalty—to be baptized."

Surely no woman's heart could have been as full of love and gratitude as Christina's. As a little girl she had divided all children into heathens and Christians, and looked with scorn upon the heathens. Since Solomon's wives were not Christians, she had not even ventured to hope their children would be children of God.

Solomon took Christina and Ethel to a department store in Johannesburg. It took quite a while and three pounds in money for the christening finery to be bought: machine-made dresses, bonnets, shoes, and socks, for children of all ages.

Christina was tired, and upon their return she was sorry to see Preacher Shwabete's four-room house full to overflowing. These were luxurious quarters which few of the millions of natives in Africa could ever hope to attain, but now with the natives milling in and out of sitting room and dining room, and even crowding the bedrooms, the house seemed to shrink and lose some of its splendor.

Five girls sat tensely in a row. All night and all that day they had waited for the King. The minute he appeared, a wild uproar broke out. Pummeling each other with closed fists, biting, scratching, clawing, wrestling and rolling upon the floor, the girls hurled insults at each other.

"What do you want here with the King?"

"What is that to you? Are you the King's guard?"

"You gave your love to David, his brother, during the King's absence."

"Are you trying to start a quarrel between the sons of Kings by giving your love first to one and then to the other?"

"Liar, liar! You know it never happened."

"I may tell lies, but you are a *'sifebe*—a harlot!"

"Oh, *I'm* a *'sifebe*! Solomon will no sooner go than you will be giving yourself to others."

Solomon settled disputes only if he had to, leaving fury to spend itself. He fled for refuge to Ethel's and Christina's room, locked the door behind him, and leaned against it, laughing, a little breathless from haste.

The King ignored a knock upon the door, but Preacher Shwabete persisted. "What is it?" the King called.

"Come and see for yourself, Ndabezitha!" urged the preacher.

"I am coming. I shall chase them all away!" The King blustered, remaining where he was.

"It is not necessary for you to chase them away; it might even be better for you not to do so. Just speak to them," coaxed Shwabete, from the other side of the door. "They are your people, your girls, and I am afraid they will try to revenge themselves against me and my daughter."

By now Solomon was ashamed of having permitted himself to seem frightened by a pack of women. He swaggered into the sitting room, gripped the first pair of shoulders within reach, and vigorously threw the women apart. Their clothes torn, their eyes blood shot with rage, they waited to see what the King would do. Habit prescribed but one procedure. He pulled out his wallet and handed out ten shilling notes which the three quieter ones greedily accepted; the other two brushed the money aside and rushed at each other again.

Shwabete whispered: "Don't you think, Ndabezitha, that it might be well to hide their handbags? I fear they may have knives in them!"

It was too late for strategy. Shrieks tore through the framework of that house! Surely this was murder! Natives came running from all directions. Two burly women had rushed to the aid of the wife of Shwabete in whatever calamity had overtaken her. They grabbed hold of the girls and carried them out by sheer force. Amid the cheers of the crowd they dumped them on the other side of the high gate.

The girls had pitted their last ounce of strength against each other in their struggle for the King, and he had scorned them. No longer was it one against the other, but the two of them against the man who had repudiated them.

They got to their feet, and slunk down the road arm in arm. With that almost unearthly quiet that comes over the fields and meadows after a lightning storm, the neighborhood settled down for the night.

The preacher and his wife spent a troubled night debating the wisdom of handing over their daughter to any household—even that of the King— where she might find herself in the midst of dangerous women.

"My child, we have heard that, when the King took you, you were a Christian belonging to the church and that your mother was against your marrying him," the preacher's wife said to Christina next day. "We, too, were against letting our daughter Ethel go with him. The King has tried to set aside our fears for her. He says she will be staying with you, as the two of you have both been educated, know good manners and the laws of God.

"Our child, we ask you, then, that you guide Ethel in the customs of the Zulus, of Mahashini, and the niceties of royal etiquette, and show her what will be expected of her in honor and respect."

"I know Zululand," Preacher Shwabete added. "I was born at Zifabeni. I know well the customs pertaining to the King and those among the chiefs. It behooves you, as well as Ethel, to ignore those who have no faith in God, who do not know Him. The King has told us you have a spirit of virtue and goodness, and that you will live happily together with our child. We put our trust in you and in these words of the King."

Christina pitied them, but her days in the kraal had taught her to temper all her impulses.

"I hear you, *Mfundisi*," she replied dispassionately. "Ethel will follow the promptings of her heart, regardless of what you have taught her, or what the King may tell her. Even though I have patience with her, she may talk about me to the others. Although I will try to do what I can for her, she may gossip to my enemies who will turn her words against me."

Shwabete's wife added her plea.

"It is in you I put my faith to protect my daughter. Ethel is our only child. In her we have laid all our hopes. I do not want money for her, nor cattle. I want only that she shall live happily."

Shaking with sobs, she fled the room and the preacher followed, trying to reassure and comfort her.

Christina moved toward the window and looked out as if for inspiration from the God she and the Shwabetes knew so well, whom so often she now forgot.

The King stood behind her. "I saw the preacher and his wife leave you. What were they saying to you?" he gently asked.

"They were asking me to watch over their child."

Solomon was pleased. "I told them Ethel would live happily with you. I realize that not only are you good and pleasant to live with, but you can live peacefully with people who know nothing of your own ways," he complimented her. "Ethel and the others will be strange to each other."

His concern was for Ethel: he had not even noticed that Christina was disturbed about what might happen to her in this new relationship.

"How do you know she will be in accord with me? How do you know she will have a heart that will listen to me?" she cried in genuine distress.

"We can see when you are together," he tried to reassure her. "I am putting my faith in you." The same words Ethel's mother had used!

And to Ethel he said, "From now on I give you into the hands of Christina. She is kind, truthful, and conscientious. Let her guide you in all matters pertaining to me and my household. If you will remember these words well, you will find happiness with me!"

It was time to go to the station. The King was leaving first, a day ahead of his wives. Three cabs carried his luggage, two cabs followed with his womenfolk. Solomon shook hands formally with each in turn, waved a general farewell to the crowd of men, and boarded the slowly moving train.

That night Ethel shared with Christina the bed that she had so recently shared with the King. At first there was constraint between them, but so great was the urge in Ethel to learn more about the King and the life which lay before her that she plunged into questions.

"Do you sleep on mats, or do you sleep in a bed?"

"I always sleep on a bed."

"What does each wife do each day?"

"The day's work is divided among the King's wives," Christina explained, and told her who cooked for him and brought him his meals, who were assigned as kitchen helpers, to do the laundry and look after his clothes, and who did the cleaning and tidied his hut.

Ethel was coming closer to what she most wanted to know. "How many girls has the King been married to? How long do you stay with all these many women before your turn comes, before you sleep with him?"

"I live with him," Christina answered proudly. "I am in his hut. I sleep with him for two nights, and then probably for two or three nights by myself, when he calls the others."

Perhaps the girl was slow in arithmetic, or perhaps she could not face the truth. "Is it the same for all the others?"

Christina passed this off with a "Yes." Why alarm her?

"You have been with him for such a long time, has nothing ever happened to hurt you, or make you sore of heart?" Ethel pressed.

"No, because he has done nothing yet that is truly wrong." Conscience must have smitten her, for she added, with some reluctance: "The only thing that I can find fault with is that he left us alone for so long; never before did I have anything to cry about."

Ethel was not daunted. "He said he would build a hut for you, and that you and I will live together in it."

"I don't know," Christina was speculative, neither optimistic nor filled with doubt. "A long time ago he said he would build a hut for me, but the hut has not been built."

Ethel felt a prick of apprehension. "Christina, examine your heart and tell me if I will find happiness with the King." Christina lied uncompromisingly. Was it to shield the girl or the King? Ethel seemed satisfied, and soon passed into untroubled sleep. But she had kindled questions and doubts which Christina thought buried; try as she would to overcome it, a wave of sadness engulfed her. She had a premonition that unhappiness was soon to overtake her whole life. Her fears magnified in the dark but she thought the pity which now racked and tore at her was for the girl who slept at her side.

Next day when natives came to say good-bye to the daughter of their uMfundisi, Shwabete spread his arms in benediction. The natives sank to their knees and Shwabete knelt with them. For one hour he called upon the Lord to bless the King and all his subjects, to bless his days, his journeys and all his activities; to bless the home, husband, children and relatives of those present, naming many of them in turn. He tapered off into a simple plea that his daughter Ethel, who was about to leave her father and mother, might find happiness in her new duties as the wife of her King. No one there sensed any incongruity in the fact that a Christian preacher was bless-ing his daughter's entry into sinful living.

As the train pulled out, the preacher, his wife, and an army of natives wailed loudly, but Ethel was so doubled up with sobs she could not see them.

The train picked up speed and rushed through the night. Morning had not come when they arrived at Kroonstad.

Msane, their attendant, found two young men drawing a small handcart, on which he loaded their baggage. The women followed on foot. He warned them he did not know what their accommodations would be like, as he had had "to choose a place by hearsay."

Arrived at the place, they had to arouse someone to let them in. A boy made tea for them, which warmed and reassured them. Their difficulties had only begun, however, for they discovered this Zulu family could speak only Sotho, the language of the native territory of Basutoland in which they now were, or Afrikaans, the language of the Dutch South Africans.

English and Afrikaans, the official languages of bilingual South Africa, are taught in all schools and printed on all documents. Natives usually know some English or Afrikaans, depending on which language is in greater usage by their white neighbors.

This family were descendants of the native who had been made home-less by Shaka's invasion many generations ago. They had been sheltered by a Dutch family, had taken their name—Bloem—and had forgotten their original tribe, name, family, and language.

Next day Christina and the two girls were taken to the doctor, a Boer. Although he neither spoke nor understood Zulu, he was expected to make a careful gynecological examination and then explain to these women how they must care for themselves. Solomon's choice of this doctor remains a riddle. There must have been a reason. Perhaps because he was willing to treat native patients, which many white doctors refused to do.

Msane could not remain while the women were with the doctor, for that would have been against all laws of modesty. The doctor told Msane, who knew a little Afrikaans, what he planned to do and it was understood he would talk to him again after the examination. Msane would then tell okaSonkeshana what had been said and she would repeat the doctor's instructions to the girls.

Nomapasi went in first. She was stiff with fright, as she had never been to a doctor before. She knew she must do as he told her, but as he motioned her to stretch out on a bed, she thought he was going to ravish her. She did as she was bidden and she made no move to resist when he examined her.

From his gestures and what okaSonkeshana told her later, she gathered the doctor said she was too small and too fat to have a child. He gave her med-icine and told her in time she would have a child. And in time she had two.

Ntoyintoyi was defiant, as well as frightened, and the doctor had to speak sternly to her before she would even get upon the bed. He won her confidence quickly, however, when she discovered that although he had never see her before, he knew that she was often in pain. When he gave her some medicine to take periodically she felt that perhaps he was as good as an *inyanga*—witch doctor—after all.

Christina was not afraid of the doctor—she had been to one once, when she was a child, at Mpandleni, near Qudeni. The doctor now gave her a drink of medicine and indicated that she was to lie quietly and shut her eyes. Then a sleep came over her that was yet not sleep, for her eyes were open and awake, but her body was limp as in slumber. All of which was very curious, but she was so tired, she could not bother to figure it out.

The doctor put into her an iron thing, hard and cold. There seemed to be a lump on one side of her, which hurt when the child pressed upon it. The pain was even worse when the doctor began moving the child to try to ease it away from this sore spot.

Christina was there a long time, for once again the doctor gave her medicine and gesticulated for her to shut her eyes and make believe she was asleep; then, just as she was beginning to be comfortable and about to go off into a real sleep, he woke her, tortured her, moving the baby first to one side and then to the other. If Christina had not known that one did as the doctor said, she would have jumped off the bed and left; this was indeed silly, to rock a baby while it was still in its mother's womb.

Msane explained later that the doctor had said it was near the time of the birth, that Christina had only a short time to go, the child had not moved yet, and he tried to move it to see if it would respond.

The doctor gave her three bottles of medicine, which the two girls envied, but they were so used to Christina's being favored they accepted the fact that even the white doctor preferred her over them.

It was fortunate Christina was methodical and could follow directions, for the doctor had said to take one medicine one day, another the next, and the third on the third day; then to start with the first bottle all over again, and the second and the third, until the three bottles were used up. There was still another medicine she was to take when her labor pains commenced, which would put her into a long untroubled sleep. The doctor assured Msane it would be a quieter sleep than she had ever known.

The medicine was a yellow creamy color, with a slight red tinge, and so that Christina would not be afraid of it, the doctor gave her a tiny taste of it to the tip of her tongue. It was bitter, but it did not sting. In this respect Christina believed the white doctor was better than the native; he so seldom, if ever, gave poison deliberately. Msane paid the doctor fifteen shillings, listened carefully to all he told him, and by a miracle remembered which instructions were meant for each.

thirteen

The return journey was most terrifying. Passing through high mountains, they expected the train to tip over any moment. They did not look out of the window, preferring when the crash came and they tumbled headlong into the abyss below, to at least be spared the sight.

They huddled against each other, and tried to keep their minds on the happy thought that soon they would be at home, where hills were high and rolling, but not threatening and ominous that made blood run cold.

At Ladysmith they saw the dawn light up those mountain peaks the way it did their own familiar hills, which comforted them a little. Also it was here they were going to meet the King.

They sat in the waiting room until daybreak of the next day, and still the King did not appear. Tired and frightened, they continued their journey without him. At Vryheid young men met them and took them to the familiar kraal of the Prince, the *uMntwana*, uncle of the King. Night already shrouded the kraal, and all the natives had gone to bed. The King's tent had been pitched for him and the women made themselves comfortable there.

Days passed, but the King did not come. The crowded tent was the scene of so many quarrels that the prince removed Ntoyintoyi, Nomapasi, and okaSonkeshana to his house, leaving Christina and Ethel alone. Ethel, a bride, was beginning to fear she would never even get to Mahashini.

The Prince began to worry lest he should find himself supporting women who, as members of another man's household, were taboo. He sent a telegram politely couched, but nevertheless demanding to know what the King's plans were.

Everyone had given up hope of seeing him, when Solomon rode up to the kraal. He dispensed with greetings, disappearing at once into his tent. He was gaunt and thin, his skin had grown several shades darker.

When one lives among the Zulus, one begins to see with their eyes the different shadings of dark skin the white world tends to lump into the meaningless classifications of brown and black. The Zulus constantly refer to "light and dark Zulus," and only an experienced eye can discern the slight variation in skin texture, for Zulus are pure blooded, of no admixture.

Christina and Ethel helped the King to bed and put his clothes away. Tired as he was, he demanded the news of the kraal from Christina, caressing her as she talked. Shortly he transferred his entire attention to Ethel, and for her his voice had an undercurrent of teasing tenderness.

Dark as it was in the tent, Christina knew that Ethel was shy and uncomfortable, unable to reconcile herself to this shared intimacy.

"Ethel," the King suggested next day in his most charming manner, "stay with Christina, and watch what she does. The time is soon coming when you will be left to tend to me wholly on your own, when she is away at the birth of her child."

Weeks of doubt had melted away through the night of passion and tenderness. Here was honor, too. The King was choosing her, Ethel, to stand in Christina's place at his side.

"You must learn to grind on the stone, and to sit upon the floor. In our huts at Mahashini, you will have to crouch as you enter the low doorway and learn to do many other unfamiliar things. You will learn quickly if you wish to, and if you love me and do not think too much of yourself. I do not want you, when you get home, to make many friends. They will spoil you. Nor do I want you to lend an ear to their lies. When you do anything wrong, you are not to try to conceal it; in that way you and I will be able to live very happily."

Solomon sent for his other wives and mothers, awaiting eagerly the report of his illness.

"I have been very sick from *imibobo*. I have a pain under the shoulder." Here he indicated with detailed gestures the location of the pain. "It travels up and strikes into the hollow of the neck; it travels down and goes behind the collar bone. It attacks my stomach, my head and my heart."

Dramatically he paused, for this dreadful news to sink in, for some sign of sympathy. There was an uncomfortable silence, which okaSonkeshana broke: "Have you seen a doctor of the white man?"

"I have been in a hospital, where the doctors gave me many medicines."

All the women shook their heads; this was serious. They did not know how serious, and would not have presumed to ask about it even had they known. The doctors had warned Solomon that so much whiskey ate away his vitality, and was the reason why he was taking nothing of food; and that so many wives, and so many girls were bad for him when he was lacking in strength.

It was the spring of the year, September, 1919. Christina and Solomon had been married four years.

Primarily Solomon had come to hold a meeting with the abaQulusi, all those people who come from Ngome to the Swaziland border. Daily, crowds of natives with sober faces drifted through the kraal. The King was always coming and going, followed by a large troop of horsemen. It was well that many oxen and goats were presented to him, for there was a multitude to feed.

When night came Solomon would dismiss the men to near-by kraals, and summon them again on the following morning. These meetings were important: the King was preaching loyalty to the government and prompt payment of head taxes, and urging quicker responses to the mine recruiting.

Taxation by the government, through hut and poll taxes, has been the necessary spur to get the natives away from their primitive hearths. Today every kraal must have its wage earners, and native labor for the mines and other European enterprises is readily available because of the economic pressure that has been brought to bear upon the natives in full force.

Government taxes are collected through European or native agents, and penalty for nonpayment is imprisonment. A parallel system of tribal taxes and fines, some known, and some hidden, are sanctioned by the government. The taxes and levies that Solomon's regime were to impose upon his people were to become a national scandal.

The women of the kraal knew nothing of tribal economics or politics: their daily routine engrossed them to the exclusion of everything else. But no matter how pressing the affairs of the nation, Solomon dealt with his mothers at all the kraals, inquired if there were enough food and ordered them to replenish staples; saw to it that his wives and mothers were supplied with an abundance of meat and beer.

Pain was beginning to overtake Christina whenever she carried pails of water from the river, or when she bent over to rub the King's clothes, or even as she stood at ease over the burning coals slowly stirring the steaming pots. Though she watched warily, she never found a moment alone with the King to tell him of this. Finally, she sent the King a brief letter, tarrying neither over salutation nor signature.

"May I ask if you will release me from my heavier duties? I can no longer do any work with comfort on account of my pain."

The King committed himself explicitly in an immediate reply. "Christina, it behooves the others to assist you in every way. Divide your work among my other wives. When the food is ready, it should be brought by Ethel. She knows how to serve me."

Ethel brought Solomon his next meal, and he sent her to the kitchen for Christina, whom he drew toward him: "Do you not wish to stay with me any longer?"

"It is just that I do not wish to be shaking myself about, or working very hard, when the pain is so great," she murmured.

"How soon is it before the birth of your child?"

"Two weeks."

Solomon burst out laughing. "You cannot know your days so correctly as to be able to say you have only two weeks. Are you then God, who alone disposes of these matters? If you want rest from me and your work I will give it to you, but you cannot make a God of yourself!"

When Christina told Ntoyintoyi and Nomapasi they were to help her, they flatly refused. Solomon had foreseen this for he had said: "I am going to have a lot of trouble about you, if your work will have to be done by these others. It would be better if I were at home at Mahashini, where there are some friendlier wives."

For two days, Christina continued without help. On the third day she confronted the girls: "Are you then in earnest? You will not help me with my work?"

Ntoyintoyi's voice cut across her sharply. "Why should I help you? Never since I have been married to the King have I cooked for him. He does not trust me."

Nomapasi had a greater grievance against Christina than the King. "I will not be told by *you!*"

"Very well, my brothers," she drawled menacingly. "I was just asking for the second time to make sure before I told the King."

She thought better of bearing this tale to Solomon, and took it instead to okaSonkeshana, who at once confronted the girls: "When the King asks about this, you will be angry you were reported to him, but what is Christina to do? You cannot expect her to protect you from the King's anger, when it makes her short of breath, her heart beat more quickly, and the pain in her womb worse to do the work which you are supposed to relieve her of."

She talked to them as if they were children, thinking perhaps once they knew the entire story in its full significance, they would want to help. They looked straight into her eyes and kept silent. Now when her own dignity and authority were involved, she ordered: "You will go at once and do the King's bidding!"

They rose, and at the door said challengingly: "We will not!"

"The King has made a very poor choice in these girls, who behave so strangely," okaSonkeshana muttered to herself.

The storm brewing among the women had its first rumble and threat when the King needed a shirt and Ethel did not hand it to him. "I want a shirt!" he repeated sharply.

"You have no shirts," she told him plainly. "I had no time to iron. I was too busy in the kitchen cooking the food."

As soon as they were summoned into the King's presence, Nomapasi and Ntoyintoyi knew they were in trouble:

"Did not Christina tell you I said you two were to be in the kitchen and help with all the work to be done there?"

"She told us," came reluctantly.

His voice carried to all the shadows of the tent, as he thundered, "What does this mean?"

"We do not serve you with food. You have never asked us to prepare it nor had us taught how to do it."

Here was defiance, but here also was appeal. Solomon ignored the appeal. "Tell me the reason, the *real* reason! I know you acted this way because of something else. Christina, herself, never prepared food for me at her home. She learned after she came to me. The daughter of Shwabete served me with food at her home, and she serves me here. If you had waited, the time would have come when I would have called upon you to serve me.

"I see through the two of you. You are rotten at heart. Ever since you started out with me you have carried this grudge, which you brought with you from your fathers' kraals. When I like one of you, show natural preference, you begin to whisper, 'that one, whom the King likes, has medicine, or love philters, and has given it to him to drink.' Today you two are united; tomorrow you will kill each other. Get out!"

As they left the tent their whispers ruffled the night air like breezes. The King tiptoed out behind them, and in the shadows heard them give their version to okaSonkeshana. "You say you have been reported to the King," she said, "but I, myself, warned you to do the work."

Next morning when Christina came into the kitchen the stove was already lit, and she found Nomapasi and Ntoyintoyi there, busily finding things for themselves to do. Ethel brought the King his coffee, hoping that he would hurry off to matters of state and that the unpleasantness of the night before would be forgotten since she and Christina had gained their point in securing the services of the other two.

Solomon suspected exactly what had happened. "Who is in the kitchen besides Christina?" he demanded.

"Nomapasi and Ntoyintoyi."

"I do not want them to go near my food. They are unwilling. They may be dangerous. Go fetch them; I have something to say to them."

"I heard all you had to say between yourselves last night," he began, when they entered. "Though you say nothing, it is as if the words were upon your mouth; only words of quarrel. I want no service from you. Leave everything of mine alone. I have Christina. If Christina's strength fails, I have Ethel.

"I do not want to put you to any trouble." The King's tone grew sharper. "Remember, though, you have put *me* to a great deal of trouble."

"We have done nothing to the King," the girls exploded later to okaSonkeshana. "It is others who have stirred him up against us. The King does not like us. He thinks we are fools, just two ignorant people of Zululand. Those others, they think a lot of themselves. They think they are of the *abelungu*—of the white people—just because they are *kholwas*, and dressed in clothes. They sleep on beds, we sleep on mats. We are made to sit on the floor, they are given chairs. When the King gets a letter, it is their letter, too. He lets them read it, and write his letters for him, too!"

"Those two, they are tricky. They told the King they liked to have him buy things for them, because the King buys things which cost more than the amount of money he gives. But they did not let us in on that secret. They tried to make us believe they let the King choose for them so as not to offend him. These Europeans! We hope a curse falls on them!"

From then on there was open warfare among the four wives.

Ethel was disturbed by the atmosphere in which she found herself. "Christina, I believed it was the blindness of the Christians, who are against a man's having many wives, when they told me many tales of how mean wives can be to each other. I believed that, in so great a household as the King's, everyone would be well looked after and glad to be of service to him. I believed it would be like Christians trying to do God's will. All this that I see with my own eyes, and hear with my own ears, frightens me."

Solomon showered attention on Christina and Ethel in the next few days. A carriage took them to Vryheid, where Christina bought a miscellany of things for the expected baby. Solomon's benign mood continued even after they reached home, when he suggested that since they were tired and it was already late they need not bother to prepare any food for him.

Christina and Ethel gratefully relaxed in the kitchen. OkaSonkeshana came in to hear about their trip. On learning they had been released from their duties, she suggested to Nomapasi and Ntoyintoyi that they prepare a meal for the King. "How can we when the King says we are not to touch his food?"

"Never mind, let the King say that! Cook the food and see if he will refuse it."

Ntoyintoyi and Nomapasi began to bustle about officiously. By this time, Solomon was hungry. He came to the kitchen to ask his wives if they would prepare just a little coffee for him. Gone was his mood of friendliness when he found Ntoyintoyi and Nomapasi there at work.

"What are these people doing here in the kitchen?" he demanded.

This was a situation worthy of a statesman's wife, and okaSonkeshana, the widow of a Zulu King, put all her wits to it. "My child, be lenient with those who have wronged you."

Her tactics failed; if anything his anger was greater. "Mother, you will rouse me to lay hands upon these people. If this had taken place at home, I would have thrashed them!"

A hush fell upon the kitchen. Never before had Solomon mentioned thrashing a wife.

Later that night, as Ethel lay in bed with Christina, she seemed puzzled.

"The King is angry and displeased with Nomapasi and Ntoyintoyi. Why should he call them to spend the night with him?" she asked.

Christina had learned all the answers of the kraal. "The King is angry with these wives in some matters; that has nothing to do with his sleeping with them."

fourteen

hristina, Ethel, and okaSonkeshana left the Prince's kraal by comfortable carriage while Ntoyintoyi and Nomapasi preceded them by a day on the slower going luggage wagon. Day was almost done when the carriage first passed the luggage wagon. The King's wives glared at each other in stiff silence.

The King and his indunas were settled merrily within the stockade of Mahashini when all the women finally got there. Everyone stared at Ethel, whom the King took by the hand and led straight to the cattle kraal where he pointed out a beast for her, so she might be promptly and properly welcomed to her new home.

Solomon had brought two bolts of dress material for his wives, but the sweet of the gift was made bitter by the presence of this stranger and of Christina, who was to apportion the gift. The wives did not stop to consider that they did not know how to measure, while Christina did; nor that she would be called upon to sew these dresses. Dark looks melted into smiles when with each dress length Solomon gave a pound note. Pointedly, Nomapasi and Ntoyintoyi had been left out in the distribution of the gifts.

"I have had a very enjoyable trip, except for my illness, and the trouble I was put to by Ntoyintoyi and Nomapasi." Solomon launched into a tale calculated to discourage rebellion. "Ever since we left here, they have been at odds with me. They cannot live peacefully with other girls. I took all the bad things they said calmly, though I felt like *striking* them, because I was on a journey with them, not at my own kraal. *I* was the wife; *they* were the husbands."

The bitter wives had been enjoying themselves at the expense of Ntoyintoyi and Nomapasi, who sat at one side, frowning. But when they heard the King speak of striking, their heads and shoulders drooped limply before him.

"I have been a sick man," Solomon continued with a more commanding air. "The pain in my shoulder moved along to my collar bone and to my neck, and then to my spine, until finally I had to put the pain to bed with me in a hospital."

The women swayed their bodies, and punctuated his words with properly sympathetic Oh's and Ah's.

Christina felt the tale had reached a good-humored peak, and tactfully asked permission to go to sleep. Ethel rose to follow her, but the King stopped her.

"You are like a small child," he teased. "You want to go with her, whose affection you are sure of!"

The assembled wives were to be made fully conscious of the importance of this new wife. "Are you not hungry, Ethel? You do not even drink beer? What are you satisfied with? What have you eaten? I will order tea and bread, which you are used to, taken to you."

Ethel, who had not yet learned how to leave a native hut, backed out through the wicket-shaped entrance, about half the size of the average door. The wives forgot themselves in unrestrained shrieks of laughter. Guffaws still burst from them, even after Solomon sternly admonished: "Do not laugh at Ethel, for where she lives in Johannesburg they do not have huts like these."

If only the laughing abandon had stopped then, a girl's shrill voice would not have been carried along with it to say: "Oh, there has arrived another European among us. She goes out of the door backward!"

"Who is the other European?" the King tore through the laughter in torrential anger. "What you say, that there are some of my wives who are Europeans, must stop at once! I never want to hear it again! And the saying amongst you that there is a well-beloved one must also stop before it causes dissension and death! There is not one of you I like less, nor one I like more. There is not one of you whom I dislike, and not one whom I love. You are all the same. The only difference amongst you is brought about by work, by the tasks you have to perform."

Nothing more was said until they were well out of the King's hearing, but then there started up talk which lasted for many a month. They kept repeating they knew it was love that made the difference, that the King loved some more than he loved others; he had chosen to tell those who had suspected for a long time that his love had cooled toward them, that he did not love them. From now on, sides were drawn between those whom he had openly spurned and those whom he had chosen to love.

The following day Christina wrote Solomon, "Where am I to give birth? I have no hut, and the time is drawing nigh."

Solomon sent for okaMtshekula who reported all the huts were occupied. Lost in thought, he made his decision to sacrifice his own comfort and prestige for Christina's. Two kitchen storage huts had been set apart for him, one for meat, and one for beer before it had been strained. By nightfall, he had the beer hut made ready for Christina by the daughters of the hereditary servants of the kraal—the *egabeni*—those humble men who had no property and could never hope to aspire to any, who did all the meanest work without even having their task named for them.

Had Christina not been engrossed with her impending childbirth she would have paid more attention to Ethel's welcome, taken her in person to call upon the mothers of the kraal, escorted her from hut to hut, warned her beforehand who were friends, and who were only pretending to be, but she was already suffering an almost insurmountable pain, and Ethel was left to make her own way.

Christina suspected that the wives thought Ethel was a loose woman from Johannesburg. They went out of their way to speak rudely to her, or their manner was causal, too offhand, with a marked look of disdain on their faces. Some looked at her with an assumed lack of interest and walked by, though they knew they should have at least spoken to a newcomer.

Unlike Christina, Ethel said she could not lie in the dark and put thoughts together so that they ran along like a path in the wood, with a place from which you started and a place to which you came. All her thoughts jumped about like bull frogs in the night, and frightened her. Ever since she had married the King, when she got up in the morning, instead of opening her head and her heart fresh and clear for whatever the day might bring, it was as if insects buzzed about in her head, and the days seemed gray and dark.

In her father's church, Ethel had learned long prayers by heart, and she found herself repeating Christina's coaching of each day as if it were a prayer.

"You will find all sorts of people, some will be kind and some will be mean; some will be toward you, and some will be against you; but throughout it all, walk among them with humility and respect."

Christina and Ethel took possession of the freshly renovated beer hut, and were joined by a newly arrived wife, another Christian girl of the Mambatheni, Cathareen. They took to each other at once.

Solomon arranged that while Christina was away having her baby, Ethel and Cathareen were to cook his food, watch his grocery supplies, and tend his kitchen hut; and that Nomapasi and Indluyokufa, a girl of the Ndwandwe, were to keep his personal hut tidy, and wash, press, and mend his clothes.

On the day Christina felt the first pangs of labor, she called to Ethel to fetch okaMtshekula, while she drank the medicine the doctor had given her. Her body became as if drunk, and she could not even hear what people said to her. No one patted her stomach with hot water, nor touched her in any way, and before she knew it, the child was there. Miraculously, with the birth of her child, her hearing returned, and her head felt as if a cool breeze went through it.

This was in 1920, but Christina, who had known her calendar in missionary days, could never remember whether her son was born in September or October, only that the Christmas festival that followed had taken place while she was still weak.

The women busied themselves about the hut, wrapped the child in flannel, but no one suggested Christina get up and go behind the hut and wash herself. All was not as it should be at this birth. Christina lay still for two days. The women lowered their voices when they approached her, and coaxed her to eat, and washed her off with warm water, but she was in such pain she could not even rally her customary gentle politeness.

The child, too, was sick. There was a big hollow from the top of his head to his forehead; he kept passing green matter and string-like worms; he would not take food. Native doctors took the child to a place where lightning had struck and gave him medicine at the spot to make him turn to his mother's breast.

Solomon came with Maphelu on the third day and asked that the child be brought to the door. Christina neither thanked him for his gifts nor acknowledged his presence. The mothers tried to pass it off but his whole manner changed. He sent immediately to Kroonstad for medicine for Christina and the child. She was not better for three weeks, but the two bottles of medicine sent by the doctor then began to make a difference in her.

The child, born big, had become very small and wizened. Even though the hollow in his head had closed, he still had trouble in eating. The doctor had told the King's messenger that the child was to be given two drops of the medicine early each morning which would relieve it of the poison in its body.

The first time the child was dosed it brought up blood. When the King heard this, he ordered the wicked medicine to be stopped instantly. Christina, still very weak, agreed with okaMtshekula that it was wiser to disregard the King, who knew nothing about children. Had the doctor not said they were not to take fright if the medicine took "severe action"? The doctor had not said, however, insisted the messenger called in for requestioning and to reenact instructions, that the child might bleed. Nevertheless, for a week they secretly, but faithfully gave the baby the medicine. He began to put on flesh, and at last lay content at his mother's breast.

The second month after the child's birth, Ethel and Cathareen rejoined Christina in her hut, and okaMtshekula returned to hers. Christina again took up her duties in the kitchen. By nightfall, she was too tired to listen to the others, whose tongues made lively gossip, for not a week passed now without the King's taking a new girl or wife.

Wives were becoming pregnant and giving birth so frequently that it was hard for Christina to keep them all in mind. And no sooner did the wives become pregnant than they developed pains like hers.

In the month when Christina's son began to sit up, Solomon called up all his children from all his kraals to Mahashini to be baptized. Christina's daughter, whom she had left behind at the Zibindini kraal, arrived and did not know her. She did not call her "Mama" but "Sibiya." She said her mother was okaNdemele, who really was her grandmother. Pain stabbed through Christina's heart not unlike that she had recently felt in her womb.

The baptism was to be celebrated with becoming pagan ceremony. The King relied on Christina to help him chart his way through Christian rites.

"Find Christian names and assign them to all the children," he ordered. Already Christina felt none too secure among the other wives. "The mothers may resent my naming their children," she suggested. "You are right," he agreed.

He called all the mothers together and explained, "Each of you must find a name for your girls. I, myself, will name the boys. If you need help there are Christians among you ready to do so."

The women broke up into little knots; some sought the advice of Cathareen, some of Ethel, and few went to Christina. They labored more than a day over their lists when they again came before the King.

"We will now decide on the names of our children, which we will tell the minister. I have the names for my boys." Slowly the King began mispronouncing the unaccustomed English names which took on a Zulu sound. "Christina's son will be Hezron; the son of the daughter of Ndemele will be Victor; the son of the daughter of Buthelezi will be Agrippa; the son of the daughter of Zungu will be Ivious; and the son of the daughter of Mambathini will be Alphison."

The five mothers of the sons, each of whom secretly nursed the ambition that this, her firstborn, would be "pointed out" by the King as heir and the future King of the Zulus, thanked Solomon prettily for the honor he had bestowed on her by naming her son.

The girls' names were simpler, and more familiar to the European ear. Christina's daughter was to be Greta, a name she had cherished since her childhood at the Norwegian mission. There were two Margarets, a Harriet, a Jessica, and an Irina. Christina and the girl from Eshowe had two children; all the others had one each; seventeen children in all.

Christina hoped the people of the kraal would be so taken up with the ceremonies that they would not notice Greta insisted on speaking of her brother as "the child of Sibiya," as a stranger might.

Solomon called his children whatever their mothers did. Pleased to see them grow tall, in later years he referred to them affectionately as *aBafana boQunga*, Children of the Long Grass.

Ordinary natives' children, the *izingane*, called their father, *Baba*, their mother, *Mama*. Solomon's children addressed him as Zulu, and referred to him as *Inkosi*, the King or chief.

Royal children were specially designated. They were the *abaNtwana*, borne by the daughter of a given tribe. They would further differentiate as the boy, girl, middle, oldest, youngest, smallest, or biggest child of that daughter.

The royal children themselves called each other by name, mixing Christian and native names indiscriminately. When they got older, they spoke of *uMntwana wakwethu,* the child of one hut, the child of us, but if you asked which child, they would be specific, *uMntwana* Greta.

The Rev. Leonard Oscroft, of the Church of England, head of the school for chiefs and sons of chiefs, conducted the baptismal service at the church close by the Mahashini kraal. Hereafter he was to officiate at all Christian ceremonies at the royal kraal, and rumor had it that neighboring missions entertained a touch of envy toward him because of this closer association with the royal family.

The sun shone brilliantly as the mothers and the children in their crisp, fresh finery, filed into the church. Humbly Christina thanked her God for finding His way at last to this kraal, and for saving from eternal damnation her children—and the children of the wives whom she liked. Tucked in somewhere was the plea that He bring back her child Greta to her.

When her son was in his ninth month, crawling and beginning to try to walk, Christina became pregnant again. Almost immediately those pains which she had almost forgotten came back. The King sent to Kroonstad for medicine for her and for Nomapasi who had had her child, and who was not seriously sick except her leg swelled out and puffed until it no longer looked like a leg but like a tree.

Since Christina's last painful delivery, seven other wives had had children, of which three were stillborn. The King and everyone in the kraal showed great concern. The Christian God had been invoked to protect the kraal's fertility, and surely His wrath had been averted by the baptism of every one of the King's children. What, then, was this curse that now lay upon the kraal? Undoubtedly it was connected with childbirth, for not only did some of the children die at birth, but almost as soon as the seed was planted, the pregnant woman suffered with pain at the root of her womanhood.

A wife among them, though she desired to have children and fulfill her destiny, now met her fulfillment with anxiety as well as joy. Even the mothers, who were supposed to be well-versed in the secrets of womanhood, could not explain what blight had come upon them.

Suspicion grew. No one was trusted. Eyes and ears were sharpened in the hope of finding the enemy in their midst. The mothers put the blame upon those wives who went to their childbirth in fear, saying that the fear rose up in a cloud and brought down the curse. If the wives would only stop being afraid, the curse would leave them.

Three wives had children in one week. Cathareen had her child and it was healthy, but it was long in being born. Now whenever the birth of a child was reported to the King, he replied to his wife by letter, congratulating her on the birth of *his* child, and promising to present her with a goat. Some of the wives were at the same kraal with him, but some were at his other kraals and had not seen him for months. Eventually, all his wives knew this letter by heart.

A few days after Cathareen's child was born, Ndebele had her child. The King had never relaxed his instructions that his wives should not be touched or held during birth, lest some of the women use this opportunity to vent their spleen upon a helpless woman. For two days and two nights Ndebele lay there writhing in agony; the child would not come and none dared touch her. If only the King had been there, but he was at another kraal, and it took time for a messenger to go and come back with change of instructions.

Everyone knew Christina had been helped by medicine the doctor had given her at the birth of her son, and the mothers came and asked her to give some of this medicine to Ndebele. Christina was in a heart-breaking dilemma. It was an inflexible rule of the kraal not to give medicine to any-one without the King's consent and though she yearned to help this girl she dared not disobey. Now when every woman suspected every other woman of a desire to kill her, or her seed, was no time to break this rule. With a curi-ous prescience she dreaded the consequences if Ndebele grew worse after receiving medicine from her.

Solomon's permission came at last. Ndebele had froth at her mouth when they poured the medicine down. But the child quickly came away from her, and it came alive. The women all gave thanks from their hearts, but they paused not for a second. Even as they began to sponge Ndebele with warm water, she fell back, the whole of her right side twitching and she became a horrible sight to see. They knew she would no longer be with them unless something special and immediate were done. If only an *inyanga*, or the doctor of the white man, could tell them what to do!

Ndebele fought them off and would not agree to any treatment. They tell of the horror of it to this day. The child had come when the sun was at its height, and when the sun was fading, and the south wind was blowing, the mother died.

The child had not cried when it was born, and now they noticed some-thing was wrong with it, too; its right side was twitching as the mother's had done. Soon after the mother's death, the child died, too.

The kraal was grief-stricken. Trouble had been expected. Ndebele's lover had not wanted her to marry the King, he wanted her for himself. He had pleaded with her father that even though he was poor and did not then have the cattle to pay for her, if only the father would have faith in him, he would some day repay such confidence amply. Unmoved, the father put cattle and position before everything else, and arranged his daughter's marriage with the King.

The lover, maddened with jealousy and defeat, had come to the kraal. They said of him, "*ugulelwa amabhugane*"——that he had beetles in his head, that he was mad.

"It makes no difference who she marries, if she does not marry me, whether King or anyone else, at the time of her childbirth, nothing will be right for her!" Shouting, screaming, and shaking his fists, he threatened the curse which had now come to pass. "If she marries the King, a curse upon him and all his women!"

"I knew this man's curses, but I neglected to do anything about them," the King was to say later. "I trusted in God, and believed this curse would have no effect. Instead I should have called out my own witch doctors."

Tenderly, the women washed the bodies of the mother and child, combed the mother's hair straight back, and dressed her in a loose white gown, quickly stitched up by Christina, and swathed her body in white flannel. The baby's body, too, was warmly tucked about with it.

The mothers removed all Ndebele's ornaments, her armlets, anklets, bracelets, necklaces, and beadwork; and it was well they did, they thought, for soon the corpse swelled and would have been bruised by them.

Two of Solomon's mothers and the mother of the dead girl watched over the body that night, wailing loudly, their wails echoing in every hut of the kraal. All the women remained wide awake and added their voices to the night air. The hut of the dead woman and her child did not remain in darkness, for already some women claimed to have seen *itokoloshe*, a sort of fey creature visible only to women. There were too many ugly spirits abroad. The King's large lamp had been borrowed from his hut, and burned brightly through the night at the side of Ndebele.

The sun had been up for a while, and the watchers were growing weary with hunger and their long vigil, when the men brought in the plain wooden coffins they had been building through the night. Gently they laid the bodies in and nailed the covers down. Then the men bore away the coffin of Ndebele, draped with black cloth, while Solomon's mothers carried that of the child.

The coffins were taken beyond the stockade, back of the kraal, to a little fenced-in place where the still-born babies were buried. A native Christian preacher conducted brief burial services, after which men began to dig the graves. These were bordered, Zulu fashion, with a ring of stones, but no cross was put upon them, for these two were not Christians. The minister said a last prayer and the mourners joined in singing a Zulu hymn.

Girls in charge of the children kept them out of sight, for it was not right for children to see the dead, and with this strong curse upon the kraal it was necessary to be especially careful.

Everyone went down to the river for cleansing. Out of sight of the men, the women took off their clothes and washed their bodies; those who had towels dried themselves; others put on their clothes while still wet. A few of the mothers went to the hut where the bodies had lain and threw water about and washed away all signs of death.

The King was not able to come for the funeral, but when he returned next day everyone went to condole with him. He was so overcome with grief that Maphelu had to answer for him. People from distant kraals came to pay their respects and offer sympathy. Messengers were sent to the store for black material, and Solomon ordered Christina and Ethel to cut mourning armbands for all the women of the kraal. What was left of the material was sent to the mother of the dead girl.

Tragedy had come to the kraal crushing the women's spirits. They believed the curse laid upon them by Ndebele's lover had come to stay and nothing but misfortune awaited the wives of the kraal.

fifteen

A lighter feeling spread throughout the kraal, when for the first time a wife was sent away to have her child at the lady doctor's hospital at the nearest mission; surely she would banish this curse that hung over them

Ethel, too, was sent to her and reported that the lady doctor had found her too fat, and had assured her that after only a few doses of medicine she would be with child.

"Here is my medicine nearly finished. What am I to do? The doctor told me while I was taking it I was to sleep with the King," Ethel complained.

Christina had neither answer nor advice, but felt the matter was serious enough to take up with one of the mothers.

"Ethel is going to stop taking her medicine because the way to the King has been blocked by many girls," she solemnly informed okaMtshekula.

That evening okaMtshekula led up to Solomon's responsibility with the most effective argument her mind could devise. "My son, you know the daughter of Shwabete has been with you a long time. Her relatives are displeased she is not with child, and they are beginning to wonder whether you are paying any attention to her."

The King read the letter his wives received before they were delivered to them, and he had seen how in each letter the Shwabetes' anxiety had increased. "Of a truth her relatives are disturbed, and think I am treating her like a person at a distance, and her heart is sore with shame before them," he acknowledged frankly.

Dutifully, Solomon sent for Ethel on four successive nights, though the nights were broken by the visits of other girls. But when he came upon her and Christina in the kitchen unexpectedly, there would not be a sound of talk or laughter. "Has someone been speaking meanly to you?" he would ask.

"No, we are just silent, that is all," they would answer.

"What are you thinking about?" he would say, trying to penetrate this wall of silence he could not understand. "I told you if anything worried you, you were to bring it to me at once and not hide it from me. You do not deceive me; my having a lot of girls goes badly with you; you think I have cast you two aside. I have not. I have so many women, so many people to attend to."

Why did the King plead with them? But he did, as if he wanted to think through his own bewilderment: "No, we Kings do not cast aside, nor can we pay attention to all around regularly. Some girls use love philters, and even if you do not love them at first you commence to do so. They cast a spell upon you! My girls work against my wives. They do everything they can to keep me away from them, especially from you two. They all whisper that I love you two, and that you are Europeans."

Suddenly Solomon brightened with a happy inspiration. "When I go down to the uSuthu kraal, I will take Ethel with me."

It was well he did not wait for the effect of these words.

"Christina," Ethel was burning with the restraint of the past few minutes, "I will not go with him! I do not want to go and live at this kraal, and at that kraal, and at every other kraal. I do not want to be separated from you. Who is there at the uSuthu who will guide me? Who will comfort me when I am homesick?"

"You did not marry me; you married the King; and wherever the King says you must go, there you must go," firmly and dispassionately declared Christina. "Your luck may change. Perhaps you will get a child at this new kraal. The King is offering you his love, and you should be happy."

Christina had not yet known continued hunger, her experience at Middleburg had been wiped from her mind. All she asked of the King was medicine from the doctor at Kroonstad, since she had given hers to Ndebele and had none left.

Solomon always countered with a joke—her child was still a long way off. Several times she tried to explain the medicine was for pains during pregnancy as well as at childbirth, but the King grew impatient and left her in midsentence.

Once, before going to the uSuthu, Solomon called Christina to him. Now when the King called a wife to his side, there might be one, two, three, or more girls waiting their turn. A wife barely got to the King's hut before she was coming back to her own to sleep alone.

Christina found it filled her body with a strange restlessness to go to the King in this abrupt way, instead of nicely drowsing with him. She was afraid of her own thoughts, when it suddenly came to her that she would almost rather not be called to her husband at all.

Ethel had been with the King at the uSuthu some weeks when he brought her back with him to Mahashini. The lonely weeks melted away as Ethel and Christina chatted rapidly, as if the short time they might have would not be enough to get everything said.

For once, it was Ethel who did the talking. "It is just the same at the uSuthu as it was here. He calls me in my turn, but there are so many of us the turns come far away from each other. He still keeps paying for other girls in cattle. And I still do not have a child."

Christina sensed she was withholding something and prodded Ethel into disclosing it. "Yes, I have a sorrow," she admitted, sighing. "It is even greater than my not being with child. Christina, the King *thrashes* his wives!"

There had been rumors of this, but perhaps Ethel was exaggerating. "How do you know?" Christina demanded, unbelieving.

"He has not thrashed me yet, but he thrashes the others when I am in the hut, and it is as if the sjambok hit my flesh!" Ethel answered with flashing eyes and a reminiscent shudder. "Sometimes the King is drunk, and maybe he does not know what he is doing. Sometimes he loses his temper about something which has nothing to do with his wives. He looks about him and sees some girl, remembers some old thing she did which she had long forgotten, and then he grabs her and beats her with all his strength.

"Once in a while when he has thrashed a girl, he forgets it immediately and talks quietly to her, even calling her to him that night. Sometimes it takes longer before he forgives her."

Neither was struck with the incongruity of the King's doing the forgiving. "He never thrashes a girl to whom he is showing favor, or wives who are with child," Ethel continued sadly. "They say at the uSuthu that for a long time he never struck anybody, then the day he started, he kept it up as if he were feeling at heart all the evil things ever done to him by his women."

Christina's mind shuttled back and forth. She could not believe this cruel tale of the King; he must have a reason for behaving this way.

"What had these girls done to make the King so angry?" she insisted.

"There have been so many thrashings, so many things done, I cannot remember them all," Ethel confessed. "Some refused to serve him; others he beat for telling lies."

The women at Mahashini had been none too friendly since the death of Ndebele, but there had been only threats of disobedience there.

"Why do the wives refuse to serve the King?" relentlessly probed Christina.

"Maybe it is jealousy," suggested Ethel, struggling to be fair, "for he calls some all the time, and some wives live there at the uSuthu as if they were strangers to him. Their hearts grow sore because the King does not call them, and they sit in their huts and say ugly things about the others. If the King in passing should hear, he leaps into the hut like a cheetah and pounces upon the girl who is talking. He strikes her one or two blows and orders her to come to his hut where he keeps his sjambok, and then we know what is going to happen. He slams the door shut behind him, so none of his mothers, nor his indunas, can put him off by praising the spirits of the departed Kings. Nothing can put him off when he is like that."

Christina could not banish the horror of these disclosures from her mind.

"I hear you have thrashed some of your wives at the uSuthu," she hesitantly said to the King when they were alone together.

Savagery seemed to take possession of him: "I am going to commence thrashing here at Mahashini."

Never yet had she suffered the full strength of his anger, and her courage was intact. "Because you started thrashing people at the uSuthu, are you going to come to Mahashini, and thrash people who have done you no wrong?"

"This Mahashini is the same as the uSuthu. The women are evil doers, the whole lot of them. I have not thrashed before because I had control of myself. I want my wives to realize they are no longer little girls, they are married, and I am *the man!*"

Seldom had she heard his voice so ugly. She knew better than to make any comment, and was relieved when his anger seemed to cool, and he spoke of routine matters.

Before the King left for the courthouse at Babanango he gave specific instructions that large quantities of beer were to be prepared. The women knew Solomon was likely to return from meetings the worse for continuous drinking. There was even a rumor among the Zulus that government inspectors had suggested to the Magistrate that he stop Solomon's drinking so much, that the Magistrate had asked how they thought it could be done; and that then white men had even gone so far as to threaten to make it a crime against the government for any white man, or native, to sell or bring liquor to the King.

There was much talk about this among the chiefs, and even those who did not like to have the government interfere with the lives of the Zulus with additional laws agreed they would not blame the government if such a law were introduced. Often when the chiefs would wait weeks for their supreme Chief, the King, to come and settle an important matter—a dispute about cattle between two men of equal rank, or which of two brothers was the father's heir, when the father had been careless and had not pointed out his Great Wife during his life—the King, whose decision was final, would arrive so drunk they would have to put him to bed and wait a good part of a day, or perhaps two or three days, before they could hold their meeting.

When the King returned from Babanango even the new wives could see that his feet were not planted as firmly on the ground as they might be. He staggered into his hut, weary of the squabbling of his tribal family. His head buzzed and his stomach ached, and though he was sick of the sight of beer and whiskey he longed for a draught of liquid which would make his tongue lie smoothly in his mouth.

Barely looking up, he asked for beer, and when it did not come promptly, he shouted: "I want beer."

"There is no beer!" one of the girls managed to mouth.

Solomon rushed to the kitchen where four of his wives were busily preparing food. "What does it mean, there is no beer?" he demanded.

Christina no longer paid any attention when the King spoke with the fumes of liquor about him. Once he had a few hours of sleep, his head would clear, that befuddled look would leave his face, and the thickness disappear from his voice. "I do not know, as it is not my duty to look after the beer," she answered simply.

"Where have you been?"

Her patience was like that of a mother with a child who does not understand very well, who must be told a story from the beginning: "Early this morning I went down to wash your clothes at the river. From there I went to get wood where the boys had been chopping. Then——"

"Didn't you go at all to the hut where they were supposed to prepare beer?" he interrupted.

"Yes, but I didn't stop to see what they were doing."

"What did you go there for, then?" he snarled.

"I went to look for my child, who was not in my hut."

This silly business of questions and answers was too much, for Christina had the right of him on every one. He strode to the door of the hut and shouted at the top of his voice: "I want all my wives to come here at once! All of you hear me calling, go find my wives and bring them here!"

Wives streamed from every direction to the clearing at the front of the kitchen hut. There were a great number of them, more than Christina could count: wives with no definite assignments, those with prescribed ones, and those whose specific duty it was to make beer.

Solomon noted who was there, too, for now he shouted, even more loudly, "All those in the kitchen, and all those who look after my hut, come here immediately! Let a young man stand guard at the hut!"

With lagging feet, they came forward. Christina locked the kitchen door behind her and came, too.

The King's voice rasped with anger, a muscle throbbed at his temple, and his face was gleaming wet. "Are all my wives here?"

No one answered. Some of the wives had cowered under blankets and sent word by others that they were sick.

Solomon made rapid mental count, "Who among you is sick?"

Since no one spoke he pointed at a girl before him, and hurled his words at her: "*You* tell me!"

"Ntoyintoyi, a girl of the Buthelezi, and a girl of the Ndwandwe," trembling, she barely managed to whisper.

"When did they get sick? When I left there was no one sick in this kraal!" He raised his voice so that all the kraal might hear him: "Those sick ones, they better come out of their huts! It will go badly with them, if I, myself, go there and yank them out!"

Ntoyintoyi walked up defiantly, but the others came on dragging feet. Hypnotized with terror, he held them there in apprehensive silence, while they waited for Christina to bring his oil swinging-lamp, his flashlight, and his sjambok. Not even a whisper passed through the crowd. Far away there was the faint sound of water trickling and dripping.

The King snatched the sjambok from Christina and curtly ordered the panic-stricken women to follow him outside the kraal to the stable. Heads bent, shoulders slumped, they filed behind him, doomed automatons from whom all hope was erased. Solomon sat down upon a box and all his wives knelt wordlessly before him. It might have been a prayer meeting; so it was, for those who remembered their prayers.

Christina placed the lamp beside him, and it illuminated him alone. The rest were in black darkness. Slowly he flicked the flashlight around to make sure, once again, that all his wives were there.

With an assumed gentleness, he broke the tense silence: "Is there any beer?"

No one answered. Power of speech had long since left them.

As if each word made a pleasant sound, Solomon repeated: "Is there any beer?"

To Christina it seemed as if that voice was speaking to her and to her alone. "I don't know!" she almost sobbed.

"I am not asking *you!*" His reply was solely for her, too. "Get out and attend to your work in the kitchen. I will thrash you in a minute, separately," he thundered.

Not even in demoniacal rage was Solomon prepared to abuse Christina. She stumbled to her feet with the habitual "thank you!" that followed any order of the King, but indeed her thanks had never been more sincere.

Solomon fixed his attention on Cathareen cowering in fright: "Who did you leave in my hut?" Before she could answer, he barked at her: "Get out! Get out to the hut and look after it!"

Common dread fused into a common hatred of the new favorite. All the wives remembered Solomon had specifically designated a young man to look after the hut; he was using a flimsy excuse to spare Cathareen the punishment they were about to receive.

Christina leaned helplessly against the kitchen hut, tears pouring down her cheeks, her knees shaking from the terror which was still upon her. As wild screams cut through the air she felt her heart tear from its roots.

Galvanized into action, without considering the propriety of leading open rebellion against the King, she ran for the kraal mothers, and as three of them came running toward her to discover whence and why came the sudden blood curdling yells, Christina, now hysterical, began to shriek: "Stop him! Stop him! He will kill them! He is like a crazy man. I will get all the other mothers and all the men of the kraal."

As she ran about, screaming for help, first these three mothers, and then a great many others, rushed with full force upon the stable door, and tried to bash it in. Desperate, inhuman cries from behind the locked door drowned their efforts to attract Solomon's attention.

"*Ngonyama!* Lion! Lion! Strong man! Great man!" they sang Solomon's praises. "The greatest of all Kings! Greater than Dinuzulu, greater even than Cetshwayo! Leave off, Ndabezitha! Leave off! Be merciful, our son!"

At last he opened the door. "What are you doing here?" he demanded of the weeping mothers.

"We hear voices crying out in death!" one of them managed to say. A chorus of wails supported her.

Solomon was neither moved nor diverted by this mention of death. "So, it is you who incite my wives to disobey me!" he sneered.

"No. We hear the words of death our ancestors are sending to warn us, so we may warn you," their spokesman answered. "Better desist, our son!"

The interruption had merely given Solomon back his breath. "Since I have started thrashing, I am going to thrash thoroughly all of them that disobey me," he announced with ugly, unswerving intention. "You shall see for yourselves, hereafter, how I shall hold my wives in obedience to me."

With a lordly gesture he pushed open the double doors revealing the sobbing, prostrate women. The helpless mothers could not bear to look at them.

"So I am not a King!" Solomon screamed. "So I am just an ordinary native. But we shall see whether my orders mean anything, whether they are to be carried out. Come out of this stable, and this very night, grind the mealies, and brew the beer!"

No one stirred.

"Come out, I said!" There was a struggling, crushing stampede through the door to escape the hissing black snake Solomon let fly from him.

The sjambok dropped limply to his side as the last girl passed him. "Any one of you who wishes to leave my kraal may do so and marry wherever she likes! I have none of you chained up," he called to the fast disappearing, bowed backs.

The crowd that had collected drew aside and made a wide path for him. No one, man or woman, looked him in the eye.

The wind had died down. The blackness of night had never seemed more impenetrable. Usually the kraal had long since been blanketed with silence. Tonight at the top end of the kraal, at the beer hut, where beer was being made, wives were quarreling among themselves. Two of them had to be separated. Others were shouting at each other: "You got hit only a little——" "I got thrashed more severely——" "You have medicine, which makes him like you better——"

Some said nothing, only nursed their bruises and their bleeding cuts.

The King could hear the row and sent for Christina to report on it. She was glad he did not press her for what the wives were saying. The noise went on unabated through the night. The King did not go out to challenge it; he sent for Cathareen, who tried to bring peace and comfort to him.

Christina lay in her hut that night and wondered doggedly why there was no comfort to be had from her thoughts. She decided maybe, when her heart had been torn from her body, her head had been, too. The emptiness and the pain which had been growing within her were swallowing her up; it was as if she were no longer alive. Every time she tried to think, to remember how it all had happened, it was as if she had forgotten how to think, and a great pain came to her head, and a great sickness to her stomach.

She tried to cry, but her mouth and body were numb, and the sobs would not come. She got up, and tried to take some beer, but she could not find the beer, nor even the other side of the hut. It was all darkness, whether she moved about or lay upon her mattress. In a desperate weariness she gave up trying to move and lay there staring at the dark until merciful sleep closed her dry, hot eyes, and she forgot about her pain.

When Christina awoke next morning she tried to find an excuse for the King's maniacal drunkenness. Her chaotic thoughts were easier to marshal than on the previous evening. The King had to be obeyed by all his subjects, she reasoned, not only by his wives. There were laws for every man and woman of the Zulu people, and men learned these laws early. If they broke them, the indunas called them before the court of chiefs, and made them pay fines in cattle or money; and the white man's courts, that were even higher than the Zulu courts, had said it was right that the Zulus should respect the laws of their King.

Even little children knew there were laws for every kraal, with a man the head of his kraal, and his wives were expected to obey him; so, surely, when the head of the kraal was the King of a nation, whom men and women were taught to respect and obey, his wives must know that punishment would inevitably follow if they did not do as bidden.

Christina began to believe in the justice of the King's anger, though she still shuddered away from the memory of his brutality.

sixteen

None of Solomon's wives left him. A few nursed his permission for future use; most of them, however, decided they were but empty words; they had nowhere to go if they did leave him. Their marriages had been the result of long negotiations and a much desired political alliance with the King, and their relatives would do nothing to jeopardize their standing at the King's kraal.

Native wives seldom left their husbands, and only when the husbands consistently and flagrantly abused them. Under such circumstances the girl's family could demand penalty in cattle. In practice the relatives seldom did this, for it is dangerous to sit in judgment on a man and suggest publicly that he has behaved badly.

When penalties could be exacted for her misconduct, a husband might send a wife with whom he had lost patience back to her family. This happened more frequently. It required open court proceedings and publicity too; and Solomon who might have sent back some of his wives, preferred like so many other husbands, not to call attention to his inability to manage his womenfolk.

Since the advent of the white courts, which were a higher tribunal than the native ones, to which any native might bring a grievance, it was known a native would be punished by the white men if he beat his wife. Most wives did not know about this law, and even when they did they were afraid to complain to white courts against their own menfolk; such tale-bearing would breed its own trail of persecution.

An abused wife of the King's kraal would have to throw herself upon the mercy of the men of her family. Suppose a father were good-hearted and it pained him to hear that one of his beloved daughters had been unfairly treated by the King, there was very little he could do without sacrifice of property, prestige, or both. If the daughter had not borne at least one child to the King when she returned to her father's kraal, no matter how great her grievance, the cattle which the King had paid for her would have to be returned.

Suppose this father had loyal sons who had worked with him to build up his kraal and his household, who chopped the wood, built the stockade, tended the cattle, and pooled the earnings from the mines with him, against the day when they wished to acquire wives with the cattle of the kraal. The cattle were not apt to be numerous, for the kraal had to be fed with meat, and each new beast cost four or five pounds. How could a just father, to satisfy a girl's whim to remain no longer with her lawful husband, pay with cattle that the sons now regarded as their own?

Sometimes there are brothers of gentler hearts, but an induna who had married his daughter to the King might have twenty wives himself, and from these twenty wives there would be sons, and the return of a wife back to the kraal of the father would be a subject for all the sons to consider and decide. It was not likely, nor to be expected, that the majority of these men, who frequently had trouble controlling an audacious wife, would take seriously a sister's grievance against her husband, particularly if that husband were the King. All this the wives of the King knew only too well.

The embittered wives declared they now had but one hope, to arouse the King's anger firmly against them. If he no longer wanted them at his kraal, then the men of their family would be compelled to take them back.

Solomon seemed rested and in excellent spirits when he summoned all his wives into his hut.

"Is there any beer?" was his greeting.

A firm chorus of: "Yes, Ndabezitha," answered him.

Some of the women had raw welts across their faces, scars of which they bear to this day.

"Who has been striping my wives' faces?" the King jocularly asked.

Casually he picked up and examined the torn knuckles, raw palms, bruised arms. A few wives grew rigid at his approach and touch. Many tittered nervously. Others were angry and failed to appreciate his good spirits.

"The person who thrashed my wives and spoiled their beautiful faces must pay a fine." The voice was gay and lilting, the face smiling. "What shall it be, a beast, a goat, or money?" he teased.

Five of the wives stood up simultaneously. "We want the man to pay a fine in money!" they chorused.

A curt nod at them indicated they were to remain standing. All the rest were on their knees out of respect to him. Spreading his legs wide apart, thrusting his hands into his pockets, he drew out a large roll, counted out one pound notes as penalty, and paid them quickly to those who had suggested the obvious way to salve his conscience. For the others he had neither word nor glance: he had made a gesture of friendliness, and they had spurned it.

Nevertheless, he announced that a beast was to be killed for them, that he was leaving immediately for the Zibindini kraal, and that there would be a great festival on his return in honor of his marriage to the well-born daughter of Nqothi. "My indunas will bring word of the day of my arrival, so that plenty of beer may be prepared!" he threateningly concluded.

Custom requires that a groom be present at his own wedding ceremony, though he need not participate in it. On the day the bridal party was expected, Solomon was back, and invited all the wives of his kraal who were not pregnant to be present. This was in the early twenties: Solomon already had more than twenty wives, but this was his first formal wedding feast.

The Zulu bride sets out from her home for that of the groom the day before her wedding, spends the night with the bridal party in a secluded spot along the way, but remains in concealment from the groom and his people until the peak of the wedding ceremony.

The wedding feast of Nqothi and Solomon commenced with the 'gqumushela, that part of the ceremony in which all the young people of the same age as the bride and groom clap hands and dance, and separately make merry. There had been some sly whispers about this for this bride was far from young.

About twenty of Solomon's men, as distinguished from those of the bride's immediate family, lined up in military precision and commenced the wedding dance. They waved their shields, brandished their sticks, and tossed their knobkerries, even in their wildest hysteria preserving a regimental unity. For this performance in the presence of the King, they had for days rehearsed patterns and forms that now fused into a smooth harmony.

Distracting not one whit of attention from the men's dances, slowly up the hill proceeded the bride. Behind her straggled long files of women attendants, bearing aloft upon their heads mats, calabashes, suitcases, boxes, lanterns, umbrellas, and hunks of raw, exposed meat, as befitted a well-dowered young woman of high estate.

Chairs had already been placed for the most distinguished guests and among them was the groom himself, looking on in a bored and cynical manner. Solomon had not only matured in the years since he had married Christina, but the change in him was that from a country boy to a slick city sophisticate. He drove about in high-powered motor cars, and wore a cocked cap of his own design and a snugly tailored military uniform, with which the government had forbidden his wearing a Sam Browne Belt. Certainly, looking at him there it would seem there might be justice in the rumor that the King took ancient tribal customs with a trace of humor.

Others beside Solomon smiled when an induna, on horseback, representing the South African government, asked the bride and groom if they loved each other, and they mumbled that they did. When the government first decreed this question would have to be asked at all native weddings, it was greeted with roars of laughter, as according to their traditions a bride and groom are not supposed to show the slightest interest in each other. The bride is marrying a clan, not an individual man.

The bride did not have the usual bridal topknot, for it was known that if she had already prepared one, the King would give orders to break it down instantly and cleanse her hair. A Zulu maiden about to marry has all the women of her kraal help build up her hair into a high edifice solidified with a dry red-clay powder. The higher the structure the more beautiful the bride; the more carefully tended, the neater the wife. From the day of marriage the wife retains the high knot.

Nqothi represented a blend of heathen and Christian ways. Her hair was clean and smooth as any Christian girl's might be, but she wore a large feather headdress and a small beaded face veil, as was proper for a Zulu bride.

Too late, some of the wives discovered that Nqothi wore the leather undergarment of the heathen state, almost like a man's loin cloth, but they knew that no sooner would she come into Solomon's presence than he would strip it from her and tell her never to wear it again; that his wives wore ankle-length petticoats, as Christian women should.

Fluffy white oxtails spread like fans at Nqothi's shoulders, waist, and knees. Crisscrossed over her body were countless taut strips of intricately wrought multicolored beadwork. At a distance she looked exactly like a large bird of gay plumage.

A brand-new knee-length skirt of a well-cured, nicely marked hide hung from her waist. After the ceremony, other girls would have had to give up so handsome a skirt for the other brides of her kraal to wear, but Nqothi's father was so prosperous he could afford to give his daughter her wedding skins outright.

Nqothi and the women of her kraal had learned how to knit, and for this royal ceremony they had made tight-fitting leggings of rainbow-colored wool, with tassels bobbing at the knees. Tied to the ankles with great big bows were butterfly cocoons threaded on velvet bands and filled with tiny flecks of gravel which rattled as she danced.

As Nqothi's menfolk advanced into the clearing and took position directly opposite the groom's party, from it defiantly strutted a man intoning loud praises of the King's household. One by one, men of the bride's household, depending on their status—the heir of Nqothi first, then his blood brothers, and then his other brothers—broke away from their ranks, leaped into the air waving their assegais and shields, stalking and challenging the groom's party, and singing the praises of their own household.

The old ladies of the bride's party crouched before the warriors in pantomime, sowing mealie seeds from their calabashes and invoking the blessing of fertility for the bride. Just then Solomon unfortunately chose to walk away. The bride, as everyone knew, was without doubt bringing fertility to the King's household, for she was already pregnant; this traditional ceremony was not necessary, and it was tactless of the King to call attention to it. But as any bride might have done, Nqothi danced in wild abandon until she was exhausted.

The Zulu concept of virgin shades in meaning, for the Zulus will accept a woman as a virgin if she has not conceived a child. If the bride brandish-es an assegai, or a metal-bladed knife, she is indeed a virgin. The bride may have had children by the groom; but, once a pregnancy has occurred, imme-diate negotiations for formal marriage are begun, and the man responsible is expected to marry her.

When a couple are engaged, a pregnancy before marriage is taken more lightly than when a girl merely has admirers. Before the advent of the white man, when only Zulu customs prevailed, a child born out of wedlock was instantly killed and so were its parents. The Zulu code had now relaxed to the point where the King took unto himself whatever girls he fancied, and frequently made alliances only when there were children, or when purpos-es of state dictated them.

The King, very drunk, reeled into his hut and immediately fell asleep. Maphelu hastened to minimize the insult by announcing that the groom's party would do their big dances the following day, and the King would parade his regiments. The bridal party were not mollified by this promise of regimental honors; many of them had not even seen the King, and appar-ently, they said, he did not see fit to remain at his own wedding.

When Solomon woke it was well into the night. Still drunk, he ordered the bridal party awakened and the festivities to recommence at once. Eventually the King wore everyone out, and in the early dawn the kraal looked like a field of battle, crumpled bodies strewn about in a drunken stupor.

All the wives of the kraal were set against the King, who had chosen so blatantly to honor only one of them. They were jealous of this woman who had a formal wedding while they had not, and they said harsh things among themselves. Their relatives were jealous, too, as they would have liked a brilliant wedding ceremony for the King and their daughters, but in their case Solomon had just taken the girl and paid later as he wished.

Christina felt as badly as the rest but, not one to join in talk about the King, she said directly to him, "Why does this one get such a magnificent wedding, and why did none of us have one?"

"Nqothi would not consent to my marrying his daughter, so I had to put her into pregnancy." He did not stop to weigh the effect of his words; "Then her father, who is a mighty man amongst us, whose anger I dare not risk, said his daughter would have to have a marriage ceremony." Christina knew he was not telling the exact truth.

For once all the wives were united, joining in ridicule and hatred of this new wife. They noted with pleasure that the King did not treat this bride as he had others. After the wedding he neither sat with her, nor made merry with her, and when the bridal party returned to their home, the King accom-panied them while the bride remained alone at Mahashini.

Christina had expected to welcome this bride graciously and with sin-cere good feeling. The daughter of Nqothi herself had made this impossible;

she flaunted before all the wives that she was born of an important man and was the first to have an elaborate wedding ceremony.

Escape from the King's kraal had begun to be openly suggested and discussed. "In our case we can return home if we wish to. Nothing can be done to us because no formal ceremony took place; no formal marriage was registered at the white man's court," Christina told Nqothi with triumphant malice.

When the excitement of the wedding was beginning to peter out, the mothers and the wives of the kraal took note which of the King's wives had stayed away from the ceremonies. Pregnant women do not come to a Zulu wedding. Sudden suspicion centered upon two wives, a daughter of the Cebekhulu people, whose kraal was near the Umngeni River, and the daughter of Zidumazile.

Everyone knew whom the King called and when. It was a matter of careful tabulation and note for all the mothers and wives. The King had not called these two wives for months; Cebekhulu not since the time her child had been born dead, over a year ago.

Ethel, who always seemed to Christina to need things explained to her a little more carefully than other people, kept repeating: "How did they ever manage to do it? Why, we are not even allowed to talk to one of the King's brothers!" Several times Ethel had seen Solomon, or one of his mothers, send for a wife and severely reprimand her for having merely greeted one of the men of the kraal.

Realities and facts transgressed theories for Christina: "They must have found a way, because everyone knows that these two, Cebekhulu and the daughter of Zidumazile are with child."

The unity among the wives lasted just one day. This fresh gossip immediately divided them into cliques again. Most of them were bent on getting full satisfaction out of making sport of the two wives, who could hardly walk across the kraal without some wife taunting: "Where did you get this from?" or "Where did you get that thing you have with you?"

Ntoyintoyi alone had nothing but praise for their ingenuity when, abandoned by the King, they were clever enough to find other men for themselves: "Now we shall all go out and commit adultery!" she gaily promised. "Those two are much smarter than the rest of us!"

Christina, Ethel, and Cathareen were the only wives who not only showed pity for the two now shunned as outcasts, but agreed this was the worst blow the King had yet received.

"Adultery has taken place in the King's kraal; it must be rooted out, and steps taken about it immediately!" was the message the mothers sent to Solomon.

Solomon ordered all the wives to report without delay to the head mother's hut. Cebekhulu was the one whose stomach betrayed her, and the mothers spoke to her first. "What have you there, inside of you?" Cebekhulu did not answer. "Where did you get that child?" demanded the mother. "I just found it in myself; picked it up somewhere."

"And where did you find the man who put this child down for you to pick up?" persisted the mother relentlessly.

Cebekhulu kept her eyes pinned to the ground, unable to face the mounting hostility in the hut. But the malice and hatred of the mothers aroused her defiance: "Do you think I had to go away to find this child, when there are so many men here who have no wives?"

It was as if the mothers were hunters and she the prey, and they were about to spear their assegais into her. All their threatening faces were intent upon her, as the head mother pressed still further: "We must know that man! We must know that man! You had better tell us his name!"

But Cebekhulu would not answer. It was sunset before they gave up, and she had told them nothing.

It was different with Zidumazile. She flatly denied her pregnancy. "How do you know I am pregnant?" she demanded. "I am only sick."

"I am sorry, my child, that we have insulted you, or accused you wrongfully; that we have slurred your father's name!" the head mother sneered.

The King, who had been eavesdropping, now shouted from the doorway: "Let all the wives get back to their work!"

Next morning, after breakfast, all the wives were called together again, and it did not take very long before Cebekhulu broke down and confessed. She accused Mbede, a young man from Swaziland, who looked after the King's horses. As soon as her condition was noticeable, she said, he had run away from the kraal.

The mothers hastened to Solomon. "I will send a telegram to establish a thorough search for this man," he declared vehemently. "As for this girl, Zidumazile, she is lying; she has no illness, she is not sick in any way. She used to go with Cebekhulu wherever she went. I will send for Doctor Green, at the magistracy, and get him to examine her. He will let me know whether she is pregnant or not."

Meantime the wives were having a heated argument. Some believed Cebekhulu was justified in naming the man who had deserted her to stand her punishment alone; while others felt she should have stood out in stubborn resistance, and had shown herself to be a coward. Most of the wives were more concerned with what would happen to Zidumazile, and whether she could manage to get away before the King and the mothers discovered she was pregnant. Chiefly it appealed to their love of intrigue to have a woman try to hide her pregnancy. But also, the neglected wives had a welling up of sympathy for her.

"Ever since the King has been married to Zidumazile he has never called her, or been near her in any way," they said. "He comes and takes girls away from boys who are in love with them and brings them here, and then plays the fool with them. We will show him! We, too, shall become pregnant as and where we can."

The King's pride was wounded, and it hurt Christina to see him so humiliated by his wives.

"Did you know that Cebekhulu was having anything to do with this boy? Tell me the truth, Christina!" he pleaded.

Discouraged by the multiplicity of his wives, she had long since given up strict count of whom he called, except those in whom she was especially interested, and for whom she hoped for kind attention. Her heart ached with pity for him but she answered truthfully, "I thought this stomach was yours."

"This girl used to stay with you in your hut. The number of times I called her would not escape your memory," he insisted.

So many wives had been slipped in and out of Christina's hut, until better arrangements were made for them, that she no longer remembered who had been sleeping there. Besides, the King's habits had changed. "I was not keeping a close watch." Again she strove for accuracy. "But anyway, how could I tell? Now you even call your wives to sleep with you in the daytime, when I am busy with my work."

On second thought Solomon must have feared the doctor's verdict on Zidumazile would commit him to immediate action, so he canceled the call for him, preferring to move slowly in any difficulty. Zidumazile was sent back to her people, presumably so they might treat her sickness, but Solomon was quietly waiting for the pregnancy to develop into something her father would have to take up with him.

Before Zidumazile left he reminded her: "If your sickness turns out to be a child, you are to tell your father where the child came from!"

Cebekhulu was to be dealt with after her child came, he announced. Later the mothers and the wives thought he had made a mistake; that prompt action and a proper punishment for these two would have saved the King from the scandal about to break openly in the kraal.

Gossip had never been so thick before. The words "*bethi . . . bethi . . . bethi . . .*" constantly fell upon the ears of the annoyed King—"saying this, saying this, saying this," that is, gossiping.

Two wives made a break for freedom. The kraals were carefully guarded, but Ntoyintoyi and a girl of the Mtshali people, who lived at Dlebe where the poisonous trees grew, were not to be found in their huts.

On reaching her home at Babanango, Ntoyintoyi sold the clothes bought for her at Johannesburg and Vryheid, and went back to wearing only her *ibayi* shawl. Her father, an induna at Zibindini, warned her he would have nothing to do with this insubordination.

When the King came to Babanango looking for her, the father swore he did not know where Ntoyintoyi was. Her lover, too, got down on his knees, upraised his arms and swore he did not know either. The King became furious at this double deception, first the father, and then the lover making sport of him.

That night the King sent men to prowl in the dark. Faint noises drew them to the bachelor hut, for natives' ears are attuned to every sound of the night. They could hear the lover fumbling for his assegai in the thatch of the roof. Every native has at least one secreted there, despite the law which forbids them to own any weapons of defense. A native may own and carry a stick with a top knob no bigger than will fit into his mouth.

With one rush the King's men broke down the door. They found Ntoyintoyi grappling with her lover, trying to make him surrender his assegai, fearful lest in a moment of madness he make himself liable for murder. Maphelu and another man separated them, and forced the assegai away from the lover.

The entire kraal crowded in, imploring: "Let this young man be. Don't kill him!"

Ntoyintoyi refused to leave her lover, but two of the men dragged her off a goodly distance, screaming and biting the entire way. The men were so exhausted that they practically dumped her before the King.

The King took in her appearance slowly. "Why did you throw away all the clothes I gave you? What are you doing wearing a leather girdle?" he demanded sternly.

Ntoyintoyi was still panting, unable to speak.

"Why did you run away? Did I not tell you that if you wanted to, you could go at any time, but that you must tell me first?" he pressed rhetorically. "You will be troubled until you die! Now I will never let you leave me."

The wives saw that in his heart Solomon forgave Ntoyintoyi and was coaxing her to turn toward him rather than against him. But she, even though he called her to him and sent her on errands in a pleasant way, as if he wanted all the kraal to see how kind he was to her, held herself rigid and aloof and her face set in hard lines. With the wives, too, she kept this unsmiling stormy face.

Solomon was finding wives increasingly more of a nuisance than a pleasure, though the trouble with Ntoyintoyi had a surprising sweetness and excitement in it.

Messengers were sent for 'Mtshaleni with orders to return to the King at once, but she refused. They reported she had already put up her hair into a topknot and had taken off her Christian clothes.

The King and his party went to Dlebe to deal with this wife in person. They arrived during a marriage ceremony in which 'Mtshaleni was one of the bridesmaids. A hush came over the kraal as they saw the King penetrate the back line of the girls and jerk 'Mtshaleni out of the dance.

All the dancing stopped. The men of the bridal party stood at attention in salute to the King. One could even hear the breezes blow, as the King took 'Mtshaleni roughly by the shoulders, as she was, without a cover on her, and marched her off to where his horsemen waited.

"Who has put the headdress on my wife?" Solomon demanded of 'Mtshaleni's brothers.

"A lover must have done so," one brother barely mumbled. Solomon had paid full lobola for 'Mtshaleni to this very brother.

"Did you send word to tell me of it?" he pressed.

"I heard, Ndabezitha, you were away."

"Did you send word to my mothers, or the head men at Mahashini?"

The man's "No" was very weak.

"Seeing I passed right here, did you send word to me?"

"I heard the King had passed, but I was ill."

"Even though you were ill, you could have sent other brothers. It is you who want your sister to marry her lover. It is you who are conniving with her. I will attend to you later. Get her some clothes to put on."

Everyone knew henceforth it would go badly with this brother in his regiment and his tribe, as he had incurred the open enmity of the King.

Solomon waited for 'Mtshaleni to do his bidding, but she sat upon a stone whimpering, immovable, as if she grew with it. With so large an audience the King could not afford to countenance such insolence. He struck her across her lap with his riding crop as one would a horse to spur it into action, but she still crouched there, crying. In hard and ugly silence he stared fixedly at her. No one breathed comfortably, as they waited to see what would happen next.

Perhaps the girl hoped someone in the kraal, her brother or her lover, or even an older woman, would speak on her behalf, but when not a voice was raised, she realized the helplessness of her position. Without another word from the King, and before he could strike her again as he was about to do, she rose slowly and took to the road.

seventeen

Christina, absorbed in personal worries, soon forgot the latest kraal scandal. "The birth of my child is almost here!" she wrote to Solomon. "But I have not seen my medicine arrive yet."

"The medicine is doubtless in the post," he replied. After two more days, when the medicine still had not come, she wrote again even more urgently, and he admitted he had forgotten it. Stung by last remnants of conscience, he sent a runner for it.

So many accidents had happened in childbirth, Solomon himself was beginning to be fearful of every confinement. He sent word to Christina that if she were frightened she could go to the lady doctor at Cibini to give birth there. Christina had no time to consider this, for on that day her labor pains commenced.

OkaMtshekula should have been with her, but Christina's son was sick and she had to look after him, for there were not enough mothers to look after all the children sick in the kraal. Once again, the women of the kraal remembered vividly the curse evoked upon the King's children as sickness raged amongst them.

During the night, while Christina was giving birth to her third child, a girl, her son became so sick it was as if his body were hot enough to cook on, and the next morning he could not get up. Christina was not yet able to care for him, but she thought more often of him than of the newborn baby, to whom no one was paying any attention.

The child of the daughter of Buthelezi died; two days later another child died.

"The King is very sad about the children dying. He has decided to send all the wives with children to other kraals," okaMtshekula told Christina five days after the birth of her child.

Christina was dumbfounded. "Mother, how am I going to leave the kraal when I cannot walk and I have one child at my breast, and one who can barely toddle, and that one sick? Ask the King to tell me how that can be done!"

Significant of Christina's present relationship with the King was that her first concern was not about the separation from him.

"The King says you must go with all the others. The sickness is becoming worse," warned OkaMtshekula. "He will get people to carry the children, but you will have to walk. Wherever your strength fails you, there you will have to put up at the nearest kraal, until you recover sufficiently to go further." Christina had never been able to walk long distances because of her unusually small feet, which were poor support for her fattening body. Up to now, the King had always been aware of this and had given her a horse to ride or a place in a carriage. When her feet were weakest, her heart heavy with fear for her son whom she expected at any moment to breathe his last, it was hard to face embarking on an unknown journey.

"Christina, you will leave today." The King's face was drawn and pale as he made this abrupt announcement without inquiry as to her health or mention of the new child. "You will sleep at the kraal which is near the uSuthu. Even if you have not enough strength to reach there, God will carry you through to Mahlabatini."

Tears were streaming down the King's face which he did not bother to conceal. "When I come to this hut, or when I go to that hut, I hear a child's labored breathing. Whatever hut I go to, I hear a child in pain, until I fear all my children are dying. I cannot understand; what is causing all my children to be sick? Why should some have died already?" The King was almost sobbing. "It must have been the wedding which brought us bad luck at this time; from the day of that wedding I have had trouble. A lot of people collected at the kraal, and they must have brought the sickness with them."

Zulus know nothing of modern theories of germ infection but they believe that crowds often bring illness. Traditional lore also dictated that if a kraal become infected with illness that normal methods could not cure, the people should abandon it for a more healthful place.

The King was a prey to wicked and dark thoughts, and Christina suffered for him. Solomon had seen very little of her in the past weeks, but he had not yet lost the current of warm sympathy which flowed so peacefully and pleasantly between them. Aware of it now, when he needed it most, he was grateful for it. "Christina, will you have enough strength to reach the Sikhwebezi near the uSuthu kraal?" he asked for he still thought of her with gentle consideration when he remembered her.

Never before had she seen the King in tears, and she would have done anything at this moment to help him. "Strength will be given me by God," she solemnly averred.

The flow of emotion between them was unbroken. It was as it had been with them in the beginning, Solomon was sensitive to her body, realizing that now, it was, perhaps, in pain. "It would have been better were it two weeks since the birth of your child, Christina," he murmured sadly.

"Look after this money carefully," he admonished her as he handed two pounds to her. "Buy yourself whatever you need. Weak and alone, if you eat whatever you desire, you will get your strength."

Her "I thank you!" came from the depths of her heart.

"Pack all your belongings. What you leave behind I will look after, and send to you by young men," he continued with thoughtfulness for her comfort. "Take only sufficient blankets to sleep, only those things which you need immediately, so you will not be burdened with too much to carry. I may not have time with you again. God will protect you!"

Ethel cried unashamedly at parting. Having had no child as yet, she was remaining behind at Mahashini. She promised to write frequently, and give the news of the kraal; tell how Ntoyintoyi was behaving, what punishment the King had decided on for Cebekhulu, whether Mbede was found and brought to justice, and whether as the months passed Zidumazile was proved pregnant or just sick.

They did not notice the unconscious use of the words, "in the months to come," nor how they were preparing for a long separation.

Once only did Christina rouse from her lethargy and then it was to say: "Write me, when the curse on the King's kraal is lifted; this curse of pain and sickness before the children come, and then this fever burning the children up!"

Twelve wives were due to go to the Zibindini and the Nsindeni kraals. Christina would have preferred the Zibindini where she had been so happy, and where her daughter Greta lived, but she and two others, whose children were the sickest, were assigned to the Nsindeni where there was a noted *inyanga* near by.

The curse was spreading, and there was no time to lose. Extra men and girls were drafted to help carry the children and baggage on the footpaths across the hills. Weary and bedraggled, they arrived at sundown at the kraal of Mkhwanyana on the other side of the Black Umfolozi River.

Natives turned out in great numbers to welcome them, and beer was brought in large quantities for all to drink, so fear might be forgotten for a while. The children seemed a little better, they took their food with eagerness, and slept well afterward.

Maphelu spent the night with them to make sure the party would be properly directed. He turned back at Macanca where the wives who were going to Zibindini and those who were going to Nsindeni bade each other farewell. That night, the larger party, for whom accommodations could not be found, slept on the bank overlooking the river.

Christina and her group arrived at Nsindeni with sinking hearts. They thought they too might as well have slept on the bank of a river, for there were only two huts in the whole of the Nsindeni kraal, and it was little better than a wilderness.

At the first signs of daylight, the *inyanga* was sent for, and came immediately, bringing medicines with him. He gave the children a dose to drink, which they pushed away but finally took, and which he promised would heal them. Medicines were set to simmer on the red-hot coals, made of herbs and plants with which Christina and the other mothers were familiar. When the pot was steaming the *inyanga* held it before the faces of the sick children so that their breathing might be made strong with it.

The *inyanga* did not *bhula*—throw the bones—nor mumble prayers, nor swagger about with a show of power, nor smell out the evil, the way an *isangoma* would have done. Nevertheless, when the mothers who had represented the King's authority, and the men who had escorted them on this trip, were about to return to Mahashini, Christina was able to give them a brief message for the King.

"God willing, the children will recover!"

Christina directed one of the King's messengers to notify her family at Nhlazatshe and her married sister Daisy, at Nkonjeni, near by, where she was now living.

Daisy had not seen Christina for a long time and not only was she overcome with emotion at their meeting, but it made her weep to see her sister, who had lived in luxury and been the King's favorite, stopping at so dismal a kraal.

Christina was a homemaker. She wanted beauty and dignity, and a realization of her own dominance; she loved familiar and well-worn things. She had to have a table, bed, hooks to hang clothes on, shelves on which to put away dishes, and a hearth nicely swept of ashes. From these she gained a sense of well-being and put down roots. With but two huts in the kraal the standard was more nearly at the heathen state than anything she had previously encountered. Depressed by the dirt and squalor about her, before another day had passed she determined not to remain in the hut of Ntuli, but to start housekeeping for herself, to live as she liked in God-fearing cleanliness.

Daisy was happy to be able to help her sister, who had been kind with gifts in her first affluent years of marriage, and she provided thatch of which a good native housewife always has a goodly supply. Christina paid three shillings to a neighboring village man for the *izintungo*—the wooden strips—for the base of the hut. A native woman hammered down the mud floor for a shilling. Daisy, her husband, and Christina worked tirelessly, and within two weeks, a record time, the hut was built.

There was no furniture, but the hut was her own, and Christina was delighted with it. Daisy ordered a door made of planks and bought firm cotton sacks, in which store goods are packed; Christina ripped them apart and sewed them together into a mattress case. Near the kraal grew a fine, curly, soft grass—*'nsinde*—almost two feet high, from which the kraal took its name. Though weak, Christina cut grass, leaving it to dry in the sun, to be stuffed into the sacks and made into a soft mattress.

By now all the children were quite recovered, and Christina and Daisy were quietly sewing in the first day's respite since the hut was built. It was the time of day when those who can pause know that even time has a rich fulfillment and that this is the moment of high noon, when the sun shines at its most radiant. Christina was sensing and enjoying the moment when they heard the clatter of hoofs and saw horses appear in the yard. When least expected, the King had come!

"My heart is filled with gratitude. I see the children are much better," the King addressed all his women. "It behooves you, my mothers, to send word to me if my wives or children fall sick, or if at any time they need anything. My wives are now your children, and I shall expect you to look after them for me."

"Ever since your father died, Ndabezitha, there have been no indunas at this kraal," one of the bolder mothers ventured. "There are no huts in this kraal. It is as though we were living like the beasts in the wood, without man-made shelter."

Solomon saw there was indeed much to be done; the desolation of the place had weighed full upon him. He had not brought a tent with him and the only place for him to sleep was in Christina's hut, which still had no door, but only a mat dangling at the entrance. Try as he would, the King could not forget that he lay in a hut without a stockade around it, without a securely fastened door, exposed to any passing enemy.

Every able-bodied man who arrived to do him honor was set to work immediately to help build a large hut that very day. The men worked silently and speedily, with no wasted motion and no undue noise. Working hours were best shortly after dawn before the midday heat and in the afternoon when the heat had spent itself. One had to hurry against the fading light, for once a purple haze began to touch the sky there would be but a brief blaze of purple and red glory, and then, like a sudden curtain, night darkness would descend.

As the building progressed, men broke into spontaneous lusty song, swaying and massing their strength in long swinging strokes. By nightfall the framework was finished and was faultlessly and strongly put together. The men worked in feverish haste, as if they knew that the day might yet hold unpleasantness for them.

Before it grew dark, Solomon called every man before him: "Why have you men neglected this kraal?" he demanded sharply. "Why have you failed to build up its fences?" Men shuffled their feet, looked down and tried to cover up their embarrassment and sense of guilt.

"The head man of this country-side will pay heavily for this," the King warned. "When I return again I want the whole of this yard chipped clean. I am going to bring cattle to the kraal to feed the children. Never again do I want to have to speak to any of you about letting a kraal of mine become so low there are not enough huts for people to stay in and no decent place for me to spend a night in if I so desire."

Though the *inyanga* had been honored in being allowed to treat the King's children, and later might boast of the King's confidence in him, and thereafter collect larger fees in his practice, the King nevertheless rewarded him with a pound.

Daisy also got a pound, and the succulent leg of a beast, and he admonished her to tend to all her sister's needs.

"I hope you will forgive me," he apologized to Christina. "I left Mahashini so troubled I forgot to bring your belongings to you, but I will see they are sent to you." She did not remind him he had promised to send Greta to her, for she did not expect to remain there for more than a short while.

He gave each of the wives a pound, and told them to buy supplies with it, meaning things like jugo beans, flour, tea, and sugar.

His last words were: "You will never know whether it was not the bad terms on which my wives lived together that caused their children to die and get sick. You few wives are now separated from the others. It behooves you to live on good terms with one another. If you are divided amongst yourselves evil will surely enter your lives."

eighteen

Ethel and Christina wrote to each other regularly, and Ethel discreetly reported what was happening at Mahashini.

Despite all of Solomon's efforts, Ntoyintoyi did not change. No sooner would she come from his hut than she would say, "I am going away tomorrow." And then one morning they discovered she had run away again.

This time she was overtaken on a train. When she was brought before the King, he said to her in a voice that froze Ethel, who was in the hut at the time: "Even though you cross the sea I will always get you. You are my wife, Ntoyintoyi. Mahashini is your home. I would let others go, but you, never, now!"

When Christina heard Ntoyintoyi had run away for the third time, she kept wondering what it was that made a woman so stubborn she would continue to refuse to accept the fact that there was no escape for her.

Ethel asked many questions in her letters, too. "Now there are only three of you does the King pay more attention to you when he visits you? Does he bring many girls with him? Do you hear of marriages we do not?"

Long since, Christina had written a letter she was waiting to smuggle with a friendly messenger, "Ever since the first weeks we have been here at Nsindeni, the other wives and I do not see the King. It is as if he never knew us."

"Though it has been a long while since I have been near the King, I think there is something in my stomach!" Ethel wrote.

Months went by. The Zulus said "*kwahlalwa-ke*"—"it was sat then"—meaning time sat still. The seasons no longer meant very much to Christina, as there were neither feasts nor moments of happiness to mark the days. The baby she had brought with her in her arms had not yet been named by the King. Christina herself named her Sishoniswapi. Like the names which Solomon had given the other children, like all Zulu names, it had a definite significance. Literally translated it meant, "Where are we being driven to?" Years later this little girl was baptized Corinna.

Christina now had three children, two in addition to Sishoniswapi: her oldest daughter Greta at the Zibindini kraal, and Hezron, her son who was with her at Nsindeni.

The one remaining contact with her former life was the steady stream of letters from Ethel, who wrote confirming her pregnancy. "It seems one no sooner becomes pregnant than she is discarded. Two girls are shutting out the rest of us. We are just sitting here. These are the girls of the Mambatheni and the Buthelezi . . . . But he keeps on getting married . . . and the wives keep on leaving him! Another wife of the Buthelezi has gone!"

Christina and the wives at Nsindeni could not understand what was happening at the King's kraal. All these many marriages! Far more significant, all these wives leaving! Had the King chased them away? Had they misbehaved? Had the King collected penalties for them? Or had the King begun to so abuse his wives the men of their families were willing to risk his enmity by taking them back? Something strange and mysterious and quite terrible must certainly be happening at the Mahashini kraal.

Whenever a letter came to Christina she and the other wives would hope it was from Solomon. Perhaps he had finally remembered them. Instead it was almost certainly from Ethel, and no exiles ever read and reread home news more avidly.

'Dumazile (the Zulus drop a syllable for familiarity), who had insisted she was sick and not pregnant, had been sent home to her father's kraal, presumably where she might get better. Only her mother knew that all this time she was pregnant, of course. The first the kraal knew of it was when they heard a child crying in 'Dumazile's hut. She had been able to deceive everyone. Her Christian garments, the full-gathered skirt she wore, a curious and strange garment at best, hid the fullness of her figure.

'Dumazile's father sent messengers to notify the King a child had been born to him. "I do not know this child you tell me of," the King said to them. "I only know 'Dumazile said she was sick, that she was wrongfully accused when my mothers insisted she was pregnant. . . . Tell her father and her eldest brother to bring her and her child before me."

It was a long way from Mahashini to Ntabankulu. Messengers returned from the King and found the child was dead. Often a child who may cause trouble in a kraal does not live. Such a child is known *as an ear out of place*, something that attracts immediate attention.

The King had no greeting for 'Dumazile and only a frosty nod for her father. His first words to her were before the full assembly of the kraal. "Who has given you this child?"

"Pikithi," she barely whispered. Pikithi was the herd boy.

"Everyone is to be quiet until Pikithi arrives!" the King told the assembly conspiratorially as if letting them all join in a game.

Beer was drunk and the waiting made an agreeable and sociable event. 'Dumazile's father and brother kept to themselves, and men and women of the kraal felt sorry for these innocent men who had this trouble brought upon them.

The indunas brought Pikithi before the assembly, struggling, frightened, and rebellious, and insistent that he was wrongfully accused. Pikithi was known as a *'phamela*, a nervous timid man who jumps at the sound of a bird. Having experienced the enmity of the kraal, 'Dumazile found her heart torn with pity for this young boy, who was tasting the same cruelty.

"He is speaking the truth," she cried aloud, "It was I who went to him in his own hut. He did not want me, but I kept coming and begging him until finally he consented."

They waited, expectant, for the King to speak. "Pikithi had no right to consent! It was your duty, Pikithi, to come and report to me when a wife of mine entered your hut to try to make you lie with her."

Men and women nodded their heads in sober agreement.

The King in a tempestuous rage ran for a gun. Men ran after him to make sure he would do himself no harm. There was general hysteria. In the confusion Pikithi managed to get away. Fortunately for him the sun had set, and it was growing dark. The King prowled about with a torch all night, but did not find him. No one knows where Pikithi disappeared.

Days later 'Dumazile's father, who was still waiting to hear how this matter was to be settled, decided to brave the King and make known his intention of going home.

The King wasted no words: "I have driven Pikithi away. Take your daughter away with you, too. Do not forget, however, I paid twenty-five head of cattle for her, and I want them back."

A repudiated wife of the King's kraal, but nevertheless a legally divorced one by agreement, 'Dumazile was now eligible for courtship and immediately married another man.

The King, as the natives say, was "selling his horse," was in a position to dictate terms. The well-born, prosperous man 'Dumazile had married, he said, was to repay not twenty-five head of cattle for her, but forty head, the difference in cattle to represent the worry he had had from her.

The full forty head were not paid until ten years later. The first time cattle were herded together to be sent to the King, an older wife fought with her husband about it. She insisted this was cattle belonging to her estate and she was not going to allow it to be wasted, the husband had not needed 'Dumazile, and she was not worth so heavy a price. The husband then paid the cattle in driblets of twos and fours; and each time as the wife protested, he would say: "There is no wife who owns cattle!"

Ethel's letter about Cebekhulu troubled the wives at Nsindeni, just as her tragic fate had saddened everyone at Mahashini.

"I do not care where Cebekhulu is sent nor what happens to her child," Solomon said. "She is Mbede's woman. Let him look after her." Such nonsense, when Mbede was a stable boy!

Accidents in childbirth lowered the morale of the kraal, so

okaSonkeshana sent Cebekhulu to the lady doctor at the Lake, and there her boy was born. It cost a pound but Cebekhulu herself had to pay it. The King had refused to clothe or feed her; she had had to provide for herself, and had managed fairly well, had had her own garden, grew mealies, wove mats and sold them.

Maybe it was because she had flagrantly disobeyed the King and brought scandal upon herself, but her punishment came shortly after the birth of her child. Though the birth was successful, Cebekhulu's stomach continued to hurt her, and finally it was her stomach-ache that killed her.

Her own blood mother came and took the boy away. If the child had been a girl, Solomon would have kept her so that when grown up she might fetch back the cattle once paid for Cebekhulu, who had not given the kraal any children and had made all the time spent upon her a great waste. It was understood the cattle paid for Cebekhulu would be returned to the King's kraal by her people.

nineteen

Sixteen long months passed. The wives at Nsindeni heard not a word from the King. Christina had begun to feel a letter was but another way of talking, and the day came when she got up with but one thought, to speak her mind to the King! She wrote with the intention of "spoiling everything," of bringing matters to a crisis.

"We are going hungry. We go with nothing on our bodies, we have nothing to put on. We do not even have soap to wash with. Was it the sickness that sent us out of Mahashini? Or were you overburdened with us?"

This produced an indignant reply. "Do you realize I cannot take up my time with my wives, and forget matters of state? Those at the Zibindini see me only because I have matters to attend to near by at the courthouse at Babanango."

A week went by. Then to their amazement, a messenger arrived, bringing Christina another letter from Solomon and *ten pounds* in notes! The letter specified a not so distant date on which they could expect him. The wives fingered the money as if to make sure it was real. The date for the King's arrival did not loom nearly as large as the banknotes in hand.

On the day the King was due his wives tidied the hut he had as yet never seen, filled it with the choicest mats, and tried to make it cozy and comfortable with the few treasured things from their own huts. Their clothes were freshly laundered and pressed; their hearths were brushed clean; beer was made and stood in readiness.

Slowly the sun dipped down below the horizon and the King did not appear. The wives at Nsindeni had not realized how much longing and energy had gone into making ready for him. Unashamedly tears of disappointment trickled down their cheeks as one of them said: "It is no use to prepare for him. We will never see the King again."

Next day when it was long since dark, and the wives had given him up for good, there was the unmistakable sound of his automobile driving up.

The King curtly ordered Christina to fetch his things from the car and put them in her hut; to wake all the others and set them to work. Fractiously he demanded a fire in the kitchen, his bed made up, and tea given his white driver before he returned to sleep at the village store.

As the other wives entered they heard an indignant and accusing mother saying: "Did you plan to throw away your wives at this place?"

"No, mother, oh, no!" he drawled, "I have not thrown them away, but I know them. They will be leaving soon, just as the others are leaving at Mahashini."

Alone with Christina, the King demanded: "Where did you get the right to write me such a letter?"

She held her ground. "I did not know I was doing wrong by writing to you."

Ever sensitive to her moods, he recognized immediately she had meant no offense, and his manner changed, his voice grew soft and tender. "What is your heart saying now? Does it tell you I have discarded you, Christina?"

Too often she had been swayed by his winning way, and she steeled herself against it. "My heart does not think of that; it thinks of the treatment under which we have lived in this kraal. Your mothers told you what it was like, living here on the hills. Even the ground here is against us and does not yield food after one toils over it. I wrote you of our need as you directed me to. I did not write you one letter; I wrote you many. For nearly two years I have never seen an answer."

Solomon's patience was at an end. "I see there are now people who are spoiling your heart."

Solomon spent two days and three nights at the kraal. By day he conferred with the men of the neighborhood. By night he took each one of his wives to sleep with him. Acting upon an impulse of renewed affection he told Christina he was planning to send Ethel home to have her child and then he would summon her to Mahashini in Ethel's place.

Christina knew her heart was no longer right. Even though she was with the King, even though he spoke gently to her, even when he sat next to her, playfully caressing her, her heart was cold and empty.

Now the days were all alike. There were no letters from Ethel and there was this coldness in her heart. There was not even longing for the King, which had had its own sweetness, for it was he who had brought this emptiness. There was also a new and horrible fear, that here in this wilderness, where there were no real friends, two small children would have to be left alone, without anyone who really cared about them.

Two months later, without any warning, the King's car came to take Christina to Mahashini. The dreaded moment of parting from her children had come. The King's orders had to be obeyed; pain and dread were meant to be hidden. Her farewells were like words in a trance.

The King had acquired so many wives at his various kraals he did not build a hut for each. Lucky wives, a few favorite ones, were established in their own huts with their own children, but many lived in a common woman's hut, presumably awaiting assignment to a hut of their own; and their children lived in a common children's hut, or were parceled out with other mothers or wives, at the same or other kraals, who tended them along with their own.

There was a big hut at Mahashini where all the King's girls slept. Christina was given a mat to sleep on in this hut. The girls were much younger, their status undetermined, and she, an old wife, had nothing in common with them. Ethel, Cathareen, and the wives she had cared about were no longer at Mahashini. Ntoyintoyi was still there and so was Nomapasi, but they had never been friends of hers. They had their huts, their children, their friends. She had nothing.

Christina resumed her duties of washing, cooking, and ironing, of personal service to the King. Daily, she went through her routine. She thought it was lucky she knew the work so well, for it was as if the work did itself. Sometimes it was as if the movement of her hands were ahead of her, almost as if she had no head. Sometimes she knew she still had a head, not because it helped her any, in telling her or showing her what to do, but because it hurt so.

Sometimes when her head hurt, it seemed that maybe it was really her heart that had the pain, and then again when she would stop and try to feel where her heart hurt, it would be her head that the pain came from. When she became pregnant again, and this was soon after she came, she decided maybe these pains came from the stomach, maybe her pregnancy was not right in some way.

There was not even joy in knowing she was about to have a child, her heart was so heavy with worry. She had had little money and little time to send gifts back to Greta for a long while. There was no one who could write or read letters at Nsindeni, and she did not hear for months about her children there. She feared, when she could no longer keep her mind away from it, that when the new child came, she and the child would be banished to some place even worse than Nsindeni.

Dark feelings and dark thoughts grew in her. She took no interest in the life about her and the new wives said of her, "She is a sad one."

When her work was finished, she would lie down to ease her pain. Only once did she have a flicker of feeling, and that was when Ntoyintoyi's child died.

Ntoyintoyi had finally had a child. Everyone in the kraal used to laugh at her because she behaved as if no other woman had ever had a child; as if only she cared about one. She never let anyone else touch it, if she could help it. When the child was far too old to be carried on her back and should have been crawling, she still insisted on having it with her all the time. And then foul things began to come out of its stomach and before they could send to the doctor for medicine, the child began to twitch, and died.

Ntoyintoyi told anyone who would listen to her that she knew one of the wives must have poisoned her child. The King was very sorry for her and had her come to his hut, and tried to do pleasant things for her, but she would just sit and whimper and no one, nothing, could comfort her. Eventually months went by and the King no longer called her to him.

Christina did not blame Ntoyintoyi, when one morning, it was discovered that once again she had run away.

It was summer, when the new, green leaves stand thick and high on the mealies. The King rushed people in every direction, into the fields, and onto all the roads. Maphelu went to Nongoma to send telegrams to all the railroad stations, and the entire countryside was ordered to aid in the search.

Ntoyintoyi escaped in the morning when it was neither night nor day; light enough to see, and yet dark enough to hide. She hid in a bushy gully, quite close to the kraal. When the search for her died down, she crawled into the mealie gardens, and there she had been for three days.

Then one of the mothers heard a little boy at the fence of the kraal, telling the other children he had seen someone who looked like Ntoyintoyi very early in the morning in the gardens; but she had heard the children talking, too, and when the King sent people there to look for her, she had fled.

They caught her about ten miles from Mahashini, on the other side of the Sikhwebezi River. As the horsemen surrounded her, she neither struggled, nor spoke, she merely turned around and walked back with them. The men told the mothers, later, they would far rather she had fought them than have come back as quiet as the dead.

Late that afternoon they brought her before the King, and they say he no sooner saw her than he threw back his head and laughed aloud, and taunted her: "You had better get wings, and fly to where I shall not be able to bring you back. Unless you get wings, my men will always find you."

Ntoyintoyi slept with the King that night and for a number of nights that followed, but anyone could see her heart had died within her. This was the last time, however, that she ever ran away.

All the others said, "Ntoyintoyi has settled down," but Christina suspected that she had found a man at the kraal with whom she was able to snatch moments of stolen intimacy. Christina knew, and by now so did everyone else, though some would not admit it, that there was a large number of wives who would always be liable to such charges.

Solomon no longer had faith in any of his wives. He had not been near many of them for a long time and he began to insult them openly: "You have taken the same road, you have other men!"

Christina knew that sixteen of the King's wives had left him already; other wives would probably leave him hereafter, but it would make no difference; the King would keep on taking wives, be attracted by the new ones, and ignore the old ones. Except for Ntoyintoyi's suffering, she would not have even paid attention to the talk of adultery. No longer did it matter to

Christina what happened to wives. Her days and nights were all alike!

As the time approached for her to have her child the old familiar pain became more intense and she sought opportunities to beg the King to send for medicine to the doctor at Kroonstad. Each time he promised and each time he forgot.

Since she could no longer tend him in his hut, he ordered her to return to Nsindeni and have her child there, assuring her a messenger would bring medicine to her. He had not remembered when her presence was a reminder; once she was gone, he completely forgot.

Three days and three nights Christina struggled to bring the child from her, and the child would not come. The mothers and the wives at Nsindeni crushed about her, and though she begged them to allow her freedom, they held her down rigidly, squeezing her stomach, and brushing aside her weak pleas. On the night of the fourth day, after it had grown dark, the child came away. When the child was born, they could not see its body, for it was covered with a thin, white veil, and the women who had been clutching Christina jumped back terrified, refusing to pick it up, crying: "It's a *'nunu*—an animal—something wild!"

The child lay writhing inside this veil.

Hatred boiled up within Christina, and gave her strength. "Better for an animal to be seen, in order to discover what animal it is!" she hissed at them.

A woman of the neighborhood, who had the most courage, grabbed hold of the veil near the head and jerked it off. Then it was that all could see it was a human being after all.

It was a boy, and was shaped like any other child. Something seemed to be the matter, however, and already the witch doctors were burning medicines in their little pots to bring strength to it. But when the baby tried to pass water, it began to scream, and that was what was ailing it, and none of the medicines seemed to help. Word of this was sent to the King.

The King, always prompt about serious illness, arrived by automobile and offered to take Christina and the baby to a doctor at once. But Christina had been through a travail not customary to native women, followed by a shock about her child, and could not muster enough strength to get up from her bed.

Pity was in Solomon's face as he watched the child continuously crying. He left a few minutes after he came, cautioning Christina it would be well for her to make ready to go with him to a doctor as soon as she could.

Though the child seemed to grow thinner and more sickly as the weeks went by, he did not cry so much. Frequently Christina thought of her previous kind deliverer, the giver of medicine, that doctor of the strange country at Kroonstad. And she called her son, Nyangayezizwe—Doctor of the Strange Country—in fond and wistful remembrance.

Christmas passed without the King's coming, and then the next month, and the next. Christina turned over on her mat, and barely paid attention to the sound of an automobile arriving at the kraal.

"Why are you practicing witchcraft and killing me? You have bewitched my wives away from me," she heard the King shouting; every word was distinct; there was no greeting. "Go to those men of yours. I will never sleep with you again, because you are always with other men. I told you when you first came here, you would kill one another with your dislike of each other. Christina, here, very nearly died because of you. You get medicine from your men, and you use it against Christina, against each other."

Once Christina would have felt sorry for him, but the strange hatred which had risen up in her when her child was born choked her sympathies. Solomon lurched into her hut, mumbling thickly: "I told those wives straight out about their evil doings; they and you are stupid. YOU ARE FINISHED. YOU WERE DEAD, A LONG TIME AGO. Witchcraft took effect on you."

Christina's heart was with the women of her kraal, as she drove off with the King and her baby. The swift car brought them to Vryheid before sundown.

Since the birth of her child Christina had not been well. She could not eat without pain, and her nagging itch was worse than she had ever imagined it could be. The King took her to the European hospital where he told the Sisters, who understood and spoke Zulu, about her sickness and that of the child.

The Sisters led Christina away and examined her. They talked a long while among themselves, words she could not understand; and then they told her they would speak to the King. None of the Sisters, nor the doctor, told Christina she had a disease which she might communicate to others, nor did they ask the King to be examined. Other wives and mothers were saying the King's wives had a disease, the *woman's* disease, which the King had, and gave to them.

The Sisters told the King the baby had a serious inflammation and would have to be circumcised.

Solomon demanded of Christina: "Will you consent to have your child cut?"

In a crisis she automatically deferred to him. "It is as you wish, Ndabezitha."

"I, myself, do not care for it. I do not see why the child should be made imperfect. It would be best to get some medicine to heal it, and cure the pain in that way."

There was no better way to smell out the mistakes of the white people than to put them on the trail of each other. "I will go to the Magistrate and ask him what he thinks about having the child cut," he told her.

Solomon seemed calmer after his visit to the Magistrate, beloved and trusted by all the Zulus. The Magistrate had pooh-poohed the matter, explaining that white people often had their children circumcised, some even when it did not have any pain. Since this was expert opinion, they yielded without further question.

Two nurses came to the room where they were waiting and took the child. As Christina tried to follow, they blocked her way. Five more stiff-white nurses, and two white-clad doctors disappeared in the direction taken by the two nurses with the child.

The door shut after them! Christina thought she heard the murmur of prayers. Then she heard rattling, as though forks and knives were being pushed about. Then there came the hush of death, with only one person talking all the time without stopping. This was interrupted by another murmur of prayers, and a bell ringing, like the table bell with which a native girl is summoned from the kitchen. The bell rang four times; there was the rattle of metal again, and then the child's voice cried out, the only familiar sound in that strange building. Then there was a horrible silence again. Once more bells rang.

Christina felt as if she could take her hard, fearsome thoughts, one by one, and lay them there in her lap to look at; she knew them so well. Each thought was about the death of her son, who was in that other room among all those strangers, with the door firmly shut.

Again she heard the child cry, and then she saw them bringing it out. But when she tried to go toward it, her head told her feet to move, but her feet stood still.

A nurse was standing in front of her, giving the baby to her. He was wet with perspiration, as if he had been washed in it.

A voice said: "Christina's support has not come; there is nothing else to wait for."

Another voice said: "The baby is to be brought back tomorrow, to be washed where it has been cut."

She heard them as if from a distance, and tried not to let them see her hands were shaking, that it was hard to keep them steady.

Just as the doctor had predicted, the wound healed within three days. It seemed so strange that not until they knew he was going to recover did they give him medicine to drink. Perhaps they did not want to waste it.

It seemed to Christina that Solomon now loved this boy far more than anyone. He bought an abundance of food and clothes for it, not one, but two small overcoats; shoes, though it could not yet walk; and a shawl to wrap it in when asleep. Almost as an afterthought he bought a rug for her to cover with, too. He seemed to want to give this son presents such as he had never given any of the other children. Once she hesitantly thought he acted guilty about him.

The child was baptized in Vryheid and named Seaprince.* That was the

---

* See the introduction, note 41.—Eds.

name reported by the natives and the one which came into general usage. Actually the minister had chosen *Cyprian*.

It was January, 1925. Christina was now twenty-five, ten years married, and the mother of four children.

Renewed vigor and courage flowed through her with restored health, and there was happiness in her heart again. The promise of winter was in the air, when in May, the King decided that since she was so much better, he would return to Mahashini and she to Nsindeni. People of the kraal came to say good-bye, and shook her hand with jingling silver amounting to two pounds, five.

Christina lacked for nothing. Her luck had definitely improved, for when she returned to Nsindeni her children there were very well, too. The King was in a generous mood, remaining at Nsindeni for three days. All the wives talked of it among themselves, it looked as if a new happiness and a change of luck at long last were coming to all of them.

twenty

Christina leaned too heavily on the passionless reunion which the illness of her child had brought about. She did not realize that the current of passion between her husband and herself was irrevocably gone after two years of neglect.

June slipped by until it was Christmas, and a full harvest was upon them. Christina had long since grown well, and yet she heard from Solomon only through short and abrupt notes. Well again, she longed for her husband. The glow of the Vryheid visit faded into memories of previous days at Nsindeni, and again she began to wonder if she were not discarded.

When Cyprian had begun to run about on sturdy legs, the King arrived with some girls, and this time he kept all his Nsindeni wives at a distance. But he would smile at Christina and ask her to perform some small service for him. The smile seemed automatic to her, prompted by convenience, and not genuine uprush of emotion or desire, which she now knew was the only safeguard in holding the King's affection.

Never did the King taunt her directly, as he did his other wives, but she heard it from them: "*All* of you have your own men here."

A saddened heart lends itself to bitterness. The fruit of her toil, patience, faith, pain, her lonely agony, was to have Solomon accuse her of adultery. Such an accusation fell with its full, ugly significance. There had been faithlessness to the King at Mahashini, but never at Zibindini nor Nsindeni. Christina felt it was the King who was planting these evil thoughts, who dressed his wives in wickedness conjured up in his own mind. If deplorable consequences followed, it would be he who would have brought them about.

At the height of this distrust and constant accusation of adultery, Solomon asked Christina to come to him. She refused on the ground of illness, and for the time evaded the issue of distrust.

Solomon had begun to forget her for months at a time, but when in sight, she had never yet completely lost a special attraction for him. She belonged to the period of his youth when he was not only deeply concerned about her, but about others of his wives, and though his sensibilities toward women had become hopelessly blunted, she still stirred within him whatever kindliness he could command. He had offered her an opportunity to come again into the circle of his heart, and she had refused. His impulses toward reconciliation were rare, and it did not further them to have them frustrated at their very inception.

Christina had steeled herself against jealousy, for loyalty to the King's creed demanded it, but when her very loyalty was doubted by the King himself, her love was shorn of its basic sustenance. With passion and daily affection gone, and now confidence going, the relationship was so barren it might better end. It had taken her many months of groping and mental stumbling to arrive at this. Now, when the King beckoned to her, she knew it was a momentary gesture, that the King had changed, and there was no friendship in his heart.

The King was always in a hurry, with little time for her, too little time to find words. No longer was it possible to talk with him, to say anything beyond greeting. Not a single nameable grievance troubled her. Great tides of unfamiliar emotion were welling within her, and pride and this new estrangement from him made it impossible to open up to him.

Had the King more time, had there been fewer women, Christina could have hoped that slowly and gradually she could find a way of reaching him, and that time together would wipe away this wall which had grown up between them. But Christina sensed that hereafter whenever he saw her he, too, would only be troubled by her. This was the last stage of vanishing happiness, this was what her mother, her relatives, and the preacher had warned her against.

*She had but one thought—to get away! However, she stayed the year out, for departure required carefully laid plans. Now she had but one fear; if she slept with the King she would probably have another child and that would tie her there.

"If God is willing that these, my children, be healthy and spared, then they are enough," she would say to herself. "They are all I can clothe, since the King no longer clothes them. They are all I can feed, for he no longer feeds them. Surely then, God, I ought not to have any other children."

The other wives at Nsindeni had begun to say, not once, but many times a day, "We are going to leave here!"

Invariably Christina, whose maternal fears would be aroused, would urge them, "Wait another little while until the children have grown larger."

Not in the memory of any living Zulu had there been a King so possessed with passion for women, or so involved with multitudes of them. Never before had a royal kraal had so many unattached girls, so many quarrels, so much intrigue to gain so flighty a man's attention.

The King's peccadilloes had reached the ears of the white men. How could they help knowing, when the King would stop his car on any highroad and pick up one of his woman subjects and take her off with him, regard-

---

* Compare here through p. 151 with the record of original interview, appendix 1D.—Eds.

less of whether she were Christian, heathen, wife, or girl! These escapades created more than one disturbance which white men and the tribe were called upon to settle.

When a man's fancy roves expansively over an area encompassing a million people it often becomes necessary for even a King to make his smile more precious by the glitter of a gift. More than one white tradesman had claims against the King for the heavy debts which mounted daily, and which worried the elders of the tribe.

Solomon had built himself a house, bought soft rugs, and easy chairs with trick compartments, in which he secreted whiskey and cigarettes, wore silk bathrobes, and surrounded himself with luxury. An organ, a victrola, a brass bed, a dining buffet, and gaudily framed portraits of the British royal family were part of his personal household effects. The gifts he felt called upon to give were of a similar standard.

Wives who had neither clothes, nor rice nor tea, nor jugo beans would hear, even in distant kraals, about some hussy whom the King was parading in finery that only white women were entitled to wear. Their hearts hardened and the seeds of rebellion flourished. Wives planned to leave the royal kraals not only because their bodies yearned for passion, but because the King's insult to their pride was almost a national scandal.

How could Christina, an ignorant native woman, trace the steps by which she first decided she must leave the King? All about her there was talk of leaving. How could she avoid linking her own grievances with this solution?

Throughout the world divorce usually entails deliberation, the overcoming of obstacles, and delay. Christina was marking time. Meanwhile, she struggled through the days at Nsindeni, as if there were to be no release from them. She sowed and tended her garden, though she did not do it easily. Daisy conserved her crops, ploughed for her with oxen, and kept the garden weeded through the many months when she was too sick to tend to it herself.

Elizabeth, who had anticipated the day when her daughter would find herself abandoned, and had pledged her God she would then work for her and her children and win them back to the faith, began to plant tobacco, and peddle it. Christina would unexpectedly get one pound, or one pound ten shillings, with the curt, almost severe admonition: "Look after yourself with this! Buy what you need!"

The goats purchased by Christina with her earnings as a teacher had been left at her old home. Whenever she was short of anything she wrote to Elizabeth, with the request that one or two goats be sold and the money sent to her. The few goats had multiplied and she was reaping the interest on her savings.

Custom and law required that Solomon support his children; Christina should have demanded it. But fierce, hurt pride rebelled. When her sister or her mother would question her about squandering her savings for the King's obligations she would say: "I want the King to realize it for himself. He should know he has to look after all of us in every way."

Christina's last shreds of loyalty were going to cost her dearly. The King was ill at Mahashini and all his wives were peremptorily summoned to him. Neither Christina, nor any of the other wives, stopped to question what all of them could possibly do for him. They answered the summons promptly as faithful, obedient wives should.

By the time they arrived, the King was much better, and the wives made a feast of it. In the midst of the feasting, a dust-covered messenger arrived. Tensely they waited for the King to order the messenger to give his news. Terrified, wretched, the man's eyes focused upon Christina. In a flash everyone knew the news was for her, and it would not be good.

"The morning after Sibiya left the kraal," he blurted out, "her eldest son, without any illness, suddenly died!"

Christina waited to hear no more.

There was no swift moving automobile to be had. The King's cars were all broken down, for few native mechanics have had sufficiently thorough training to understand automobile machinery. Usually one of the cars would be out of order, and then the King would buy a new one, as his patience could not survive the repairs' delay, and then this car would break down, too. A white man would be called in to act as driver, to avoid these incessant breakdowns and motionless lapses; and then the King would become irked by his superior ways and dismiss him. Then all the cars would stand idle, as they were now, until the King would make up his mind what to do next.

Christina started out on foot, and slept three nights on the road. She felt neither heat by day nor cold by night, nor weariness nor hunger. Every waking moment she trudged, praying to God she might get to the kraal in time to see her son Hezron just once again. When she reached Nsindeni, fainting from weariness, they had already buried him.

The full torment of her agony crushed down upon her. When she had left the kraal, her son had been perfectly well, not a thing the matter with him. Friends reported that without any warning, Hezron's head had started to ache. The afternoon she was driving to the King's kraal, Hezron had begun to grow feverish, his head to ache more insistently, and the following morning early, he had died!

The boy had been old enough to herd cattle. Christina decided somebody had put poison at the gate of the cattle kraal, and when the boy crossed the path below it he had inhaled the poison secreted specifically for him in the line of his duties; the fumes had gone to his head and killed him.

Weakened by illness, the King acted even more slowly than usual, but hardly had Christina arrived at Nsindeni when messengers caught up with her, bringing his sympathy and money with which she was to buy black clothes for mourning.

"This is a terrible thing!" he wrote her. "The child dies without having been sick! I will consult medicine men, and find out what it was that caused it."

Christina settled down at Nsindeni in permanent terror for herself and the lives of her other children. At night fear continued to stalk her dreams, invariably about her dead son. She would wake up trembling, soaked with perspiration, trying to recapture the dreams, hoping they might give a clue as to who was the enemy near her, who had resorted to murder to punish her.

Women, and everything connected with them, were an ever-growing maze of bewilderment to Solomon, and though he should have long since pointed out his Great Wife to the elders of the tribe, so her son might be known as his heir, he had shrunk from his responsibility.

Among the wives, and in the tribes where there was naturally much speculation about this, it was generally agreed that since Solomon did not have as much veneration for position as some of the other Kings, and was embroiled in severe rivalries, unless he definitely pointed out another, he might yet formally designate Christina as his Great Wife. There was the accident of her being his first wife; it would avoid tribal rivalry, as she had no position of her own; and in the absence of a favorite, since knowing so many women nowadays it was impossible to cultivate one, he would rest his hopes for a good heir in the sound qualities she might transmit to her son.

Fragile as was her hold upon him, nevertheless the King's affection for Christina, and even his respect for her, was believed to transcend any passion he had for any of his current fancies.

Everyone in all the kraals speculated whether the King had pointed out Christina's son as his heir, and whether somewhere this secret had leaked out and the boy had been killed so that some other woman's son might have his chance to be the King's successor.

Solomon went to three native medicine men and to a fourth, an Indian, in Durban. All of them pointed to the same culprit, and he was satisfied they spoke the truth.

Solomon came to Christina with his discovery. "One of the mothers here at Nsindeni poisoned our son!" he told her. "The medicine men said so. They said it was a daughter of Ntshangase, who dislikes you, and was angry to see me love you and the child so much. They said the daughter of Ntshangase had heard from some people in Eshowe that I had pointed out this boy as my successor. They told her when the Prince of Wales had asked me if I had an heir, I had pointed to this child!"

Christina listened with dry throat, too pained by her loss to take in the full meaning of what he was saying.

"No such thing as this indication of an heir ever took place! Nothing of the kind was ever discussed! It is all lies! It did not happen at Eshowe, anyway. The Prince of Wales never asked me who was my heir. None of the natives in Eshowe were ever close enough to the white men and the chiefs who surrounded the Prince to know what either he or I was saying. And why should Ntshangase have feelings about my indicating your son as my heir when she is not even a wife of mine? She is my mother! There might have been some point to it if she were a rival wife."

Trapped in a tangle of counteraccusation and suspicion, Solomon was determined to ferret out this secret murder. This was an ancient Zulu problem, one which required alertness, wariness, and concentration. What *umthakathi*—the witch doctor who casts spells and poisons, the evildoer—had cast the spell upon the child? Solomon had gone to three *izangoma*—native medicine men who throw the bones and smell out the evil done by the *abathakathi*—but the mystery still remained unsolved.

Smelling-out ceremonies are held in strictest secrecy, as the principals are subject to fine and imprisonment by the white authorities. Nevertheless, on all important occasions, rumor has it that even Christian natives believe it is well not to ignore the indicated testimony of their own wise men.

A group sits within the cattle kraal in a wide circle, expectant, hushed. A woman moves into the circle, as plaited grass and fine gravel markers at her ankles make a scarcely perceptible noise against the dark night. In the faint light her swishing skirt of black and white oxskin pleats beating against each other, can barely be seen. Fluffy oxtails give her a feathery look, almost as if she flies through space.

The silence shatters with deafening shouts. "Hear, *mngoma!*" "Listen, *mngoma!*"

The *umngoma*, stony, impervious, unaware, starts a formalized hypnotic dance, toes pointing, body rigid, firmly flexed foot to the front, one stiff arm extended directly before her and the other behind her, oxtails suspended from each taut hand. Not one movement escapes her onlookers, bewitched into a trance. Those hands and feet are ever before them, pointing, pointing; the many eyes are glued to them, as all too soon they will point to the enemy in their midst.

Finally the *umngoma* stops. Not a whisper disturbs her. "You asked me why Hezron, son of the King, sickened and died?" she says in a low-throated voice.

"Hear, hear, *mngoma!*" comes in hoarse reply, a group cry not quite human, charged with horror.

"It's a female," she announces, each syllable drawn out for dramatic effect.

This time the shouts come growling, unrestrained. "We hear you! We hear you, *mngoma!*"

Gently, almost as if she were hissing, she bends and inquires: "Shall I hit with my ox's tail?"

In quick, thunderous repetition, they scream: "We hear you, we hear you," their swaying bodies and nodding heads clearly declaring their whole-hearted approval.

Again she dances round and round that waiting circle, until the tension seems to crackle through the night. Faster and faster she whirls until it is but the fragment of a second when she is suddenly and abruptly still before a horror-stricken woman. Across that terrified face she sweeps her flying oxen tail with its full force. All the others are on their feet, pushing, jolting, crushing in upon the woman. *Umngoma* shouts over their heads: "Look in her pleats!"

Someone pushes clenched, hard, quick fingers into the woman's most intimate sheath of kilted skins and draws out a dirty piece of paper, folded over. All eyes are now on those rapidly moving fingers as they disclose the paper's secreted powder.

"Eat it, eat it," they scream in demoniacal rage, but the woman leans away in horrified refusal. Terrified, but stubborn, the woman still refuses. Then they know that she harbors poison to use on others but protects herself from her own evil. She is the evil among them and her they must cast out. No use to kill her, to tear her from limb to limb, as once they would have done, for the white people will only punish them, the innocent ones who have already suffered.

They curse her, shove and maul her, stone her, and chase her from them. Why doesn't she deny their charges, or coax them to bring another *isangoma*, her traditional right to another's indication of where the guilt lies. Either she fears them, is truly guilty, or has been hypnotized into believing she is.

There is always the possibility that the *umngoma* planted that piece of paper, framed her victim, and produced her own evidence. No one will ever know. A cloud of mystery hangs over the unproved guilt, but forever after that woman is considered an *umthakathi*, is ostracized, mistrusted, particularly by her own family who have been called upon to pay a fine. Miraculously, no more kraal children die.

Solomon may have been informed in that way, for such a ceremony was known to have taken place at an unnamed kraal.

Or it may have been, and most likely was, a private session of Solomon, his attendants, and the *isangoma*. The *isangoma* walks about, waves his arms, and then settles to the business at hand. His clothes are normal; probably, if a man, a white man's shirt, hanging full length over fringed skin kilts. He produces a worn bag, about the size of a two-pound bag of salt, and a whisk brush of elephant's hair attached to a long brown handle. With a flourish, he empties the bag, from which roll many bones, animal and possibly human, largish, small, and fragmentary; strikes the brush and bones against each other and vigorously spits on all of them; jumps up and gets a pinch of ashes from the hearth and sprinkles them upon the bones. He picks up the bones and rolls them as if they were dice, crooning and bending over them in rapt attention. To roll the bones is to *bhula*—pronounced boola, as in the Yale song.

Every *isangoma* has a collaborator who nods and agrees in rhythmic response, performs *ukuvuma*—the routine accompaniment. No doubt the grapevine report of the murder had long preceded Solomon and the *isangoma* knew what was on his mind. Otherwise, the *isangoma* would have asked the King to help him solve the trouble by thinking only of it, *concentrating* on it.

Drowsily, as if in a trance, yet with ever-increasing rapidity of pace, the *isangoma* rolled the bones and kept repeating: "Something has taken place, something has happened."

From then on it was like a game of twenty questions, each one preceded by more detailed information until the fact of the murder had been established, and bit by bit the evidence piled up, until on a crescendo of almost unintelligible staccato mumbling, the perpetrator's unmistakable description, or actual name, was blurted out.

Mental telepathy, suggestion, a slip of the tongue of the interested party, previous knowledge, it might be any of these; but the stories of crime and mysteries solved by *izangoma* are so numerous that one cannot fail to understand native fear and respect of them.

Christina was bereft of her son. The loss tended to dull her faculties, to take the edge off her interest in smelling out the enemy. She looked to the King for sympathy, for some emotional anchor in this great trouble, but instead of a tender husband she found a hunter avid to stalk his prey.

"My heart has become tired," she told him listlessly, "with the little that you have done. Even though I have lost my son, I cannot do anything to the evildoer. I have to live with her."

The King tried to make allowances for her, to explain to her: "In the case of all my children dying, I do not go searching to find out what has killed them! But I am doing this for you. This case has struck me deep!"

She begged to be taken away from the kraal, to protect herself and her children from this evil which hovered over them, which might be lurking at any step they might take. The poison might be in their pathway, or in their food, and at any minute might kill them; and yet, with this threat of death about them, she had not been able to win the King to the need for immediate flight.

Aware that something more was expected of him, he began to bluster: "This dreaming of yours, this dreaming about your child, is nothing to worry about. Women often get that way. I will get an *inyanga* to come and cure you of it."

Solomon called up all his mothers of that kraal. They came in looking guilty and apprehensive, fearing suspicion had been cast upon them. "I know now how it came about that my son died!" Solomon announced. Breathing came with difficulty as he continued: "I know who killed the boy!"

No one moved, no one dared to speak! In ancient times once suspicion was directed toward a person, that person was immediately put to death. Frequently the innocent paid the penalty of the craftier murders amongst them, who knew how to build up circumstantial evidence to point away from themselves. Often, however, natives have been able to depend upon the stirrings of guilty conscience to indicate the truly guilty one.

The daughter of Ntshangase became visibly uncomfortable it seemed to Solomon. She fidgeted, let her mouth sag open, opened and closed her hands, tensed her toes, and coughed nervously. From that day she began to say she was going to leave the kraal, though no one openly accused her.

Solomon did not name the guilty one, he merely wanted to confirm his suspicions and frighten her. Christina was convinced it was the daughter of Ntshangase even before he confided to her that suspicion pointed there. Ntshangase would never meet her eyes; she acted always as if there were something within her she did not want revealed upon her face, as if her body knew her evil secret and might betray her.

Christina did not confront Ntshangase with her crime. She began to fear she, too, would die because of this woman's hate; and she was fearful for Cyprian, because the King loved him so. If this cruel woman wanted the King's other son out of the way, how much more would she want to get rid of this one?

Rage burned within her, intense yet powerless. Due to her continual dreaming, she had become very thin, could not eat and was lying down most of the time. When she saw that the King was making ready to leave without publicly accusing the murderess, nor taking any further action, she demanded: "Do you no longer care for me? I am sick. I have just lost my son. You have told me of the evildoer, of the killer who has killed my child, yet you do nothing to get me out of her power."

"You must not let these dreams of yours cloud your vision," he said, belittling her fears. "You can see nothing but death around you. The evildoer knows I know her. She will be frightened to do anything else. She knows she is watched and would be caught. I will get you a doctor. I will see to everything."

The King left and with him went the last shred of Christina's courage. She waited for that doctor. Three months passed, and she heard neither from the doctor nor from the King. Three months in which there was never a moment when she did not believe that perhaps the very air she was breathing had been poisoned by her clever enemy. During this time the horror of her days and her nights piled up until, if it were not for her children, for whom she was even more fearful than for herself, she would have lost the urge and the strength to live.

Only they who have known intangible fear which they could not banish can appreciate the drain in facing unknown dread, night and day, with no relief. Finally, Christina appealed to her family. Her brother recognized this to be a crisis. He left his crops and his kraal, and brought Christina medicine prescribed as a certain remedy. If she were adroit enough she was to arouse herself immediately the dreams appeared and drink this medicine; she would instantly vomit, and from her body would pass the evil of her dream.

A week passed while Christina took the medicine, as directed, and she continued to dream. Toward the end of the week she found she did not dream every night, and she felt her body beginning to recover its strength. She could eat food, and there was more hope in her heart. There was also a fresh determination that she would never again appeal to the King.

When the medicine was finished, she sent for more, because it had been so helpful. A conference of the Sibiya family gave thanks that Christina had recovered. The brother came again with more medicine. This time the *isangoma* had directed she was not only to drink it, but she was to get up and wash her body with it.

This was sharp in taste, and she did not like it, so she did not take it, but eventually the dreams stopped. The most frightening ones were always alike; she would be sitting, talking to her son, just as when he was alive, and then he would pound upon her hut door, and shriek frantically: "Open the door!"

Gratefully Christina felt the door had at last opened to him, and she no longer barred him from where he was trying to go.

Out of this horror from which she was just emerging, she carried within her, deeply imbedded, the full realization that in her hour of greatest need the King had failed her.

twenty-one

Christmas passed, a holiday period which always carried Christina back to her childhood, to the kindliness, gentleness, and warmth which prevailed at the mission in Christ's name. This year she remembered it only vaguely, and that in past years Solomon had not forgotten her on Christmas day. With the same lack of emotion and interest she heard Solomon had sent word that on New Year's Day beer was to be prepared for him, that he was coming to Nsindeni.

Three months had passed since the death of her child. Christina was now a woman of twenty-seven.

Directly upon the King's arrival, for the first time in her life with him, uncontrolled tears poured down Christina's face. No man likes to be greeted with tears, especially a King, to whom it is an insult to have one of his wives so far forget herself.

"You cry before me? Why? Am I the evildoer who killed your son?" demanded Solomon indignantly. "You a Christian, should not always be crying ever since your child died."

His other wives and children were there, too. The eyes of the wives deliberately traveled over the children before them, all standing on their feet, walking; there should have been others at their breasts, but there were none. The King realized this, as he looked at them. "My wives have a big case against me," he admitted. "They have grown children, without another child following. The last to be born, I now find grown-up!"

Always eager for laughter, gaiety, approval, and flattery, he was piqued into repeating: "I have come to celebrate Christmas with you!" This produced not a single smile, and he dismissed them abruptly.

As Christina remained alone with him, trying to keep her tears from overflowing, he offered her the only consolation that he had: "You will sleep with me."

He was amazed at her answer: "I have not the time."

"What is this work you do at night," he bantered.

There was no answering laughter in her voice: "I think."

"What do you think about?" he asked, still good humoredly.

No snake ever charged its poison with more ferocity: "I think of you, and how you discarded me when I was sick."

He took refuge in his prerogative and ordered sharply: "Do not splash me with tears!"

There they remained, he at a loss for an answer, she determined to say nothing more. Soon drowsiness crept in on him and finally he slept.

Long she sat there, until she, too, became sleepy: then she lay down, reached out and snuffed out the light. Later that night he awoke, and in the dark he called: "You still refuse to sleep with me?" Grateful for the darkness, she called back a firm "Yes!"

The King woke in a quarrelsome mood. He demanded immediately: "Christina, why are you fighting with me?"

She, too, had slept and was more than her usual self, "Fighting with you? What have I done?"

He hastened to refresh her memory. "You refused to sleep with me. Who is it that has spoiled your heart? I am as sorry as you are about the child. Just as I have told you before, there is a large army against you. They are setting about to kill your love. I am always being given secret potions to affect me where you are concerned. I heard about this when I was searching out the cause of the death of your child. There are six wives who have combined against you."

Childishly he thought with this explanation she would try to resist this mysterious power and would join forces with him to banish it.

"I hear you, Ndabezitha, but I do not understand," she replied sadly. "It was not your wives who separated us, or hurt me in my heart. It was you who spoke angrily to me, saying there is somewhere I am getting satisfaction."

First stubbornness, and then vilification. This was more than any patient man should be called upon to stand. "Have you then all this time been watching my tongue, so that you could trap me?" he asked.

For years she had been waiting for an opportunity to have a heart-to-heart talk, and now she had it she was not going to hold anything back. "I remember everything you have said to my ears, your first words to me when you first saw me. How then can I forget your words of last night, or today, when in our life with one another we have become as two people born of the same person. It is as if we had grown together, almost as if I said the words instead of you, and so I remember all of them!"

"Ethel's heart is the same as yours," he interrupted. "She refuses to come back to Mahashini. It seems no sooner does a child die to either of you, than you can no longer get on well with me."

All conventional reserve in the King's presence fell away. "We have not combined against you so we shall be of the same thought. You are the one who does the same thing to all of us, neglects and forgets us, so we all act in the same way to you!" she charged exasperatedly.

"You are twisting and turning my words against me!" he shouted furiously, grabbing a sjambok. "You want to jail me. You know if I were to thrash you now, I would give you a serious wound, and that would enable you to have me jailed."

As quickly as his rage had flared up within him, it died down. His voice became very tired, almost vanished. "Get out, otherwise I will strike you. Do whatever you wish to do."

Weeks passed. The King wrote Christina from Johannesburg: "I am ill. Tell your brothers and my mothers my knees are so swollen I cannot walk . . . a car will arrive to fetch you to come and look after me."

Promptly she replied: "I cannot go. I am afraid to leave my children at this kraal where I have been so badly used."

Before her letter could have reached him the car came for her. The mothers surrounded her and insisted she should go. Their faces looked ugly, wicked, and menacing and she saw her answer in them. "I am staying here to look after my children," she wrote, and the driver returned without her.

"I understand your fears for your children," the King replied. "Ethel and another girl are now looking after me."

Two and a half years had passed since Ethel had left Mahashini, gone home to Johannesburg to have her baby, and refused to return. While the baby was still very young, and its novelty strong upon her, she had written often to Christina, but with the current gossip of the King unavailable to both of them there was not much left to write about. Then, just as the baby was beginning to walk, it died, and Ethel rallied enough courage to write Christina about it, but had not written since.

The King used to visit Ethel whenever he went to Johannesburg, but her father and mother no longer respected his position. Christina wondered how he had persuaded Ethel to rejoin him.

When Solomon stopped at Nsindeni some weeks later he looked so ill and seemed so weak Christina did not notice he had only weariness for her. Hardship and deprivation had been her lot wherever she had gone for so long that she was not inclined to be overoptimistic, and she had never been wasteful, so although she had often said she would do anything to get away, when the King now offered to arrange for her to go to the uSuthu kraal, she mistakenly asked: "Give me a little time to reap my crops."

Ethel had come along with Solomon. She and Christina slipped away and fell into each other's arms, the sentences flying between them.

"The King pressed me to come, my baby was dead; the days and nights were empty, so I decided to return to him," simply explained Ethel.

"Not only his knees give him trouble. He has a disease he picked up in Johannesburg, which is very painful to him," Ethel reported. "The doctor warned him to stay away from his wives as long as the disease lasts and he was to keep away from all women for four months."

"They say all the King's wives from the time they marry him now have complaints, that the King has the woman's disease, that women give it to each other and that the King's wives have made each other sick! Do you think the trouble at the kraals is because the wives are sick?" anxiously asked Christina.

"No, it is because the King grows tired, has no strength, and does not really want his wives at all," Ethel declared.

Over and over again they compared the ugly rumors with which the King's name was now inevitably linked. Though it is still supposedly a secret from prying Europeans, the entire district of Nongoma knows that European doctors have for many years visited the King's kraal, and regularly "stung with needles" the King's wives and children, inoculating them against the spread of the venereal infection that apparently has never disappeared.

When Christina reaped her crops she wrote the King she was ready to move on to the uSuthu kraal, but he did not reply, and 1927 began to pass, until eventually she prepared another garden, and still there was no word for her.

Christina now meditated: "When he says he will do a thing, he never fulfills his promise.When he is with me, he likes me but when he is away, he forgets me. I no longer have the heart to love him. I would go, but there is no way to leave. There are my children."

When the weeding of the garden had commenced, the King passed on his way to Durban bringing with him a girl from Eshowe, and stayed for four days. Christina cooked for him and served him his food, but he never mentioned why he had not sent for her. It was as if he were a stranger who did not inquire about the health of his children, and she, a stranger who was not even interested in the state of his health.

Another Christmas passed, with the King in Durban, at the doctor's, because his knees were troubling him again. The year 1928 was ushered in, and this time there was no Christmas festival at Nsindeni, but the King wrote Christina, and sent a little money for all his wives.

The Christmas money had long been spent, it was March, and the weather was beginning to grow crisp and dry, when without any forewarning the King's car drove into the kraal. Christina did not even know of the King's presence until a surly voice ordered, "Open the door immediately!"

Framed in the doorway was the King in a drunken tempest of rage, flashing an electric hand light around the hut.

"Who are supposed to sleep in this hut? Are you all here? Are Khithakhitha and Makhukhuza in their hut?" he demanded shrilly, making no pretense of greeting.

Christina had to control the sudden pounding of her heart to reply evenly. "They must be in their huts, for it is now night."

Solomon lurched awkwardly, zigzagged to their huts, found them there, and rushed back. This time he thundered: "What woman did I see by the lights of my car in the mealie garden with a man?"

"We do not know, for we have been asleep," Christina answered, still the only one among the terrified wives and mothers with enough courage and control to speak.

At one time he would have been disarmed by her simple sincerity. But now his voice was reaching an hysterical peak, as he shrieked: "You *should* know!"

Hurriedly everything was being arranged for Solomon by the frightened women, while he drunkenly muttered: "I am tired of all this putting to rights. I want to know who was in the fields near the kraal." Hatred and viciousness gleamed in his eyes, when no one answered. "I am not idly curious. I insist on knowing which of my wives was in the mealie field!"

"We do not know," one of the mothers managed to mumble.

"I am not asking my mothers. I am asking my wives! Let them answer!"

Christina felt as if every word burned into her, as if each word were meant for her, and her alone. This was the accusation he had been harboring against them these many years. "Say which one of us it was!" she challenged.

"The brave person talks . . . I know who it was," he screamed, in a crescendo of range.

Across Christina's shoulder a bright stripe appeared as the sjambok cracked down upon her. Everyone rushed out, leaving her there alone with him.

The pain of her shoulder was not so great as the pain in her heart. Only once she moaned: "What have I done?"

She did not notice her body; it was her heart that was bleeding. She did not hear Solomon's mother at the door pleading, "You will be put in jail if you hit a person as hard as that without cause."

The sjambok's rhythm had not ceased. The mother implored, "Pray stop! There is no reason for this beating. Remember, you have neglected Christina and your other wives for a long, long time."

Another mother came to the door and intoned an explanation. "As it is wet outside with dew, and all these people wash their feet before going to bed, and it is now dark, and they could not have got water since you were here, call them to you, examine their feet, and you will be able to tell who has been outside in the mealie field, for her feet will be muddy."

Christina's shoulders heaved with sobs not unlike an animal's cries in torture. Solomon's brutality had so numbed her body, her mind had only begun to function, to telegraph to her the tardy realization she ought at least to make an effort at escape. But she was not quick enough. He caught her and hurled her back into the hut.

Regardless of what the mothers may have thought or felt about her in the past few months when she had held herself aloof from them, they now rallied their loyalty.

"Stop! We command you, stop!" they demanded in a solid phalanx of rigid disapproval, their bodies drawn to full height, their eyes flashing indignation.

Solomon turned on them. "She refused to sleep with me when I called her. She has other men."

The boldest of the mothers fixed him with an hypnotic stare. "I do not know of these men, and I live with them here at this kraal. You are only trying to shield yourself because you have discarded them."

She had succeeded only in focusing his attention on herself. "It is you mothers who spoil my wives," he screamed shrilly. "Get away from this door, and go to sleep, you! And you! And you!"

Everyone slunk away. Not one Zulu man, not one brave warrior, member of a race famous for its courage in battle, ever dared to challenge the King and protect one of his women against him.

Christina was shaking with sobs. Her crying only maddened the King. "Are you offering me the blood of your body?" he shouted wildly. "Do you want me to kill you?"

Nevertheless his rage was abating. "I have not enslaved you," he roared more coherently. "I do not have you in bonds, nor chains. You can go whenever you like."

Her body was a mass of raw wounds; yet she was conscious that Solomon was now definitely suggesting she leave him. This was a moment for escape, but still true to native custom she conventionally murmured, "I thank you," and fled.

Solomon, left alone, suspicious, and antagonistic to all his wives, sent a guard to fetch his sister Trifina to serve him. A mother reported she was not there. He then sent for another sister to make him some tea. Suddenly he brightened with an idea. "Do you think perhaps it was Trifina whom I saw in the garden near the kraal? Does she have a black skirt and a white coat?" he asked the sister.

He had to repeat the question before the terrified girl was able to mumble, "Yes, Ndabezitha."

Investigation proved it had been Trifina in the mealie field and not a wife. Trifina, unmarried, was privileged to indulge in unconventional dalliance, provided she did not produce a child.

Whimsical, impulsive, living only for the moment, thinking neither back nor ahead, Solomon felt an urgent need to see Christina. Drunkenly forgetting the last half-hour with her, he yearned for her friendliness, and ordered that she be sent for immediately.

When Christina appeared in the doorway, staggering, her matted clothes clinging to her, memory came back with a rush to him, and it was not pleasant. Guilt almost overwhelmed him, but a man, particularly a King, showed no regret for the wrong he may have done his wives.

There was an audience, and he had to play up to it. Oratorically he reviewed what had passed that evening. Christina swayed, and he saw her endurance was almost at an end. He had sufficiently justified himself, but there was still something he had to say quickly, for soon she might be too ill to hear him: "Christina, I ask your forgiveness. I have thrashed you for a thing of nothing, of no importance."

A man was apologizing to his wife—a King—and with other wives present! If ever a male of the Zulu people offered full penance, Solomon did. He offered Christina his male pride, and she spurned it without even a quiver of acknowledgment. Quickly he turned and poured himself a drink and dashed it down his burning throat, his head thrown back, so none should see the shame which had risen upon his face.

But he handed some whiskey to be passed to Christina. One of the wives caught her as she was about to fall, poured the drink down her throat, and she was able to file out with the others as they were dismissed for bed.

By now Solomon was exhausted and sent for his bedclothes. While he was waiting he had more liquor, and though anger had died within him, he was no longer repentant. Drunkenly he muttered: "Go back and tell Christina to prepare a fowl for me instantly."

When they brought this message dutifully to her, she could barely answer them: "I cannot do any work now. My hands are swollen. Look at them!"

She fell into sleep even as they were standing there, but the King sent back instructions he wanted to see those hands which were unable to work. Christina stumbled into the King's hut in a state of fever and exhaustion bordering on delirium.

"Show me your hands," he commanded. He had finished the bottle of liquor but was still able to see how swollen her hands were and how her arm was still bleeding. He made no comment but ordered: "Sara, you go prepare the fowl, and be quick about it."

Christina thought this meant she was dismissed and started out, but he shouted, "Sit down!" She tried to sit down, but discovered her legs would not bend! Violently sick, she was about to vomit. Blindly she fled to her hut and fell down upon the bed, and resolved there she would stay, and only the King, himself, would drag her from it.

Early the next morning she was summoned to him. Stiff and swollen she could not bend to get through the hut door, but had to inch in slowly. In full daylight the King saw the blood stains upon her dress. "Take off your coat," he roughly ordered. "I want to see how badly you are hurt."

"I cannot," she groaned. "My clothes have all stuck to me."

He tried to take her swollen hand and hold it in his own, but she withdrew it. He groped for it again and found it.

"Christina," he pleaded, almost whispering, "truly I am very ashamed of myself. I ask you to forgive me. I do not know why I thrashed you."

Christina's child brought hot water, and a flannel sponge. Solomon took it and waved her aside. Christina managed to get her coat off. "Cover it over," he pleaded.

"What has my sister done?" asked Beauty, coming in and breaking the tense silence. "Christina has done nothing," he sadly said. "I have been wrong."

Not even the King's admission of guilt could banish the young sister's horror, who but a few hours before had been so proud to be chosen as his companion on the trip to the kraal. Later that day the King told his assembled wives, "I want you to go to Christina and comfort her."

Dutifully the wives filed in and their spokesman stiffly said: "We have come to help you, Christina. Tell us what to do for you."

"You can tell this to the Ndabezitha. It is well he has done what he has done, for now I can leave him. His heart is his witness I have done nothing wrong, but now, even if he says my reason for going is another man, I do not mind."

This was real drama. They hurried to repeat her words to the King. The King, himself, promptly came to Christina's hut, but not to quarrel. His words came haltingly, as if he were waiting for her to say she no longer had any bitterness, but he left without knowing what her heart harbored.

twenty-two

Ethel welcomed Christina to Mahashini, murmuring pitying phrases over her recent beating, word of which had traveled to all the kraals.

Briefly and curtly the King told Christina: "Plans have been made for you and Cyprian to live at the uSuthu kraal. Later I will fetch the child left behind at Nsindeni and bring it to you. We are to start at once." He did not mention their last meeting when he had pleaded for her forgiveness; it might never have happened.

Driving in the car, everything seemed to be blowing at the now habitually benumbed Christina, and yet it was as if nothing touched her; even the breezes did not seem real. When they reached the uSuthu, Solomon announced to the gathered kraal: "I have brought Christina and her child to you so that she may forget the death of her son."

They hardly saw him before he was off again, taking two of his uSuthu wives back with him to Mahashini.

This was in July. The rainy season came and passed. The fall harvest was upon them and Christmas, too, had come and gone, and still Christina remained at the uSuthu as a temporary visitor, without Corinna, the daughter anxiously left behind at Nsindeni.

Months later when the King came on a visit it meant nothing to Christina except an opportunity to state definitely and formally she was about to leave his kraal, to leave him.

"Christina says she is going home to Nhlazatshe," was the explicit message okaSonkeshana took to the King. He showed neither surprise nor emotion. "If Christina wants to go, she may. Get an induna to find men to carry her belongings."

He had an afterthought, "Cyprian, is he accustomed to staying here?"

OkaSonkeshana broke into smiles. "Ever since he came here he has become very attached to a cousin of mine, the daughter of Manusi," she assured him heartily. "She shares the same hut with him and Christina. She never had a child by the King, Dinuzulu, and it is as we had hoped it would be; it is as though she is the one who bore Cyprian."

Christina had but one question to ask of okaSonkeshana. "When did the King say I was to return?"

"He did not state a time," okaSonkeshana honestly answered.

Cyprian's clothes had been mended and put into excellent condition. All her clothes had been packed neatly into a suitcase. Final preparations, food for the journey, had been made. The prospect of freedom made Christina heady, almost arrogant. When she heard two boys had been found to carry her luggage, she insisted she required three, and the induna immediately asked: "What are you going to do with three boys? You are taking all of that? Aren't you coming back?"

Gardens were being weeded. Months before when the gardens were being seeded, Christina knew she would not wait to harvest this crop and had not planted one. Without saying good-bye to anyone except Cyprian, whom she held close and long to her, she left. It was January, 1930, the first winter of the world-wide depression. For Christina, it was the hopeful beckoning of a new life.

They made the trip in easy stages, sleeping three nights on the road in the veld before they reached Hezekiah's, her father's kraal, at Nhlazatshe.

Friends came to grieve with her over the child who had died, and to tell her how surprised they were by the ugly rumors of the King's brutality. This evidence of sympathy was deeply comforting, and she wanted to show she was not unmindful of it, "I told the King I would never do anything in his kraal to besmirch my father's name." The relatives nodded and swayed their heads in marked approval.

Christina remained with her father for two weeks, and then he said they were very hard put for food and perhaps she would go to her brother Abiot and stay with him. Hezekiah had moved from his own kraal and was a squatter on a Dutchman's farm, who was none too generous with his food rations in return for work.

Dutifully Christina packed, and went to stay with her brother. He and all his family, too, eagerly inquired about the rumors they, too, had been hearing. Then for two uneventful months, Christina took her place as a member of his household.

During the third month, the King appeared unannounced. His presence in that humble kraal after all the gossip about him and his wives created a great stir, and the grapevine telegraph whirred.

The King sought out Christina and demanded sternly: "Have you come here to stay?"

Christina was not prepared to take a definite stand. She had had more than three months' experience as a discarded wife, come back to her own people. Forced to share with her, they did, but after the first novelty of the exciting stories had worn off, she had been made to feel in numerous ways that she was a burden, a woman with no place of her own and no place to go. Remembering this, she temporized. "Ever since I was a child, and married you, I have never had a holiday, nor visited anywhere. Now I am having a rest."

It was absolutely unprecedented for a native wife and mother to suggest she have a rest in the full prime of her life when there were duties to be attended to. A day or two, or a short visit was unusual, but a three months' rest was beyond the boundary of sanity! Solomon treated it accordingly. "You had better return home!" he sternly admonished.

Solomon preempted Christina's hut for himself, while she found herself a place to sleep in the kitchen hut, where Zazeni came, eager to talk. As all the men in attendance upon the King, he was desperately engaged in saving the King's face before his own people. "Christina, do you not remember your children?" he asked indignantly. "How can you leave them?"

All over the world women have had this question thrust at them when situated as Christina was. She had only her own convictions to go by, but in her answer there was a hint of universality, too.

"It is worse if I stay with them and have only bitter thoughts. It is better for me to go away from them, than to live with them as if I were dead."

Christina lay awake, pondering long after Zazeni left. So many years had passed since she and the King had last been here. Elizabeth, her mother, who had predicted one day she would find herself friendless and alone, was dead. Her sister Daisy, who had helped her build a hut at Nsindeni the first time the King had abandoned her, was also dead. Her sister Beauty was on her own, working in Durban. How changed everything was, all about her, and within her. The change in her heart seemed the greatest.

It was now four years, the beginning of the fifth, since Christina had slept with the King. Twice during these years, he had made an effort at reconciliation, but she had rebuffed him.

Next day the King had Zazeni bid good-bye to everyone for him. He did not ask to see Christina, did not leave her any money, but avoided creating an issue by specifically ordering her to return at a definite date.

Since food was also scarce at her brother's kraal, and there seemed to be no definite place for her among these people with whom she had grown up, but from whom she had long since parted, she decided to go elsewhere.

Immediate action was suggested by a letter from Ethel, who told of three more wives who had run away from the royal kraal; serious cases, for they were pregnant. She feared discipline on all wives would tighten up, and that it would be presumed that she, too, was not returning for amorous reasons, and someone would be promptly sent to fetch her.

Her suppositions proved fact. Two men arrived with the King's instructions to come with them at once. Stubbornly she insisted: "I do not wish to return!"

Nearly all night the men of the kraal sat with her and tried to persuade her to do her duty, while she muttered repeatedly: "I do not want to go! I am still resting!"

The burden of inviting the King's displeasure by harboring his runaway

wife was too much for Abiot, and the other men who lived near by. They
went to Hezekiah to consult with him.

Hezekiah lost no time in returning with them to talk with Christina. He
called up all the men of the neighborhood to come into counsel with him.
With all these men, none of whom had been overly friendly though all of
them had probed her for full details of the King's brutality, Christina grew
franker, and remained firm: "I am not going to return to the uSuthu. I do not
want to!"

Passionately she reiterated her grievances and explained why it was
intolerable to her to go back. Once her father said sadly: "I know all about
how you have been treated, but you must return."

As a concession Christina phrased it differently: "I do not *yet* want to
return."

All morning long the men sat there and discussed what should be done.
When the sun stood straight above them, burning down in the strongest
rays of noon, Hezekiah announced: "The matter is closed. Let whatever
come, come!"

Christina sold more of the goats for which she had saved so carefully in
the days before she married, and got two pounds for her trade. Secretly she
sneaked off to the Post Office and sent a telegram to her sister Beauty at
Durban, telling her she wanted to join her. Beauty wired back that she was
now working in a hospital, that she would be delighted to see her, would try
to meet her at the station, and would gladly help her get established.

It was April, the beginning of the fall, with a slight tang of coming winter in the air. The need for hurry drove Christina relentlessly. The King's
messengers might return or the King himself might come.

In the middle of the night she slipped away to where her hidden luggage
was waiting for her. Two girls stealthily went with her to the road where the
bus passed, helping her avoid discovery, leaving her there alone in the darkness. Shapes and sounds became clearer in that dark! A lot of others were
waiting, too.

She hurried on to the next stopping place to avoid detection, as here
everyone knew her, and she feared some over zealous friend of her father
or brother might prefer to sacrifice his own planned trip and exercise his
authority to make her go back to her kraal under his escort.

The sky was reddening when the bus appeared. Only three others got
on with her, none of them apparently recognizing her. The bus kept stopping and picking people up until it was full, and at each stop her heart
missed a beat.

When the bus dropped her at Vryheid she hid with an aunt living there
and waited tense with fright to take the train that night. As the train pulled
out, fear that she would be arrested was making her ill, for she expected
that, once her disappearance had been discovered at the kraal, telegrams

would be sent in search for her, as had been done when Ntoyintoyi was caught and taken off the train.

Never before had Christina traveled alone. All that night she slept fitfully, her mind never free of disturbing dreams. Every sound of the train seemed to hold a special threat. Years seemed to have passed before they arrived at Durban at ten o'clock the next night.

Except at Johannesburg, she had never seen so many people, or witnessed such confusion and commotion. The surging mass, the noise, the smells, the very bustle about her, strange and terrifying as they were in themselves, comforted her. Where there were so many people, nameless evil could not lurk.

Beauty, who had been a long time in Durban and had made a number of friends, met her. "Take me to the Rev. Mpanza, who taught me when I was a child and is now here! I will be safe with him," Christina suggested.

A warm welcome was waiting for Christina. The Rev. Mpanza and his wife, her old friends, listened breathlessly to the tales about the royal kraal, promising that they would do all they could to protect her from discovery by the King. When she asked them to get her whatever work they could, they insisted that for a while she was to rest and forget her painful memories.

twenty-three

These days Christina took almost everything for granted. How or through whom Beauty knew that there was an Indian shop where someone was needed to keep accounts did not matter, but she protested: "I don't want that sort of work because they are still watching my trail. I want task labor—day's work—to work for someone without their knowing who I am."

Beauty was disappointed. Such pleasant and easy work and Christina turned it down! However, through friends, they tracked down a vacancy for a task laborer wanted by a European who had just had a baby.

"No one else has applied," the tired-looking woman stated flatly, "and the clothes have collected. If you finish washing and ironing that pile over there, I will give you six shillings."

Christina approximated the amount of laundry with her eyes and agreed to come the next day. The mistress liked her and arranged for her to come regularly at two shillings a day.

It was almost a year since Christina had seen her daughter Greta, and more than that since she had seen Corinna, but she heard about them periodically and sent them newly made clothing regularly. She asked Beauty to write to Ethel to inquire how her children were, realizing that if there were anything wrong with them it would be reported. Beauty also corresponded with a girl near Nsindeni and Christina asked her to inquire about Corinna.

"No one knows where Christina has disappeared to," Ethel wrote. "The King has fought with all his wives because of her. . . . He says they chased her away and they all will go, too. . . . He is certain there is a man she has gone off with. We hear it said, but we are not sure that the King went to Nongoma and had telegrams sent for Christina to be looked out for everywhere. . . . Do you know where she is? Have you seen her? If she is in Durban, write me a letter in English in case the King opens it."

"Do not tell her I am here!" Christina gasped: "Remember! If you write now that you don't know where I am, they will believe it, for they will open all of Ethel's letters, expecting her to get some word about me."

Christina heard the King had been in Durban, had been told no one knew where she was and made no further effort to locate her before he left the city. She was becoming accustomed to the pleasant routine of her life. Her appearance and language began to change, English words slipped in, with a quaint Zulu modification: as *ihofisi* for office, *ihotela* for hotel, *ipoyisa* for police, *itikithi* for ticket, *iwashi* for watch, and *usheleni* for shilling.

Her friends were no longer people who came from her own village, or her own kraal. They were from all parts of Zululand who accepted the fact that she was an unattached young woman living in a town, and many proposed to her. Still bruised and crushed in spirit, possibly fearful lest the King's messengers find her, or possibly still considering herself the King's property, she refused to favor anyone. Just being unwatched and undirected made her feel gloriously free and happy, and she would have drifted along, letting each day take care of itself, had not Mpanza advised her to get permanent work. The same European woman took her on a monthly basis for one pound ten, and she left the Mpanza's and began to live in service.

Joyfully she planned all the things she would buy for her children out of her abundant wages. Compared to the conveniences made available to her as a kraal housewife, this Durban housekeeping seemed like play. No pain settled in her back from dragging pails of water from the nearest stream; the water was there on tap. Her feet did not swell from the weight of carrying fuel long distances, for the wood, in neatly sawed lengths, lay feet away from the stove. At night there was a bed and mattress to rest upon after the day's work, and plenty to eat. Her spirit settled into a daily litany of joy.

Two months of happy, busy routine, and then suddenly Beauty came bursting in with a native policeman.

The policeman took charge. "You are wanted at the police station!" he barked at Christina. "You are a runaway wife!"

The day she had dreaded had arrived. It was as if she were walking in a daze, almost as if she had taken medicine; she knew there were certain things she ought to do and she did them mechanically but it was as if an outside power compelled her.

"I am wanted at the police station!" she told her mistress with an unashamed quiver.

Instinctively the mistress felt there must be a mistake, there could be no criminal charges against this woman. She came out into the kitchen and began to hurl questions at Beauty, as if the native policeman were not there. "Who is this policeman? Where is he from?"

"I do not know myself. He made me take him here."

Lest Christina think she had been disloyal, Beauty added quickly: "I think he heard gossip from Simpson Bhengu."

All these details were unimportant. "I will go with the policeman to the charge office," wearily Christina declared.

Beauty had already sent word to Mpanza's wife that Christina was in trouble. Rev. Mpanza and his wife were educated natives and knew how to deal with the law. Mpanzas' wife found them still arguing in the kitchen.

"You are not to tell any lies," she admonished Christina on the way to the charge office. "It will not go well with you unless you tell the truth."

At the charge office Christina told them her name and her surname, where she was born, and where she paid her head tax.

The questions became more rapid.

"When did you arrive here in Durban?"

"I have been here three months."

The officer leaned forward a little. "Do you know Solomon, the King of the Zulus?"

If he expected a lie he was mistaken. "I know him. He was my husband."

"And what are you doing here?"

Everyone waited for the answer.

"I ran away because I didn't like his kraal."

A shiver of excitement at her boldness passed over the watching natives. The charge officer went right on asking his questions, methodically, except for a faint flicker of surprise.

"But were you not his wife?"

The law presented a definite pattern covering just such a situation as this. "How did you marry him?" the officer demanded.

"I arrived at his kraal and stayed there until I bore him children."

He frowned. "But the King says you were his first wife."

Christina agreed: "The King is right. I was the first one in his kraal."

The officer frowned still more. Puzzled, he had to clarify this: "But the King says he was wedded with you."

"No, the King was never wedded to me!"

The charge officer pressed his questions: "Did he pay cattle for you? Did he pay lobola for you?"

"He paid six head on account to my father."

"Did he *qholisa* you? Did he pay a special beast to your father so that you are truly wedded according to native custom?"

Christina's "No" could be heard throughout the room.

According to native custom a girl marrying a man may not partake of curds or milk from the cattle of the husband's people unless she has been *qholisa*'d. *Umqholiso* is the beast the groom gives to his bride's father and people immediately after the wedding ceremony, as a token or symbol to indicate she has now become one of his clan.

"Why is it when you were his first wife, he did not *qholisa* you, and did not pay the complete number of cattle for you?" demanded the charge officer.

This was their problem. "I don't know! Perhaps others do!" she said, without any intention of sarcasm.

The case obviously required more investigation. "That will do! You come tomorrow. Come to court and we will hear more about this!"

Another officer explained: "You are to return to your employer. It is our duty to detain you, but we are not going to. We will trust you. You will be breaking the law if you try to escape or hide. If you are not here tomorrow, we will know how to find you very quickly, and then we will punish you severely."

She murmured the conventional "I thank you," and left the court.

The mistress, eager to hear what happened, was amazed, then thrilled. Her native servant was not only the wife of the King of her people, but a runaway wife wanted in court for her escape! Forgetting she was a member of a presumably superior race, and that convention dictated at a time like this she should be moral and righteous, helpful if need be, but coolly indifferent and detached, she too savored the full drama of the situation. "Will they put you in prison for this?" she asked excitedly.

Of the two, Christina alone had poise and control. Her dignity reminded the European woman that her servant was facing serious trouble, and she ought to do something to help her. "If they put you in prison, I will try to get you out," was all she could think of as comfort.

"It would give me a lot of trouble, if you were to leave me at this time!" she truthfully said, and with a sudden inspiration born apparently of her own need, added: "I will give you a letter to present at the courthouse tomorrow."

While Christina was trying to make up the household time she had lost, a group of young men arrived at the kitchen door. "Escape from here. This is your chance," first one voice and then another urged, in a hoarse whisper.

It exasperated them to hear her repeat: "No, I do not intend to escape, and break the law of the court."

"Perhaps you should take *amakhubalo* with you," one of them reminded her. Zulus put a charm in the mouth before testifying, in the hope it will endow their words with the desired effect.

Next morning when Christina appeared in court the room no longer frightened her, for wherever she looked there were friendly faces. Expecting to find the King there bringing his charges in person, for a moment she suffered the pang of disappointment that any star might, robbed of her best audience.

Simpson Bhengu stood in the King's place, delegated to present the charges. Court was held in the Native Affairs Department, conducted with due process of law and all its dispiriting atmosphere.

Christina did not understand all the things said, nor the reason for all the things done. When she was ordered to get into what looked like a wooden tub, face everyone, lift up an arm and one finger, mumble something, and then swear she would "speak the truth and nothing but the truth," it all seemed a little silly to her. Surely everyone there realized when a person was telling the truth and when they were not. Surely these high-placed white men knew that, since they could put you in jail for not telling the truth, you would not dare to lie to them.

They asked her exactly what they had asked her the day before, as if they did not know the answers already! They asked her if she knew Solomon, if she had accepted him, and if he had taken her, if he had paid lobola for her, if he had paid down half and promised half; if he had qholisa'd her. Again, the court officer frowned and insisted: "But the King says he was wedded with you!"

Christina respected the wisdom and education of white people but this court seemed extraordinarily stupid. Even the most ignorant natives would have understood by now, and yet she had to repeat almost as if she were talking to a child, slowly and clearly: "But I never went through any ceremony with him!"

By now she suspected that perhaps many times, day after day, they could go over these same questions and answers until they could tire her out and make her change her answers that way.

"What was it that made you leave him?" the charge officer suddenly asked with a hint of exasperation.

She decided to make answers as plain and easy to understand as she could for these somewhat dull men: "I no longer wished to stay!"

"Have you no children?" the court asked.

"I have children. There are three of them."

There seemed no way of breaking through the phlegmatic calm of this woman who answered so intelligently. Parental authority might be the stimulus to rouse her.

"Does your father know you have left your husband?"

"No," she briefly admitted.

A proud, modest Zulu, one of the better type, thought the Magistrate, so he tried a new angle.

"Were you living like a prostitute in the King's kraal? You say he did not pay cattle for you and he did not qholisa you."

Let them call her what they wanted. "Yes," she acknowledged.

The court decided only the King could challenge his wife's statements, and offered her two alternatives. "Do you want to go up to Solomon or would you like to have him come down here and take the place of Bhengu?"

Christina had never lost her Zulu sense of niceties. "I would rather go up than for the King to come here on my account."

The Magistrate was not yet through, her personality interested him. "Did Solomon ever thrash you?" he inquired, looking at her so long she felt as if his eyes had bored within her. "Was that what caused you to leave, or was it because he no longer took any notice of you?"

After all these were white men. What concern was it of theirs to gossip about the King and his kraal. "No. I just didn't wish to stay," Christina lied for the first time. The instinct to protect the King from outsiders was automatic. From his vast experience with natives, the Magistrate knew at once she was lying. Perhaps she was covering up part of a story it would be amusing to hear, or which would clear up some of the ugly rumors reaching white ears these days about the King and his kraals.

"We have heard," he slowly drawled, "Solomon is always thrashing you wives whenever there is a large gathering. They say it is the many pots of beer!"

"He does not do that," she hotly denied.

The Magistrate was beginning to enjoy himself, but they were getting nowhere. For everyone's benefit, he explained: "We would have given this woman a policeman to escort her, but, as you, Bhengu, have asked us to hand her over to you, we are going to do so. You are to look after her, and see she gets to the King. We find there is no case against her. It is between her and the King. Let them settle it."

The court detained Christina, handed her a note, and told her, with eyes on Bhengu: "If this man does not look out for you properly, if you go hungry, or if he does not put you up in decent places, you are to take this letter to the nearest police station. If there is no police station, take it to any European, and he will see that you are treated fairly and justly."

Christina's mistress was indignant. "I cannot do without you. What will I do with all this work? I don't see why they should take you at this time. I wish I had gone with you and seen the Magistrate and explained to him what a good and faithful servant you are, how much more I need you than that mean, nasty old King does. He already has more wives and women than he knows what to do with. I don't see why you are going, Christina. I don't see why we don't send this man away, and you stay here with me and let them see what they can do about it. I bet they never would do anything."

All the time she was talking, however, she was pulling things out of drawers and closets and brought forth two pairs of worn-out shoes, and an old coat. Once she stopped briefly to give Christina a pound in wages for the time she had worked. This was generous as she could have stood upon her rights and given her nothing since it was not yet the end of the month and she was leaving without notice. Christina tried to thank her. The mistress interrupted: "Here is one of my old dresses. As soon as this silly matter is settled, you put it on and come straight back to me."

There were tears in Christina's eyes, and a suspicion of tears in those of her mistress. Christina went upstairs to bid the children good-bye but could not bear to look back at her kind mistress and at this home, where for three months she had lived and worked in peace.

twenty-four

"**I** am coming, too," Beauty was saying, "the King told Bhengu to bring me."

On the journey Christina behaved like a spoiled child on an outing with indulgent parents, and kept reminding Bhengu: "I was told to ask you for anything I want! I want some fruit!"

And later: "I want something to drink!"

And then: "I want some sweets!"

So often did she taunt Bhengu with the Magistrate's admonition to look after her, trapping him into buying something for her, that in final exasperation he cried: "I came to put you in jail, but you have put me in jail, instead!" Ironically, Christina's return coincided with the peak of a wedding ceremony, that of an Ndwandwe girl to the King.

Solomon had become so bored by his weddings he usually put in a formal appearance at the beginning of the festivities, and then retired into a drunken orgy. At the hour when bridal slumber should have come upon him, he was usually courting the prettiest girl who had arrived with the bridal party.

His first wife and his latest wife, who had been married to him but a few hours, were far from Solomon's drunken mind. Bhengu was new in the royal service. Confronted with the King's indifference at midnight, at the end of a hundred-mile exhausting drive, he found himself pleading: "But Ndabezitha, I was told at the courthouse this person was to be well treated. She has traveled a long way. She is tired. What am I to do with her?"

The King ordered him out of his sight. Back at the car Bhengu's voice was a fine blend of humility and a bid for confidence. "There are a lot of people here for the wedding and all the huts are full. I don't know exactly where you are going to sleep."

With exasperated determination, Christina got out of the car and ordered Bhengu to follow with the luggage. They stopped before a rondavel that was dark and quiet, and Bhengu flashed a light into it. Unconscious men and women, stupefyingly drunk, lay upon the floor. Guided by the path of light Christina nudged an acquaintance of the Ndebele people, who awoke startled. "Can't we find a nook to sleep in?" Christina asked her wearily.

"See for yourself, there is not even sitting room on a mat," the woman mumbled.

At least her head and tongue were clear, while in the next hut the people were fighting and ugly. Christina undid her blanket and rolled it out on the floor, pushing and shoving bodies to make room for it. There she and Beauty squeezed in, leaning upon their luggage, and finally sleep crept in upon them.

*At daybreak they sought out okaMtshekula, who sobbed aloud at seeing them, then bustled about getting breakfast, meanwhile pelting them with a running fire of questions.

Christina's eager questions prevailed: "Have you heard about my children? Are they all right?" OkaMtshekula reassured her, and added wistfully, "Long ago I asked to have Sishoniswaphi brought to me but the King refused."

Some of the mothers crowded into the hut, jeering: "Where does the wandering woman, the loose woman, come from? She, an old wife, sees others leaving and then follows herself. Hah! Oh, how good you were! All the time you were concealing an assegai. You are like a chameleon. So you creep along slowly do you? When there was discontent among the wives, we never heard from you!"

"Your effect was tremendous!" another said, enjoying her words as if she rolled each one over separately on her tongue. "When it was heard you had gone, the King was struck by a great fear!"

"Even now I have not returned!" she defiantly announced. "I have come only to speak to the King, mouth to mouth, so I will not carry with me the fear of one who was escaped. I have come to clear my name."

The sun was setting when Christina asked Bhengu anxiously: "Did you see the King? What did he say?"

"The King said: 'When the bridal ceremony is finished, and the bridal party has gone, then this case will be brought forward.'"

For two days Christina and Beauty remained with okaMtshekula, eating of their own food. On the third day, okaMtshekula went to the King and demanded: "What do you think these prisoners in my hut are eating?"

Rested somewhat from his drunken orgy, the King was contrite. "I had forgotten what Bhengu told me. I will send meat and jugo beans."

Having disposed of the practical details over which the mother was so exercised, he inquired hesitantly: "Is Christina just the same as ever?"

He had almost whispered, and okaMtshekula fell into the spirit of conspiracy, and whispered, too: "She is as big as an elephant, and as white, as white can be."

This excited him. "I must go and see her!"

OkaMtshekula returned in high spirits. "The King is going to send you food! He is coming himself to see you!"

In a short while the royal car arrived and parked outside okaMtshekula's

---

* Compare here through p. 174 with the record of original interview, appendix 1E.—Eds.

hut, a trip of only two or three hundred yards. Somewhat heavily the King lumbered out of the car, and called in a teasing, bantering tone: "In the hut, here, there is a smell of white people from Durban!"

Then suddenly, turning abruptly, he stamped off in great anger to the car, followed by Zazeni, who did not seem to understand this performance any better than the women did, for there was a look of bewilderment on his face, too.

When the bridal party left, the King went to the uSuthu without having spoken to Christina. Everyone in the kraal whispered about her return, and his bitter, unforgiving mood.

Four days later, when he returned, his motor car passed right by Christina and Beauty. Christina thought: "We walk like people from a strange country, with a swaggering gait." Solomon was not unaware of this, and had his own way of pricking that conceit. He called to Beauty, put her in the car, and proceeded with her to Dlamahlahla, the royal residence.

As the car drove out of sight, Christina walked slowly, shoulders drooping, feet dragging. Long after dark, when the driver brought Beauty back, she was still sitting alone in her hut, with no fire, and no sign of having had food.

"What is the King going to do with me? How does he feel about me?" she inquired eagerly.

But Beauty was so drunk, she hardly knew what she was doing. There was a funny leer upon her face. "The King wishes me to return to Dlamahlahla and live there. He says this is not a fit place for me, that I am not strong!"

Christina watched Beauty pack, zigzagging from one side of the hut to the other, heard her airily call good-bye. For the second time that day, the wheels of a departing car drove across her tightened chest.

Dimly she realized Beauty had answered none of her questions, had been absorbed in herself, in her own prospects with the King. Clearly the King was punishing her through her sister; her last hope of getting fair and prompt treatment from him died within her.

Next morning while she went about her duties in a hopeless stupor, Beauty staggered in. In contrast to the night before, her words tumbled over each other. "The King asked how I knew you were in Durban. I said I heard of you from Rev. Mpanza, and then I went to see you where he was preaching. There you told me all about how you had come down to Durban." Christina realized that Beauty was trying out her alibi on her.

"The King asked whether there was any man with you. He said, 'She has grown so stout, who has been looking after her?' I said, 'She has been that way since she came home at Nhlazatshe.' He argued, 'I too found her quite fat at Nhlazatshe, but she was not as big as this.' Then he wanted to know, 'Was she working for a white man or a native?' and coaxed, 'Tell me, my friend, what is it that sent Christina away from here?' I explained 'Christina says she no longer wished to stay.'"

Believing that Christina did not see through her divided loyalty, Beauty continued: "Wait, there is more. 'Christina went behind my back. She has belittled me before the whole country. However, I understand she has a sore heart, a grudge against me, for I mistreated her at Nsindeni.'"

"When did he say the trial was to take place?" Christina interrupted harshly. "Didn't you remember to ask him that? That is what I most want to know!"

Irritation crept into Beauty's tone. "I did ask him, and he answered, 'I will send for my Uncle uMnyayiza Zulu, the *uMntwana* of Minya, prince of the Minya.'"

Christina felt more hopeful. The King must be planning for a trial, for he had sent for the Prime Minister.

Two weeks passed. Christina did not see Beauty, who was living in luxury with the king. The days were heavy with monotony and impatience, broken only by a brief, stolen visit from Ethel. There was a rumor that Ethel, too, had made known her intention of going, but the King had as yet not given her permission either.

Now Ethel was saying: "I am just waiting for money from home, otherwise you would not have found me here."

Another week went by, solitary, pointless. Lonely and desperate Christina burst in on okaMtshekula: "Go to the King and demand 'When, then, is this matter going to be attended to?'"

OkaMtshekula tried to pacify her, and finally admitted: "I am afraid to. I do not dare to go to him when it is so plain to everyone he is taking his own time to bring you to trial."

How could she get to the King? How was she going to remind him forcefully she was there waiting for her trial? Her only chance was through the regular channels of one of the mothers who could seek the King out, or through some woman he favored.

Beauty was only three hundred yards away, but was now avoiding her, so she sent her a note by messenger. "Can't you tell the King? I insist that my case be dealt with immediately."

Beauty, too, sent a note. "The King says he is waiting for the *uMntwana* of Minya."

A month went by, thirty days in which there was nothing to do but sit and wait, in which impatience and anger tore and gnawed at her so that sleep would not come at night, and ugly thoughts spilled over where sleep should have been.

There are some who hold that a woman's emotional cycle follows that of the moon. At the end of a lunar month Christina found herself talking to the head man, Mphimbo, with neither modesty nor respect. "Go to the King, and tell him I am going. I do not see what I have been brought from Durban for."

Mphimbo had many unpleasant duties as head man, some of which had no precedent, but he found this one particularly difficult. He knew full well if he did not have the right answer for her, since she had so far forgotten herself as to confront him about this, Christina would pursue him relentlessly until she got one. Best to be frank. "Daughter of Sibiya, I have no authority to take this to the King."

All her fury concentrated in her voice: "It is not meet I should speak for myself to him because I am a prisoner! It is not meet I should disobey him, because he is the King. It is not meet I should harken to this thing which is troubling my heart! Then, you, Mphimbo, the King's head man, you tell me what I am to do!"

Easy enough for him to say: "You had best leave it until he speaks of it."

Mphimbo had not put in more than three months of impatience that grew into a fever. "I may wait forever," Christina cried in exasperation, "There are still wives who made known their intentions of leaving before I went away many months ago, and they are still here. I don't want to stay here until my money is finished. I earned this money in Durban. What will I do when the money is gone? The King gives me none."

She hoped if she explained her position thoroughly maybe she would win his sympathy and understanding. She succeeded only in irritating him. "I am surprised at you, Sibiya," he snapped back. "Do you not even remember your children? Do you not love them?"

This trick of playing upon her emotions through her children had been tried on her just once too often, "Mphimbo, don't *you* start trying me! It is a trial I am asking for."

In helpless anger she walked away, as Mphimbo called after her: "I am not going to the King. Remember that!"

Her imagination was exhausted. She no longer knew how to reach the King; every avenue to him was closed. She lived only for her letters, her only contact with the outside world. The King and his advisers were on the lookout for a man writing to her, for if they could prove she was involved in a love affair, which as every decent person would understand she was not entitled to have, then she could be punished until she realized how a wife of the King should behave.

The white postmaster had orders to scan his list with the names of all the King's wives, and lay aside any letters which might come to them. On this list, Christina's name had been especially underlined. Since she now had no regular duties, she did not arouse suspicion at the kraal by her many trips to the post office and village store. Had the King or any of his council seen the letters which a Harriet Khuzwayo received they would have learned exactly what they had hoped to, that Christina had now begun to love a man whom she had met in Durban, and it was from him she heard, and to him she hoped to return.

Christina had given her love to Alfred Msimang, a van driver, whom the natives referred to as a man who went with the travelers. They had been to school together at Maphumulo. He lived in Durban, but his real home was at Ngoye, in a triangle between Eshowe, Empangeni, and Mthunzini. He had told Christina he was not married, but she suspected that he was, and that his wife was at Ngoye. They had not been in love very long, he always traveled with the van, and Christina had only visited with him three times. All these past months at Mahashini she had feared he would forget her.

It was hard to lie alone at night and long for a man who had wanted you, and know that a man who did not care about you could hold you to his side out of sheer spite.

Two more months dragged by. Not once did Beauty come to call upon her. Christina spent all her time writing impassioned love letters to Alfred, and looking for his. One day she forgot to tear up an envelope and she heard people at the kraal whispering about a "Harriet." Frightened, she immediately notified her lover to address her no longer by that name, but their letters crossed, and one more came to "Harriet."

When the post boy came with his packet of mail, she was at the post office waiting for him. While the postmaster was putting the letters for Europeans into their private boxes, and before the messenger from the King's residence arrived to fetch the kraal's post from the tray, she stole her letter.

"This time she chose a man's name. She called herself: "Mr. Joseph Mnqibisa." During the empty days that followed, the trick of getting a letter past the postmaster, Bhengu, the King and all his spies, made quite a game. To put the postmaster off the scent she went to him again and again, and asked for letters for "Harriet" and begged him to give them to her rather than to the King. Regularly, when his back was turned, she stole "Joseph's" letters from the native General Delivery tray.

When the money she had earned in domestic service in Durban gave out, Rev. Mpanza and his congregation sent her ten shillings and Alfred Msimang sent a pound note.

The King often saw her going to and from the post office, but he never spoke to her.

"How do you get your letters?" Beauty coaxed. Anyone would have guessed she hoped to ingratiate herself with the King by betraying her sister, and Christina ignored her.

Christina paved the way for Ethel's escape by suggesting that she, too, call herself by another name. They picked a nice sounding one, one they liked, "Clemie Mtshali," and roared with laughter over it. "To think that you, Christina, are now spoiling the King's wives!" murmured Ethel.

Nevertheless, Ethel tried to justify herself even with Christina: "I have to do this, because I never get the things I write home for. When my letter comes, the King may be in Durban, may stay three weeks. Not until he returns, and reads my letter, do I get it, and sometimes he forgets to give it to me, or post the ones I write." Her next words ended almost on song: "I am going to write home and tell them about my new name, and ask them to send me money!"

Ethel was the King's cook, in charge of the royal commissary, and she filched choice bits and brought them to Christina. If anyone asked Christina where her lovely food came from, she would say: "You see me going to the store all the time. I buy my food there!"

Of course no one believed her. Ordinary natives do not buy chicken, eggs, or succulent vegetables at the native store. If they suspected Ethel, no one disliked her enough to betray her to the King.

The King had been away, at Zibindini, for quite a while, and Beauty began coming every day to see Christina.

"Now the King has gone, you remember me!" Christina said indignantly.

"Please, Christina, won't you give me a little money to buy some food?" Beauty wheedled shamelessly. "The King is not here, and I have nothing to eat."

"Where do you think I am going to get money from, dying as I am of starvation, while you people are sitting under the King?"

The natives have a way of saying people "sit under" as do chicks under a hen for protection.

"If the King were here, you people, you, Beauty, and your friends up there at the King's house, wouldn't give me even the bone of the wing of a fowl."

twenty-five

Unexpectedly the King brought back Christina's two daughters with him. Was he trying to save his face with the community by making one last effort to keep Christina from leaving because it was known no man had ever had a more loyal or docile wife than she had been? Or was he still devoted to her, sorry to have hurt her, and hopeful of softening her heart toward him and the kraal by bringing her children to her? Almost hysterically happy to see her children, Christina did not stop to consider his motives.

Finally it was necessary for okaMtshekula to demand of the King: "What do you think Christina eats? What do you think she washes with? I thought she came with a letter from the courthouse at Durban which instructed you to look after her properly."

Even though she was a mother with privileges, it took courage to say this, but okaMtshekula, too, was beginning to wonder whether nearly half a year was not enough time for even the King to make up his mind.

The King ignored her, and she left defeated of her purpose to rouse him to just consideration of Christina's case.

Eventually Christina settled down to a long wait. She sent to Durban for wool, and knitted scarves, caps, and men's socks, and found that with the sale of these to less skillful and enterprising natives she had enough to live on.

Bhengu had brought her to Mahashini in August, 1929. Christmas had come and gone, unnoticed. The summer months had burned by, and passed into the cooler ones of winter. Spring was full upon them in November, 1930, a whole year's cycle had been completed, and a new year's cycle would soon commence and still the King had done nothing about releasing her. She knew he was trying to wear down her patience until her rebellion would seem ridiculous, and it would seem normal to remain.

Possibly the stirrings of spring were stronger than reason. She was just turned thirty, and it had been more than five years since she had known any man's love or passion except in her three visits with her lover.

Christina burst in upon Mphimbo in a hysteria of fury. "Go and tell the King I am leaving! I don't know what I was brought back for! If a person is guilty of misconduct, he is fined, and allowed to go free, or put into prison, if there is no fine big enough to pay for the crime. But when that person is put in jail, he is given food, soap to wash with, and blankets to sleep under.

What sort of prisoner am I who doesn't have this done for her? You go with these words! Take them to the King and don't hide one of them! Better go while I watch you and see you truly get to the King!"

Mphimbo set off with her eyes boring into his back, but once there, he remained drinking beer and chatting idly.

In no mood for any further dalliance, Christina started for the King's residence. The King saw her coming and shouted to Greta: "Tell your mother to return from where she came!"

Accustomed automatically to obey his orders, Christina turned back sharply toward her rondavel. The King then signaled petulantly, she was to come along anyway.

Christina joined with the other members of the kraal in a social gathering such as she had not participated in for many a month. Under cover of the festivities she asked Zazeni whether Mphimbo had said anything about her to the King, and he truthfully answered: "Mphimbo did not even mention your name to him."

Next day when Christina heard the King was about to leave for Johannesburg, she confronted Mphimbo, who hedged and stammered.

"Very well, Mphimbo, but don't you follow me if I go while the king is away" she warned him.

But again she thought better of leaving with the dreaded black mark of scandal against her, and continued to wait for the King's permission.

Time dragged on. In March, Ethel left. They learned she was gone, for she was no longer there. No one knew how she had gone, nor when. No one but Christina, who knew money had come for "Clemie Mtshali."

When the King returned in April, Christina was again hopeful. But May and June went by, and July came with its cooler breezes and chillier night air and still no mention was made of the trial that he had promised her.

On a particularly blowy day in July, Christina stood in Mphimbo's path. He always avoided her, but he saw her too late to slip out of her way. "Today I have packed. I am going!" she announced.

"What are you punishing the King for? All right, he hasn't tried your case and fined you. But he hasn't punished you, he has just ignored you. You had better drop all this foolishness!"

"I know! You, also, are married to a lot of wives, so you take the King's part. Besides, you have the privileges of a head man here at this kraal. You have to side with the King." She tried another tack. "If your wife had done wrong, what would you do to her?"

No deacon ever made a more righteous pronouncement. "If my wife went home to her people, I would fetch her back."

"And when you brought her back what would you do to her?"

Such a thick-headed woman, but at least she was asking his advice instead of scolding him in an unbecoming and immodest way. Still righteous, but a little heartier, he continued: "I would bring her back and try her. If I fined her, she could go home and get a beast from her people, and pay her fine to me."

"And when she paid her fine to you, what would happen?" she persisted.

"Then I would call her to me, and the trouble is finished, and she is again my wife."

"Then what are you telling me? I have been back a year. Nothing has been done. Nothing has been said. Why don't I get a trial? Why doesn't *my* husband tell me what he thinks about all this?"

"But he is the King!" Why did Christina fail to see plain facts? "I am only an ordinary native. You must stay and wait his pleasure."

Easy enough for Mphimbo to talk this way. He did not have long nights of loneliness, when his body was feverish with an aching longing for love, with sharp need for the King, or for any man; for after a while, even when you hated these men, this female longing came upon you and you were helpless before it.

"Mphimbo, what is the King frightened of in me? I waited four years for him when I was his wife. Here I am again waiting for him when I am not really his wife. Why is it, and what is it?"

There was entreaty and pleading in her whole bearing. Quick to respond to the true appeal in a woman, where she had failed with scolding and threats, she now won Mphimbo completely.

Mphimbo faced the King. Foolishly he had let a woman's lonely plea betray him. Distress, akin to pain, gave him the wit with which to present her case in the best light.

"Call Christina before me!" the King ordered.

As she hurried to him her thoughts were in a scramble. If only the pounding of her heart, the shortness of breath, would not prevent her from speaking her mind. So strong was this determination within her, that in her first words she found courage. It was as if they came from someone else, yet they were her own, for she had so often rehearsed them.

"I say that I am going!"

"Where to?" he indulgently inquired.

"I am going wherever I want to!"

Quite emotionless, he disregarded her defiance: "You are to wait, Christina. I am going to call up all my mothers and the *uMntwana* of Minya —my father. Long ago, I reported this matter to him, but it is he, my father, who has done nothing about it."

Once she would have mumbled, "I thank you," and left his presence. Not any more. While she was there she was going to make the most of it!

"You put this matter into your father's hands? Is he the one who came and fetched me from my people? None of the people whom you are calling upon to decide this for you were there! It was you who brought me!"

"When I took you I put you into their hands."

"The *uMntwana* of Minya—when will he arrive? This matter is now old."

Her manner was offensive to him. "You act as though I were a child in your talk with me. I will send for the *uMntwana* today!"

The very next day the *uMntwana*, the King's Prime Minister, arrived and went into secret session with him. Rumors grew and spread throughout the kraal. Some said they knew definitely the King had made up his mind to give Christina a trial, while others said this was only more of her arrogance, to think she was entitled to one.

Never before had a King's wife been given a trial at the instigation of the wife. Wives had been tried. Wives had had charges of adultery brought against them. Wives had borne children in adultery. Never, though, had a case been brought up of a wife who simply wished to leave the King, and wished to have the case tried publicly to decide that issue, and that issue alone.

On the fourth day after the *uMntwana* had arrived, the King called together the whole of the kraal, and everyone knew that at last Christina was to have her trial.

The trial was held at Dlamahlahla, the royal residence. The overflow from the sitting room spilled over into the dining room and into the hall. All the wives squatted upon the floor. Christina sat apart in front of a window that looked out onto the wives' quarters, opposite the wide door opening into the passage, could see all who came and went, and had a full view of the entire room. The *uMntwana*, too, sat facing everyone.

The King stood at attention, near by and looked down upon his people. It was not necessary to call the meeting to order, for as soon as the *uMntwana* started to speak, there was an instant hush.

Christina's heart pounded so rapidly within her she wondered if she might not really choke. There was not a stir, a whisper or a gesture she did not note. Some of the wives giggled and nudged each other. She could not hear what they were whispering, but she felt their hostility and ridicule.

Not unlike men elsewhere confronted with an unpleasant public situation, these men, by their very questions, were going to indicate the slant they wished to place upon unseemly behavior.

The Prime Minister opened the session by demanding: "Daughter of Sibiya, where have you been?"

All her courage went into a voice that carried out beyond the dining room: "I have been there where I wanted to go!"

Few men of any nation have brought before them the variety of problems this man had been called upon to solve as Prime Minister of his people, and there was dignity, wisdom and the promise of justice in his voice.

"Answer me nicely. I am not fighting. You are my child."

Christina and the *uMntwana* might have been talking alone, for their voices and eyes were only for each other.

"No, Ndabezitha, I am not answering you nastily. I say of a truth, I have been where I wanted to go."

Some of the women could be seen pinching each other.

"Where was that—what place was that?" the *uMntwana* persisted.

"Durban."

A woman giggled nervously.

"When you left here, what made you go to Durban?"

Christina corrected him. "No, I first went home, before I went to Durban."

The *uMntwana* was making a point as any district attorney might have done. "Was it your relatives who said 'Go to Durban?' Why did you not go straight from here to Durban if it was Durban you wanted to go to?"

They were trying to trap her into admitting she had gone to meet a lover and she well knew it.

"Now that you have been and come back from Durban what are you fighting about?"

They wouldn't focus on the trial, on the point which she wished to have considered.

"I am not fighting with anybody. I am talking to the King who came and took me from my people."

Mphimbo signaled to the Prime Minister and got permission to ask the next question: "Did you then have a man in Durban?"

The room grew so still the previous fragmentary whispers were almost like remembered shrieks.

"That Mphimbo is trying to pay me back for the way I dogged his foot-steps, but he is just a coward currying favor with the King, and it will never be Mphimbo who can trip me up," Christina thought. But she answered in her most ingratiating way, "If I had a man in Durban, would I have returned? Did I run away? I came here of my own desire. I wanted to walk in your hands, to do the right thing."

The *uMntwana* nodded further permission to Mphimbo, who demanded: "What is it then that is causing you to be restless when you have been back such a long time?"

"I stayed here to abide by your wishes, thinking my desire to leave would be discussed and finished with."

The *uMntwana* decided to shame Christina into a true awakening of her womanly position. "Do you no longer love your children left behind you?"

This was no place to remind them that whenever the King wished he had torn her away from these children, that it was he who had first assured her a mother could love her children and yet live apart from them. Yet now it served his purposes, he and everyone else kept bringing up her love for her children as if she loved them any the less! If she said what she felt, there might be tears in her eyes and a catch in her throat, and it was important she keep her voice controlled. Steadily, her words must march before her eyes, each word along the pathway of her goal.

"Yes, I love my children. I am happy if they are well, but I came upon them later. I did not bring them with me from my home. Even had there been no children, I would have stayed here quite happily if the King had treated me well."

It seemed too good an opportunity not to remind them of the King's attitude to these children they kept emphasizing, when for years he had forgotten them and left her to fend for them, and for herself as best she could. Passion crept into her voice. "I might have found those children in the hills. What about the years their father no longer looked after them properly?"

No one there liked the turn the trial was taking. After all here were the King's head men, and his mothers, permitting one of his wives to hurl unpleasant charges against him; and in the presence of other wives! Quickly one of the mothers cut in: "What is your wrong now? The King has not tried your case? Is that all that is pushing you to make known your intention of going?"

Christina recovered her composure: "Yes, I have waited here thinking the King was going to try the case."

The *uMntwana* pondered for a moment, and then sadly began to speak: "I am beaten. Some wives have gone, but I never thought that you, daughter of Sibiya, would go. It is not right."

Since the *uMntwana* paused as if it were her turn to speak, she replied: "They were caused by their hearts to go. I am caused to go by mine."

Instantly another mother with pursed lips challenged, as if her mere statement would be enough: "It behooves you to stay."

It was easier to fight another woman, especially one who covered up her antagonism so poorly.

"I have done no wrong. I went away without having done a single wrong thing. Had I stayed here, treated as I was, I would have done something to be sorry for."

Early in the trial the King had grown uncomfortable and left the room. Perhaps he feared Christina's rehearsal of her grievances against him, and preferred to leave her trial in the hands of those he knew were unswervingly loyal to him. But now he returned, stood opposite her and spoke directly to her: "It was meet, Christina, that you should complain about me to my fathers and mothers if I had done anything wrong. But you hit me from behind with a stick which I had not seen. You never made a scene, and I never thought you were jealous."

No one there could believe it was the King talking, never had they heard him speak with such sadness: "I admit all the charges against me, but you must remember your children, Christina."

Abruptly, the King left the room and since formal etiquette required that once the King had spoken, his should be the last word, everyone else rose, and followed him out.

The first session of the trial was over. Nothing had been settled. Christina had barely explained anything, nor had the King, nor anyone else, definitely asked her why she had left; but it was generally known her charges against the King were that he had discarded her, that he had accused her of adultery, and that he had neglected her when she was sick and had not given her proper medical attention. Beating is excusable under native law.

A short while later, Mphimbo came to Christina in her hut. "The King sends word to you, Sibiya, 'Nevertheless I have not said go in peace.' He says he is still going to think up a plan of what to do with you. He says he knows all that you are doing is not of your own accord. Something or someone has set you off. He will talk to you all about it at another time. Now he is going away to the abaQulusi!"

Bitterness surged up within her. "No, Mphimbo, I know how you people settle matters. I know a little thing takes a long, long time for you to decide. Therefore, I am going away now. I have waited too many years for the King to say all that was in his heart."

"No, no, my child," he interrupted. "Leave all that. Drop it!"

"Drop everything, Mphimbo? Whom am I going to marry in this kraal? Who is going to provide for me? The King no longer loves me, his love has gone forever."

Aware of the irrevocable truth of her words, Mphimbo said nothing.

"You people would force a person to commit adultery, and then all of you would insult and punish that person."

"No, my child. The King says just stay here like the others. They are committing adultery. You would not be the only one."

The head man of the King's kraal was openly suggesting that if she put a face on things she could hereafter commit adultery and protection would be found for her!

"No, no Mphimbo! *I cannot love two people—the King—and a native*! And then when the King is sick, you people will say it is I who have brought him the sickness; that this man I go with is the cause."

"The King says it is meet you should provide yourself with love philters," Mphimbo interrupted, "just as the others have done."

"When the King first loved me, I didn't love him because of philters, nor he me because of them. When the King is sick, when his knees are swollen and his blood is out of order, you people immediately say 'It is the woman's sickness!' I have nothing that worries my heart when the King is sick; I have never slept with another man."

Mphimbo backed out, mumbling that the King was waiting for him. The King left for the 'baQulusi without any further message for her.

Christina spent a week sewing and mending clothes for Corinna. She went on a quick visit to Cyprian. Greta was now living at Mahashini and Christina explained her grievance to her. Greta, who had never known anything but kindness from her mother, assured her she would love her regardless of what the King or anyone might say. No longer a child, she had noted the King's treatment of his wives.

Christina held Greta and Corinna against her in tight, wordless hugs, and then, her head held high, her eyes looking straight before her, she walked out of the gates of Mahashini never to return. This was in June, 1931. Christina was thirty-one years old.

twenty-six

Christina had not expected to gain her freedom and was not prepared to take it, for she had neither plans nor money. She would have liked to return to Durban, where she could get work to do, and where she had known happiness, but she had no money for fare. Instead she went to the nearest family kraal, that of her uncle at Nongoma, Jeremiah Sibiya, about eighteen or twenty miles from Mahashini. He drove her away with curses, while demanding where she was going. His mother caught a flash of Christina's hurt bewilderment, and laid her hand upon her son's arm and gently urged that he give her the welcome that would be expected of him. Ashamed, Jeremiah explained: "The king will quarrel with me if I harbor her."

A native woman must live with members of her family, unless she is in domestic service. Even if a woman should deny the authority of her nearest male kin, they and the rest of the native community affirm it.

Instead of resenting Jeremiah's lack of hospitality, Christina tried to point out the absurdity of his fears. "If I have run away from the King's kraal, you will soon know, for a messenger will be sent to get me. But as I stay you will see no one will come seeking me, for I have left with the King's permission."

Jeremiah's curiosity was aroused and he prodded her for details. "I have been walking all night long," Christina protested. "You are full of fresh energy and strength because you have had a night's rest. I will tell you anything you want to know, but now I must go somewhere where I can sleep."

Again the mother interfered: "Let her go in peace," she suggested. "She will tell you when she has slept and eaten."

Grudgingly her uncle let Christina remain, and she took her place as a member of his kraal, helped with the cooking, for she was a noted cook, and with tending the children. No one asked her when she planned to leave, and because she had undergone a great strain waiting for her trial and managing her own case, she could not muster the necessary urge to go.

In order not to incur the King's enmity, Jeremiah sent formal notice to him that Christina was at his kraal. In the third month, when she had settled down to the routine of once again being an unattached woman, the King sent two men to fetch her. Fiercely she turned upon them and passionately listed the grievances she had hoped to air at the trial.

"I will not go. I waited a year and a half for my trial, for my case to be settled. I swore on oath I would never return to Mahashini!"

Jeremiah, now in the position of Christina's father, and so regarded by her and everyone else, insisted: "You had better go!"

Christina stubbornly refused, and the messengers, who had already heard more than they wished, left without her.

More weeks went by. Then one day Christina and the King met by chance at Adams' store. They talked for days about how the King stared at Christina, took in every one of her features, then looked through her as if he had never seen her before. Nor did she greet him out of turn.

One woman said she heard them whisper to each other, but she was shouted down by a chorus: "He never spoke to her". . . "He never gave her a chance to speak to him". . . "He spoke to everyone but her". . . "He looked at her as if she were a poisonous snake". . .

When Christina got home, she reported, like an excited child: "I saw the King at Adams' store." More sadly she admitted: "He did not speak to me. It was as if we had never seen each other before."

"Now I am satisfied," Jeremiah admitted, beaming. "If you had done anything wrong the King would have spoken to you about it immediately. He is hurt and angry with you for having made him seem ridiculous to the other women of his kraal."

Christina was not happy. The letters of Alfred Msimang had stopped. All she could learn was that he had long since gone to Johannesburg with a European traveling man and had never returned. There could be no new romance here, among her family, and she clung to her old one and charged its failure against Solomon. "He gave me no happiness himself, but he destroyed what happiness I could find elsewhere."

Circumstances had taught Christina what women learn the world over, how best to adjust themselves into a society in which they no longer have a place as wives, how to sharpen their wits, and find the best way to make a living offered in their group.

There were only about sixty white people in Nongoma and they had all the domestic servants they needed. Occasionally Christina was able to sell some knitted scarves or caps, but the demand for them among the humbler natives was not so great as at the royal kraal. She looked about her at the Sibiya kraal and the Nongoma neighborhood, and decided that there was indeed a special local opportunity for her, to make and sell beer.

In an effort to cut down native drunkenness, innumerable laws and regulations have been passed in South Africa prohibiting and limiting the sale of liquor to natives. One would suppose that in a pastoral society there would be no demand, especially, in remoter areas, for the sale of liquor, that wanderers could stop at any kraal and be offered a hospitable draught of liquid refreshment. In actual fact, even in a village the size of Nongoma, which

has a small European hotel, two or three boarding houses, and a native eating house attached to the butchery run by Europeans, all with their attendant quota of house boys, errand boys, and general workers, there are a
number of unattached native men living in service without hope of getting
kraal-made beer.

Christina never made too much beer, only two paraffin tins at the time,
about eight gallons, for if native beer stands too long it gets stale, flat, and
ferments. When she mixed nothing but "pure maple," which she bought at
the village store, the supplies cost her about three and six, and she got a
return of about eight and six. She figured that one batch of beer brought her
about five shillings' profit, or about twice her cash investment.

Some people drank their beer there at the kraal, others took it away
with them. If the men had money they bought the beer; if the women had
money, and they had not made their own beer, they would come and buy;
and then there were always those customers who were passing by, travelers.

How did natives know there was bootleg beer on sale, and who was selling it? They used to "just hear," Christina said, and that was how she developed her trade. Christina became not only a full-fledged business woman,
she became a bootlegger.

When people came to buy there was laughter and gossip, and it seemed
a very pleasant way of earning a living, but Jeremiah could not see it that
way. "I do not want you to make beer in my kraal," he kept grumbling. "It
causes a lot of people to be always coming here. There is no getting away
from them now. It would be better for you to get married, Christina."

Without any warning, one day, Jeremiah grabbed the tin and dumped it,
so there was neither the beer nor the money spent on it. Christina had lived
too long without any money at all, so that the waste of it, as well as that of
her energy, maddened her. Distressed and angry, she went to another member of the Sibiya tribe to ask if he would find a place for her to live. He suggested she stay at his kraal, and she moved over immediately, and there she
continued to ply her trade peacefully.

No sooner, however, had she left Jeremiah's kraal, than they, too, started making beer and selling it. Those who had heard what he had said and
done to Christina were surprised. She was not. All along she had suspected
he envied her her prosperity.

Christina heard the King was pleased that she was now staying with one
of the Falaza, a member of Cetshwayo's crack regiment. She made no effort
to go to Durban, nor Johannesburg, nor any of the big cities, for as long as
she remained here, she would be cared for, could get word about her children, and should anything be the matter with any of them, go promptly to
them. After a while she made no further effort to make and sell beer, for it
was feared so much rivalry and competition would undoubtedly bring it to
the attention of the authorities.

Months went by and Christina was content. It was a full and busy life, she had almost forgotten what it was like to know a man, and anger at the King began to fade.

Her present father of the Falaza Regiment entered into secret negotiations with powerful allies of his, friends of the King, to see if Christina could not be reinstated in the King's good graces, so she need not live, while still in her prime, the life of a neglected woman. As long as the King lived, no other man dared approach her, though she, herself, insisted she was now a divorced woman.

twenty-seven

Solomon had helped weld together the uSuthu and Mandlakazi tribes, previously antagonistic for forty years. When his knees became bad and his health began to fail, his interest in women dimmed and he again became more alert to the tribal disputes around him. There were some who said the King had begun to realize that unless he cultivated the men of his nation more strongly, he would never get the financial support he needed to pay off his stupendous debts.

The abaQulusi were having a dispute which reached such proportions that only Solomon could settle it. It was only proper the leaders should have come to the King, but instead, because of the effect they hoped it would have upon the whole tribe, Chief Kambe prevailed upon Solomon to come to his kraal with him.

While Solomon was in the heat of argument at Kambe's kraal in the Ngotshe district, he was taken with violent cramps, and asked for tea. Everyone thought he would be better in just a few minutes, that it was only a passing pain. True to his life-long antipathy, he refused any medicine. He refused to send for a doctor, even when the pain persisted. Before the day was over, Solomon died in agony.

Then it was believed that the abaQulusi would pay dearly for his death, for they had violated native sense of decency in bringing the King there in the first place, and his unexpected death would unquestionably point to poisoning. Who could tell what had been in the tea? But when the abaQulusi appeared at the funeral and a beast was killed for them it was taken as a sign among the Zulu people that their explanation had been accepted.

The King was brought home to Mahashini where he lay in state upon his brass bed, in a room hung with photographs of the British royal family. The funeral was delayed for several days because his brother Mshiyeni had to arrive to be the first to throw up a spade of dirt for the King's grave.

Mshiyeni used a royal spear to dig the grave, and this, and everything of value belonging to Solomon, was laid in his grave to rest with him. Some thought it unfortunate they could not put in the American player-piano which was the late King's proudest possession. He had been very fond of music and had a phonograph and many records which he often played.

After the six grave diggers had washed their bodies, they lowered the mattress, upon which the King was to be placed. A few stood in the grave to receive the body. They were terrified for fear they would be buried alive, as they would have been in olden times, but the presence of the Bishop of Zululand, who officiated on behalf of his church, reassured them.

Some say the King, who had luxurious European tastes, was buried in an expensive coffin, but they do not know native ways. The King was wrapped in a white oxskin, the most beautiful to be found in all Zululand.

In tribute to his modern tastes, they sang the hymns he liked, for as a boy, he had been educated by the daughters of the famous Bishop Colenso, and from them had acquired favorite Christina tunes.

They built a stockade nine feet high around the mound of piled stones atop the grave. Green branches were carried by the mourners, most of whom had come for many miles. The stockade fence withered in time and turned a dismal gray, but at the head of the grave they planted one tree that would ever be green, the euphorbia, a wide-spreading variety of cactus, known to the natives as the *umhlonhlo*. All Zulu men of rank and importance have this tree growing green above their graves.

The natives, tens of thousands of them, stood in the pouring rain and chanted:

> *The fish has been dried of its water*
> *This death has cut our strength*
> *We are like sheep without a shepherd*

Christina stood among the other Zulus and uttered up her prayers that the King, whom she now believed she had loved unswervingly, would be welcomed into the protection of his Lord.

Solomon is known to have wanted to be buried near the home he had loved so well. Many of the other Zulu Kings, Dinuzulu, his father, and Ndaba, and Mpande, before him, are buried in the Babanango Magistracy at the Dingana kraal, in that spot where Dingana effected the famous Zulu military coup, the Piet Retief massacre. For more than twenty miles around this is considered hallowed ground, and Zulus dare not touch it even with their walking sticks lest they be asked, "Dost thou stab the King?"

The inscription on the expensive coffin which was sent for Solomon, but which was not used, read:

> King Solomon kaDinuzulu
> Died at the age of 40
> Born 1893
> Died 1933
> Reigned 1913–1933

Who was the heir to the throne? It was generally supposed Solomon had left a will in which he stipulated who his heir would be, and that the elders of the tribe knew whom he had appointed as his Great Wife, whose son would be King.

One reason why Christina had recently remained content was that she had hoped her son Cyprian was to be named the heir, and she and all her family did not want to jeopardize any benefits that might accrue to them, nor so offend the Zulu elders that they would have to cast her son aside because of the scandal which beclouded his mother's reputation.

Solomon had not designated his Great Wife or his heir, but the tribe, in a secret session, had pointed out the heir and had communicated the name to the South African Government, who had registered it. No one else had been told, for fear the boy, who was still young and defenseless, would be poisoned. Each mother hoped it was her son, and acted as if it were, thinking she might gain prestige anyway and fool other women, and perhaps other people, into believing she was the mother of the heir in actual fact.

Christina's family continued to hope Cyprian was the heir. Some of the newspapers got hold of his photograph, published it, and reiterated the rumors that Cyprian, whom the King had always especially loved, probably had been chosen heir. But even the natives knew they had no facts to go on.*

The Zulu nation would go into mourning for a year, at the end of which time they would hold a cleansing ceremony. All the Zulu wives, except Christina who had been divorced and was not properly of the King's household, would then be eligible to remarry, provided the King's brothers did not want them, or that their future husbands paid the King's heir the price in cattle demanded for them.

Christina had friends at Mahashini, Zazeni, the King's bodyguard, Gilbert Zulu, and Mnyayiza and Mathole, the Prime Ministers. All of them spoke kindly to her, respected her as they had in the beginning, and never called her a loose woman, for which she was grateful. But no matter how much they might want to, without the consent of Solomon's brother, Mshiyeni, they were powerless to find a way of looking after her and her children, even if she were the mother of an heir.

Whenever Christina met Mathole or Gilbert, they would say: "Why don't you return to Mahashini and look after your children?"

Christina, who would have liked to live again in the security of the royal kraal, since she had established her independence there, would reply: "What would I live on? I can't enter the King's kraal and live there on the strength of your invitation. How much better it would be if my Greta were

---

* Christina's son Seaprince, officially known as Cyprian, was in actual fact designated future King, and is now openly acknowledged the heir apparent. When the King and Queen of England, with their daughters, Princess Elizabeth and Princess Margaret Rose, visited South Africa in 1947, Cyprian was a leading figure in native welcoming ceremonies.

a boy, for then he could invite me to live with him and build a hut for me. He could insist on it."

Mathole and Gilbert looked at her sadly the last time she talked this way and said: "We hear, Christina. You are a wise woman. What you say is true."

Mshiyeni, who had been Regent since the death of the King, was monogamous, married to a devout Christian, and it was generally agreed Elsie would not tolerate her husband having any other wives. Solomon's wives would either have to be taken by the other men of the family, or marriages arranged for them with the men of the countryside who could afford to pay for them, and who would be glad to have a wife in such close connection with the royal kraal. This, despite the fact that everyone for miles around suspected the wives and children of the King had a malignant contagious disease.

Fifteen months after Solomon died, they held his *ihlambo*—cleansing ceremony—and Christina was sent indirect word that it would be regarded as unseemly for her to participate as a mourner, or even to come as a private citizen to mourn for her King. More than anything this established her complete isolation.

Nowhere is it recorded exactly what the *ihlambo* should be, and throughout South Africa there were conflicting newspaper reports of this one. Christian missionaries of every faith, as well as government officials, and thousands of natives, gathered at the royal kraal and made official obeisance to the departed King. Hundreds of Europeans, travelers, tourists, scientists, artists, and camera men looked on.

All through the night the Zulus waged their traditional hunt. Warriors dipped their assegais into a huge steaming cauldron. The witch doctors had prepared this brew and they continued to pray and chant over it. As the fire lit up the clearing, gruesome and distorted shadows emphasized these primitive rites on the bank of the Black Umfolozi. At previous *ihlambos* men killed each other at the ceremonial hunt, but at this one they killed beasts and dipped their assegais in animal blood. Despite every precaution, two men were seriously injured; perhaps intentionally, perhaps accidentally. There were no human sacrifices, but screaming, maddened men rushed about in the dark killing every living creature in the woods.

Mshiyeni carried Solomon's assegais and battle axe, heading the procession of warriors. Men of rank followed and then came the regiments, the Regiment of the Mountain of Heaven, the Regiment of Lions, the Regiment of the Elephant Tusk, and the Regiment of the Black Bull. Men dipped their spears into the witches' brew to ward off the evil that had come upon them with death. A great purification ceremony was completed.

Next day the women, except the widows in seclusion, dipped their brooms in sacred water and swept the kraal clean of death and all its evils. They went to the stream and burned their mourning clothes, and washed their bodies free of the aura of death. Now they could begin to grow their hair and face a new life.

In the afternoon, as dignitaries of the Zulu state and the South African Government made weighty speeches, black-robed widows gathered behind drawn shades in the bedroom of the late King. Doleful wails blended with the unceasing whir of the sewing machine, as without waiting for the ceremony to be over, the wives were taking turns at making their fresh white clothes. Shut up until almost dark, they began to file out, on any pretext, one by one, hungry and bored.

Men danced all that night, the day after, and the night following. The hills resounded with the old historical chants: at first, pretentious ones— the Shaka and the chant of Glory—that compared the King to Shaka and the more heroic characters; and toward the end, those of a homelier nature, sincere and deeply moving:

> *We are the tribe of the big animal*
> *We are the tribe of the big elephant*
> *The greatest of them all*
>
> *Solomon was the big animal*
> *Solomon was the elephant*
> *Solomon was the greatest of them all*
>
> *The fish has been dried of its water*
> *This death has cut our strength*
>
> *We are like sheep without a shepherd*
> *We are a broken people*
> *Our staff has been broken*
> *We have nothing left to lean on*

Christina had married as a girl of fifteen. She had known love, passion, and the bitterness of faded love, and the futility of variable and undependable affection once passion had died. She had borne children she dearly loved, and whom she wished to have with her, but for whom she could not provide.

She was a woman without status, for only a husband could provide that for her. When she had had a husband, once he no longer cared for her she had left him. She had been the first wife in the royal kraal to force a trial which did not grow out of adultery nor her misbehavior in marriage, but because she could no longer tolerate the condition imposed upon her. She had insisted upon her right to leave the King when she no longer wanted to remain at the royal kraal, and though she had won her freedom on a technicality, when that technicality was long forgotten she was remembered as the woman who, of her own free will, had left the King's kraal and yet gone from it in no disgrace.

And so Christina, who had gone through a twenty-year cycle of married life with its joys and disappointments, found that she, a royal Zulu, would rather go into domestic service among strangers than remain in her own village, living in the hope that some man might purchase her from her family and make her his wife and so provide for her and her children.

Without any background of formally organized or acquired knowledge, without the comfort of knowing that other women faced the same problems that she did, or behaved as she did, Christina had worked out the possible solution of her own life, based on what she, herself, believed was right, and on what she personally wanted to do. Living alone in the hills of Zululand, steeped in the traditions of an ancient and pastoral tribe, Christina was a twentieth century modern.

epilogue

Christina lies in state next to her husband, Solomon kaDinuzulu, the Paramount Chief, King of the Zulus, in the royal enclosure at Nongoma, in Northern Zululand, at last and forever the acknowledged Great Wife, Mother of the King. Arrangements for the twin tombs were one of the first royal acts of Cyprian Bhekuzulu, Christina's son, who ruled over the approximately three million Zulus for about twenty years, until he died in September, 1968.

A Zulu King designates his heir, and all his sons are eligible to the succession. Throughout Solomon's life the keenest rivalry between his many wives centered on each one's hopes that her son would be the chosen one.

When Solomon died he apparently had named no heir. Cyprian, Christina's eldest son, was a son, by his first wife, and, therefore, his natural heir. However, the elders of the tribe, met in Council and designated another son heir apparent, appointing a regent to serve while the heir was still a boy. Christina and Cyprian were ignored.

Later Christina was to claim that she carried on her person the letter Solomon gave her designating her son Cyprian as his heir to the Kingship.

As Mother of the King, Christina would have been an honored and privileged woman, no longer an impoverished outcast. How many women would have remained silent, withstood the temptation to declare their son's rights and establish their own glorified status? But Christina was primarily a concerned mother, and as always was governed by her own code of what was right. For she feared for Cyprian's life, was convinced that she had lost his eldest brother because jealous enemies fearing he was the designated heir had poisoned him.

Christina reasoned that if a boy of twelve were named King he would be trapped in a web of intrigue that would inevitably surround him, and she would be helpless to protect him as she had no powerful friends at Court. She decided to bide her time.

When Cyprian reached the age at which he could serve as King, Christina took her letter to the government authorities. News of a conflict about the rights to the throne spread like a bush fire throughout Zululand.

What I now relate I pieced together from what had been told to me by Europeans and Africans in Nongoma, Durban, Pietermaritzburg and the Cape, after Cyprian had been made rightful King.

The South African Government, the ultimate authority in Bantu affairs, convinced of the authenticity of Christina's letter, announced there would be a Court hearing for all the evidence to be presented. When the case came to trial in Nongoma, seat of the Magistracy and headquarters of the royal kraal, there was no building large enough to hold the interested throngs.

Under a blazing sun, before an estimated crowd of 4,500 persons, the trial was held outdoors, the improvised judicial shelter barely covering the principals. Testimony, often heated, was heard from many people. The Magistrate ruled in favor of Christina and her son, confirming that King Solomon had indeed provided Christina with proof that he wished to see her son Cyprian as his successor.

Cyprian owed his Kingship not only to the prompt action of the government authorities but to his mother's loyalty, perseverance and determination to make him King. Such is the story told to me.

But are these the facts? I am not sure. The South African Government offices in New York, and the Department of Bantu Administration in Pretoria, after months of correspondence and effort on my part informed me that regrettably all matters pertaining to Cyprian's succession are *classified material.*

Was there ever such a letter? What was its date, and what were its contents? Did the Government lean toward Christina because Cyprian and his followers were amenable to the official plans to make Zululand a Zulustan? Is this a sensitive political area enshrouded in political intrigue as Zululand traditionally has often been? I do not know. The story told to me seemed to fit in with Christina's character as I had know it, to emphasize her essential nobility, and on that basis I accepted it.

Cyprian did not appear to have been overly influenced by his mother's life or suffering. When I was in Nongoma in 1951 his second wife was in the local jail sentenced to three months for committing one act of adultery in his absence. Her plea of neglect and loneliness was disregarded.

When I asked the European Magistrate, if the European jails would not be overtaxed if similar punishment were meted out to Europeans, he replied, "It is a case of maintaining law and order. We must uphold respect for the King."

afterword

"Let all the stories be told": *Zulu Woman*, Words and Silence

The call that serves as the title of this afterword is drawn from Njabulo Ndebele's essay "Truth, Memory and Narrative," which was published in a collection entitled *Negotiating the Past: The Making of Memory in South Africa.*[1] Another writer in the same collection speaks of "memory as a means of excavating silence,"[2] and certainly the silences around the lives of women have been deafening. This seems particularly true of the public sphere, where the public stories of men have been represented as the sum total of a community's, region's, or nation's history. Nation, one needs to remember, is an extremely slippery, even treacherous word in the South African context, particularly if one considers its intercultural meanings.[3] Yet even if we take into account the slipperiness of the meaning of nation, it seems fair to assert that the stories that underpin any concept of the nation, in any number of nations, have been the stories of men. South African history, in all its multiple strands, is thick with the names of men, some honorable and some dishonorable, but of women—even the women of the honorable/dishonorable men—much, much less is known: their stories have not been told.[4]

Christina Sibiya's story—that of a marriage to an eminent man, himself caught in a tangle of contradictions, in a society saddled with its own inherited patriarchy as well as that of the white settler state—pierces the hermetic space of the public. It also foregrounds the often silenced themes of marriage, sexuality, and domestic violence, and suggests the need for redefining the domains of the private and public, for regarding them as densely overlapping rather than distinct.

Rebecca Reyher's factional account of Christina Sibiya's life as first wife of the young uncrowned Zulu king, Solomon kaDinuzulu, set within its double frame of Christina Sibiya's own selecting and arranging of her material and the subsequent rearranging and reauthoring by Rebecca Reyher, is one of a number of double-filterings of South African women's lives. Perhaps the best known of these texts is Elsa Joubert's *The Long Journey of Poppie Nongena.*[5] More recent examples are *The Calling of Katie Makanya* by Margaret McCord and the doubly mediated story of Paulina Dlamini,[6] who in her youth was a member of the Zulu King Cetshwayo's[7] retinue of young women before becoming a devout Christian.

Like *Zulu Woman*, these texts show black women's lives refracted through the subject position of white authors: in the first two texts, other women, and in the latter, two white men, who, we are told, transcribe, translate, and edit rather than reshape the subject's narrative. Joubert's telling of Poppie Nongena's life story has received both praise and criticism. David Schalkwyk's reading of the work illuminates Nongena's "double bind" "as a woman within a violent society that systematically subjugates and marginalises women, shaping them in the images of passivity and obedience."[8] Schalkwyk also refers to the difficult role of collaboration between the two women, and points specifically to Joubert's struggle for an appropriate form for the original testimony. He quotes Joubert on her struggle:

> I had to create a form and experiment in styles. I tried to write as an objective white woman and that didn't work. . . . I tried writing only in her words but that was dull. I had to get into her mind and write in her idiom: Stay in her key.[9]

There are, of course, many significant differences between the writers and initial narrators of the texts of *Poppie Nongena* and *Zulu Woman*. Reyher was not a South African but a passionately investigative, feminist visitor; the settings, too, are different in both time and space: Nongena's testimony in its spatial sweep covers great swathes of the Cape—from the remote, northerly fishing town of Lambert's Bay on the west coast, abutting the cold Atlantic, to the squatter camps on the edges of Cape Town, to the kitchens of white homes in the city—and then "repatriation" to the bleak township of Mdantasane in the Eastern Cape, with a final move to Herschel.[10] Christina Sibiya's movements, in contrast, are far more circumscribed and cover a tiny area of what is now called northern KwaZulu-Natal, with a single journey north to Johannesburg and another crucial journey south to the city of Durban.

Taken together, the two accounts take us from the turn of the century to the crucible year of 1976 and the Soweto uprising. Christina Sibiya's narrative begins with the year of her birth, 1900, and takes the reader to 1934, the year after Solomon kaDinuzulu's death. Reyher, following the broad pattern of Christina's own testimony, accents the structure of the original narration. Reyher sets near the opening the cleansing ceremony for Solomon kaDinuzulu's deceased father, Dinuzulu, which serves as a counterpoint to the beginning of Solomon and Christina's new love. Reyher closes her account with a description of the very same ceremony for Solomon, the abandoned royal husband, a ceremony from which his estranged wife Christina is expressly excluded. Nongena's *swerfjare* (years of hardship) span forty years, and begin almost exactly where the earlier narrative ends, taking as their starting point the year 1936.

Together, these two accounts of women's lives cover a great geographic sweep of South Africa, and three-quarters of the twentieth century, while sharing a focus on the family, family politics, and domestic struggle. Each articulates the intersection of family and national politics, and each shows women negotiating sets of power relations, "systems of relationships in which individuals are embedded."[11] Both accounts place individual agency within the context of larger social and cultural influences. Thus we see Nongena endlessly negotiating ways around the harsh circumstances of her life until the events of 1976 overwhelm her and her only recourse is to tell her story—an act of agency and resistance, which is also meshed with the other testimonies of her family and the reworkings of Joubert. Christina Sibiya's sense of agency emerges more slowly, through time, as she works through the years of her marriage in the chaotic and claustrophobic domesticity of a royal household that is neither traditional nor modern yet, at the same time, attempts to relate to both tradition and modernity. In a rare reference to the domestic domain in his study of Solomon kaDinuzulu, Nicholas Cope describes the Mahashini residence and the way in which it fitted with Solomon's attempts to fashion himself as "a twentieth century Zulu king":

[The] initial renovations included building a few rectangular wattle and daub "kholwa houses," set slightly apart from Mahashini, which were called KwaDlamahlahla. Then, in the early 1920s, Solomon set about having a substantial stone house built on the site. . . . The new KwaDlamahlahla added the final—and most crucial—touch to a unique combination of cultural elements brought together by Solomon . . . from the original beehive huts and royal cattle kraal where traditional ceremonies were performed, through the rectangular wattle and daub "kholwa houses" with the royal stables nearby, through the small church and school where the royal children received their primary education, and finally to the imposing house, KwaDlamahlahla with the Buicks in the forecourt. There was at least something here with which every Zulu could identify.[12]

What this description cannot tell us, but what Christina's narrative illuminates, is the chaotic internal domesticity of Mahashini, where she shares her living space "with four other wives."[13] The contrast between the imposing appearance of Mahashini as Christina first sees it and the dangerous—particularly to a young wife—sphere of its internal domestic politics is well captured in the text. What is also clear, though, is the way Solomon, too, must pick his way carefully through the morass of tensions, alliances, and counteralliances that constitutes his modernizing yet tradition-bound domestic world. The year is 1918, the year of the worldwide Spanish flu epidemic. The description of Mahashini has the mark of Reyher's "othering" mediation, but the spoken dialogue, with its vivid rendering of Solomon's words, is undoubtedly Christina's.[14]

> Within the kraal there were the usual huts, but they were surrounded by a tall stockade, neatly made of saplings, fronted by a tall green-growing hedge. The only concession to European custom was an enormous shed built of corrugated iron for Solomon's ever-growing stable of horses. . . . [Solomon speaks to the assembly of women, and then publicly to Christina:] "I have already separated Christina, while young, from her mother, and again from her child, which is still a baby. . . . If she is badly treated now, her heart will be very sore." . . . [Turning to Christina, he continues,] "Whatever happens, whether for good or evil, you are to tell me. You have always spoken the truth. I know that here you have arrived at the source and school of lies. It is here they are nourished and here they flourish!" (pp. 72–73)

Solomon speaks here as son and husband rather than, or perhaps as well as, king, and behind the phrase "the school of lies" and the sentence "It is here they are nourished and here they flourish" are the echoes of another poetic and discursive tradition brushing close against the English. These are the echoes of the voices of women, set in a long tradition of the poetry of women, expressing the discomforts and dangers of the polygynous household. The pain of such situations had long found expression in the praise poems of women and in the poems they composed for their children. Thus Solomon kaDinuzulu's paternal grandmother, Nomvimbi Mzimela, was known in her praise poem (*izibongo*, or praises about the self) as

> *The Slandered One,*
> *Slandered by men and women,*
> *Little Wagon that is a nuisance to the big carriages.*
> *The Desired One, she went on her wedding journey;*
> *The married women went [too], a bunch of conspirators.*[15]

Solomon's mother, Silomo Mdlalose, had composed praises of infancy (*izangelo*) for her daughter, Solomon's sister, Constance Magogo kaDinuzulu, which similarly mark the excoriating antagonisms within the royal female household:

> *I wonder, Father, if the deceitful creature over there hears*
> *   my words?*
> *The broad-lipped woman pursued me unmercifully, the one*
> *   with labia like a puffadder.*

They plaited for me a rope of mutual disdain,
All the royal household turned in disdain from me.
I have come out with the great mother of the royal line.
The day I walked out to the harvest gathering
I was mocked by the vultures,
I was mocked by the cuckoo shrikes.[16]

Praises like the above give some indication of the way in which women attached to the royal house through blood or marriage had access to a genre that allowed for self-expression, self-defense, and self-validation within a wider set of cultural practices that did not encourage such "writings of the self" on the part of women. Rather, women's personal, private selves were largely silenced, subsumed within the genealogies of male lines in which women played their part as bearers of children but not markers of lineages. Nevertheless, through the *izangelo* (praises for infants), like the above example, which were usually poetic, confessional statements about the mother's life as well as comments on domestic politics, and also through *izibongo* (praises of the self), women, whether royal or not, had access to a coded art form that allowed them some means of self-affirmation and self-remembrance. Solomon's reference to the "school of lies" is both an acknowledgement of the practice of such domestic eloquence—of the power of his wives and mothers to disrupt through words—and an arrogant downgrading of such words.

Christina Sibiya, daughter of a devoutly Christian mother, her childhood spent largely in the austere household of the Lutheran missionary at Nhlazatshe not far from Mahlabathini, gives no hint in her narrative that she ever had any direct access to such expressive forms and the cultural epistemologies they embodied. Reyher herself almost certainly did not know of their existence; they are unlikely to have been passed on to her by her white informants, often ex-magistrates, missionaries, or other officials who would have had little access to, or even perhaps interest in, such submerged poetic forms falling largely in the discursive domain of women. Nevertheless, what the story of Christina Sibiya's married life gives the reader is an overwhelming sense of the company of women, their presence in Zulu—and more broadly South African—culture at the particular moment of history of which Christina Sibiya herself is a part. In this way, the story—Christina Sibiya's and Rebecca Reyher's—brushes "against the grain" of history, as Walter Benjamin has put it, and presses the reader to reconfigure both past and present.[17] The text is a web of women's stories and voices, and the tales are often full of both pain and resistance. Although Christina's is the main story, many others lie half-submerged in the text. These stories, captured in the text of *Zulu Woman*, provide a counterpoint to male history and hint at earlier presences of women—ones that have since been erased.

Rediscovering these voices pushes us to question traditional histories: to reshape the past, to comb and reread it for lost voices and perspectives.[18]

Christina's co-wife, Ntoyintoyi, who went with the small royal party on the journey to Johannesburg and to the farm called Thengisa in Middleburg, is one of these resistant figures. Women's desire—a powerfully present topic in Zulu women's poetic discourse but largely skimmed over otherwise—finds a voice through Ntoyintoyi's story and is indeed a part of the wider history of Christina, the marriages of Solomon, and his neglect of his wives. Ntoyintoyi longs for sexual fulfilment and rages against Solomon's neglect and inability to satisfy her sexually. Her "defiant honesty" (p. 82) on this occasion, as the small group waits at Thengisa for Solomon, absent in Johannesburg, is about sex:

> Ntoyintoyi would become so restless with unashamed sexual hunger that Christina wondered if there was some way they could get her to a doctor, even without the King's permission, so if ever she did sleep with the King again she might become pregnant and this fever die within her. (p. 82)

Ntoyintoyi attempts to escape on two occasions and each time is hunted down and brought back. On the second occasion, when she runs away after the death of her only child, the account echoes attempted escapes in African American slave narratives and is very close to the interview notes taken by Reyher, although the latter are more graphic in the details of Ntoyintoyi's physical suffering than the finished text. Reyher's rendering of the event is full of subdued power and pathos:

> They caught her about ten miles from Mahashini, on the other side of the Sikhwebezi River. As the horsemen surrounded her, she neither struggled, nor spoke, she merely turned around and walked back with them. The men told the mothers, later, they would far rather she had fought them than have come back as quiet as the dead. (p. 138)

More chilling than the capture is the King's remark to her on her return: "Unless you get wings, my men will always find you" (p. 138). Another wife, Zidumazile, is able to leave, formally, and remarries; another, Cebekhulu, is less fortunate, and, having borne a son from another man and having survived the scandal, disgrace, and withdrawal of any support, dies as a result of birth complications (p. 134). By the time of the birth of Christina's fourth and last child, she "knew that sixteen of the King's wives had left him already" (p. 138).

The other voices and lives of women that speak to us are those of "the mothers," the widows of Solomon kaDinuzulu's father, Dinuzulu. Two

mothers in particular seem to have played an important and often support-
ive role in Christina's married life. They are known in the text only as
okaSonkeshana (daughter of Sonkeshana)[19] and okaMtshekula (daughter of
Mtshekula). Both are present at the birth of Christina's first child, and
okaSonkeshana accompanies the three royal wives and the King on the
long, awkward journey by way of Vryheid to Johannesburg and the farm
Thengisa. The royal mothers also intervene as Solomon turns to group wife-
beating (p. 113) and later, when he thrashes Christina and the other wives
living at the lonely and neglected Nsindeni royal kraal near Mahlabathini, it
is the mothers who call Solomon to order, and it is one of their number who
openly challenges his drunken suspicions of adultery:

> "Stop! We command you, stop!" they demanded in a solid phalanx of
> rigid disapproval, their bodies drawn to full height, their eyes flash-
> ing with indignation. . . . The boldest of the mothers fixed him with
> an hypnotic stare. "I do not know of these men, and I live with them
> here at this kraal. You are only trying to shield yourself because you
> have discarded them." (p. 158)

Such recorded moments, giving some sense of female intervention and
authority at moments of domestic crisis, are very rare in Zulu history. On a
wider South African canvas, it is hard to find another dramatic rendition of
domestic violence like the two accounts of Solomon's drunken beating of his
wives. It has been, indeed, another area of silence.

The mothers' presence weaves in and out of Christina's story. Their
shadowy presence is briefly marked much later in the March 1945 Enquiry
Concerning the Zulu Succession.[20] This was, one could say, a conversation
between collusive patriarchies, that of the male Zulu elite and that of white
male Natal civil servants and public figures—and here again the names of
okaSonkeshana and okaMtshekula appear momentarily amidst all the other
briefly appearing oka's (daughter of). OkaSonkeshana, when summoned,
identifies herself as Solomon's foster mother and ventures the opinion that
since Cyprian was the only child to be circumcised, it was a sign of his having been marked as heir. Solomon KaDinuzulu's former secretary is called
to testify and recalls that after the king had apparently called in Christina
and called her "ikhanda lami" (literally, my head), she, already intent on
going, had requested okaMtshekula to approach Solomon kaDinuzulu and
to ask, "will my position be kept after I go?"[21] It is only in Christina Sibiya's
story that such figures are given a measure of life of their own and an entry
into a wider narrative linking together the private and the public, punctur-
ing the smooth carapace of a body politic in which there is no place for
women.

If the Zulu body politic of the 1920s and 1930s was conceived of for all intents and purposes as "male," it may not always have been so. Certainly the regiments that performed for the young Prince of Wales and for Solomon in Eshowe in 1925 were men's regiments, as were those present at the Zibindini homestead after the washing of the spears for Dinuzulu in 1915. The presence of these regiments in the early romance of Christina Sibiya and Solomon kaDinuzulu is registered by Reyher in Rider Haggard-like phrases of the exotic and the savage, reminiscent of passages from *King Solomon's Mines*. Reyher sets their presence against the couple's own barely consummated sexual passion: "the stirring panorama before them . . . pointing up their aloneness, drawing them into a mutual passion and delight they could hardly restrain" (p. 43). However, until Cetshwayo's rule and the destruction of the Zulu kingdom, female regiments, even though they may have had no military function, played a role in the function of the state and were a crucial part of the way in which the Zulu monarch controlled the sexuality of his subjects. The story of the awful fate of the young women of the Ingcugcu regiment who were ordered by Cetshwayo to marry the men of the Indlondlo regiment is well known:[22] the women refused the order as most had lovers from the younger Tulwana regiment. A few managed to escape across the boundary formed by the Thukela River into Natal (known then as *Esilungwini*, or the Land of the Whites), and the rest were put to death. At that time, all young women were enrolled in regiments prior to marriage. Dinuzulu's mother, for instance, was in the Isitimane regiment that preceded the unfortunate members of the Ingcugcu regiment.[23] An informant of James Stuart, Ndukwana, stated that in Shaka's time women were called up "like regiments of men . . . and as a body given a name . . . Kenyane, Inzwa, Imvuthwa, Ikwana."[24]

Besides the presence of young women in regularly formed regiments there was also, until Cetshwayo's reign, the presence of royal women as figures of authority connected to the military quarters of various regiments. The formidable Mnkabayi, kingmaker and aunt of Shaka, was in charge of the Quluseni kraal, which housed the Belebele regiment. From here she "guarded Shaka's northern and western borders . . . commanded more than 10,000 warriors and gave orders for Shaka's death."[25] Mkabi, one of Senzangakhona's wives, had charge of the Jubinqwanga regiment at Esiklebeni. In the next generation, Baleka, daughter of Senzangakhona and sister of Mpande, was *induna* (person in charge) of the Nodwengu kraal.[26]

Although the enrollment into regiments marked a royal control of sexuality and the reproductive capacities of his subjects, it also signaled the existence of a certain freedom and equality in the expression of sexual desire. Thus another of Stuart's informants, Mtshapi, recalled that the "girls" of Cetshwayo's Tiyane regiment "were taught by us how to *soma*" (to have sex without penetration leading to male orgasm).[27] Mtshapi also, after listing the regiments of women, mentions the Umcekeceke, who used to carry thick sticks with them that they would throw into the huts of their lovers as a way of announcing their arrival "to *soma*."[28] Ndukwana, who was so knowledgeable on the young women's regiments of Shaka's time, also noted that it was "a common thing for a girl to have three lovers each belonging to a different regiment. She would give one lover one month, another the next month and so on," and, Ndukwana adds, "when pregnant she would be married off to an older man."[29]

Besides this remembered evidence of a clear space for women's fulfilment of sexual desire before marriage, poetic language also allowed for its expression after marriage, within the difficult circumstances of polygyny. Mtshapi quotes for Stuart a verse to show how wives could bring their husband back into line through song by "stabbing their husband with words":

O! We love our husband
Why does he sleep only in one house?
Look at the husband who sleeps only in one house![30]

There were also ways, through language, of singling out a wife especially liked by her husband: "So and so's daughter who hits right on it," as well as words of mockery for a wife who turned her back to her husband.[31] Perhaps such a discursive space allowing women commentary on their sexual rights and the need for sex was never operative in quite the same way for the wives of kings or highly placed chiefs, who in addition to wives had their *isigodlo* (a term glossed variously in English as *attendant female retinue, harem, concubines*). Yet the weapons of language seem to have been able to make more than a virtual space for women to have their say. Another instance of the insistent if rarely publicly acknowledged discourse around sex and women's voices is the body of songs around the *ukwemula* rite, which marks the onset of puberty. Celebration of the body—both woman's and man's—and of the sex act has its own special place in these songs.[32]

Zulu Woman provides little sense of the existence of this body of poetic and women's discourse. Instead, the early part of the narrative hints at the silence around sex in Christina's own Christian upbringing and her inability to respond to Solomon on their first night together: "Maphelu, it is all a darkness. It all seems wicked to me. I am a Christian girl. I cannot do the things the King wants me to do" (p. 34). Yet even if the language of the body was silenced in Christina's upbringing, desire, both her own and that of her co-wives, plays a major part in her story.

This expression of female desire coexists with the erratic seesawing of the King's sex life, including his transmission of venereal diseases to his wives. And the narrative gives the sense, as his marriage to Christina unravels, that alongside this profound domestic disarray runs the deep confusion in the King's public life and role: his increasingly untenable position as an aspirant Zulu monarch, as a figure of modernity, and even as a subordi-nate—if ambiguously so—civil servant of a wily and racist state administra-tion. If, as Shula Marks has written, ambiguity was an essential means of Solomon's survival,[33] the politics of his personal life showed all the signs of increasingly desperate disarray. Yet perhaps nowhere is Solomon's ambigu-ous position better displayed than in his attitude to marriage. He expected his wives to wear Christian dress, thus enrolling them into some kind of semblance of modernity often against their will; yet he also married reck-lessly and repeatedly, both on whim and sometimes for political reasons,[34] and he also filled his *isigodlo* incessantly.

Christina's story shows us that the politics of the family is also part of the politics of the state. Her account of her life with Solomon suggests that a crucial early marker of his attempts to sign his way into modernity—and into a certain way of handling love relationships—was his use of the letter. The letter is the mark of the literate or aspiring-to-literate individual, "the *kholwa*," "the modern." Letter writing and letters feature prominently in Christina's narrative. Letters may well have been a way in which Christina organized her own memory and constructed her own telling of events to Reyher. Christina seems to have privileged the place of letter writing in her account of her relationship with Solomon, and letters serve as a structuring device in her account. These qualities hint at the great importance that "the letter," as a complex instrument of influence and at the same time an open-ing into modernity, had for Christina—and for Solomon, too.

The letter that makes its first entrance is a declaration of love from Solomon to Christina (pp. 25–26). When it comes in the form of a love let-ter, the letter can also be seen as a conduit. It had to carry the flow of pas-sionate communication that for those who worked outside literacy would have found expression through song, dance, and the socially sanctioned language of bodily desire that missionary and, more broadly, Judeo-Christian teaching, with its "fundamentally dualistic vision of man . . . an often uneasy alliance of mind and body, psyche and soma," seems to have driven out of bounds.[35] Within this tradition the body was presented *not* as a site of passion and desire but as a sacred vessel. Passion became trans-posed into the language of the letter, which functioned as a way of channel-ing what was traditionally expressed in so many sung and danced forms of bodily expression. The love letter was also, perhaps, a kind of status symbol for both writer and receiver, and, like other letters, a marker of modernity.

Solomon's first letter to Christina, as recounted by Christina to Reyher, was both formal and intensely romantic; it used both English and Zulu, and ended with the royal and slightly schoolboyish (and perhaps ominous) post-script: "To me reply with soft or gentle words, also with respect" (p. 26). The romance continued through letters, and Christina's consent, after two weeks of daily letters, is given in written form: "I am completely overcome.

I consent. I surrender" (p. 26). The emphasis on writing as both an instrumental and expressive bond between Solomon and Christina punctuates the narrative and also marks the decline from romance to estrangement. Yet, far from signifying a simple slide into disillusionment, Solomon's correspondence with Christina, as well as the letters that Christina wrote to and on behalf of Solomon, gives a strong sense of Solomon's continuing reliance on Christina, and allows us to understand the logic of his final letter to her: the one that existed outside Christina's narrative to and as told by Reyher, and the one that became the cause célèbre of the 1945 succession enquiry concerning the Zulu throne.

In the course of their marriage the formalities of naming their first child are conducted by letter (p. 51). In the early years of the marriage, Solomon remarks, "She is the one who knows how to . . . write for me" (p. 62). As the narrative frame of Christina's story moves from romance to domestic tragedy, the letters continue. They are not always answered, and toward the end of the book they are not between Solomon and Christina but between herself and a secret lover, or between herself and her educated friend and co-wife Ethel Shwabete. And the final letter from Solomon to Christina, which played so dramatic a part in deciding the successor to the Zulu throne, does not feature in the text of *Zulu Woman* at all. Christina gave no hint of this letter in her interviews with Reyher in 1934: it was simply too secret. It was written by Solomon to Christina on 26 March 1930, and sent after her departure from the royal household to her by way of her uncle. It was that letter which she kept a secret for fifteen years and revealed with such dramatic effect in March, when accounts of the enquiry over the royal succession vied for space with reports of the last battles and troop movements of World War II.[36] Only at this moment, in a public tussle between men, does the voice of "Mrs Christina S. Zulu" or "okaMatatela" surface for a brief moment in the public domain. Only the presence of a letter, marking perhaps Solomon's last desperate attempt to make some just sense of a chaotic marriage and a chaotic life, allowed that to happen.

Solomon kaDinuzulu's story is often told in his *izibongo* (praises) declaimed eloquently on public occasions marking Zulu (and national) history. It is quite clear, however, that Christina's account of her marriage to Solomon radically alters the way in which one reads the very public life of her husband. It exposes the inadequacies of public histories, biographies, or autobiographies that erase the dimension of the domestic and the domestic politics of their male subjects. More specifically, through the act of its telling, Christina's account breaks through the discursive power blocs that colluded in the silencing of any kind of disruptive story of—or by—women. Both the story that Christina had to tell and her action in leaving the king in 1924 and attempting to make a new life for herself in Durban highlight what was dissident and rebellious and usually hidden in the wider "stories of men." Her action challenged the antiquated patriarchy of royal men—for example, the figure of the royal "father," Mnyayiza kaNdabuko—whose presence pervades her story. But, more than that, her flight and her subsequent defense of her decision threw into relief the entire structure of continuing patriarchal control by Zulu men of women's sexuality—both their desire and their reproductive capacities.

There is a moment toward the end of *Zulu Woman* when Christina's whereabouts in Durban have been discovered by Simpson Bhengu, the man sent by Solomon to find her, and she is urged by a group of young men to escape while she has the chance. What is briefly illuminated is a momentary alliance of the weak—women and young men—in the face of a more powerful group of older men representing a beleagured patriarchy and backward-looking "tradition" opposed to the emergent norms of the proletarianizing city. [37] Two early works by the author R. R. R. Dhlomo, who himself played a crucial role in the succession hearings, show the conflicting ways in which ideas around gender, freedom, pollution, and the city were being culturally interpreted and debated. In his first English-language novel, *An African Tragedy*, the sexually polluting figure is that of a man, with the eponymous name Robert Zulu.[38] In his later Zulu-language novel about the city, *Indlela yaBabi* (The way of the wicked), the polluter and deceiver is a woman who is contrasted with a "pure" and unpolluted woman.[39] The cultural trope of the "loose" (and loosened) city man and woman was to feed writing in all the South African languages (except perhaps Afrikaans) for the next three decades. It had its roots in flights by women and young men to the city in search of an independent life beyond the bounds of the rural homestead head, or, also at times, in the case of women, to escape the oppressive demands of brothers vis-à-vis their sisters' marriage arrangements. Indeed, the cultural trope of flight from an oppressive patriarchy has an even longer history in the region. Consider again the lovers who fled together across the Thukela to escape the royal command that women choose husbands from certain regiments, on pain of death.[40]

Christina Sibiya's flight can thus be seen not only as a singular, personal act of courage but also as part of a long history of dissidence by members of oppressed groups. Her story, surfacing again through this edition, at this time of ardent debate over gender rights in post-apartheid South Africa, is intensely topical. The right of women to be heard in the domestic sphere is as contested as it has ever been, and the voice of "okaMatatela" speaks to us with the same urgency now as it did to the young journalist Rebecca Reyher in the hot winter days of August 1934.

Liz Gunner

Pietermaritzburg, South Africa

August 1998

NOTES

A note on the treatment of proper names in this afterword. When full names are known, they are provided at first mention; last names—or the preferred cultural shortenings—are used thereafter. When Christina Sibiya and Solomon kaDinuzulu are being discussed with particular reference to the text of *Zulu Woman*, the simple names Christina and Solomon are often used. On occasion, for clarity, transition, balance—or to suit the context—full names have been used after the first mention.

1. Njabulo Ndebele, "Truth, Memory and Narrative," in *Negotiating the Past: The Making of Memory in South Africa*, eds. Sarah Nuttall and Carli Coetzee (Cape Town: Oxford University Press, 1998), p.27. I am indebted to Pippa Stein for our conversations on memory, language, and autobiography. See her "Reconfiguring the Past: Performing Literacy Histories in a Johannesburg Classroom," *Tesol Quarterly* 32, no. 3 (fall 1998).

2. Andre Brink, "Stories of History: Re-imagining the Past in Post-apartheid Narratives," in Nuttall and Coetzee, eds., *Negotiating the Past*, p.33.

3. In Zulu, just to take one example, the word *isizwe* can mean *nation, tribe, clan,* or *state* according to its context, and a phrase such as *isizwe esimnyama* (the black nation) can have an assortment of meanings according to its immediate context. For the meaning of *isizwe*, see C. M. Doke and B. W. Vilakazi, *Zulu-English Dictionary*, 2d ed., (Johannesburg: Witwatersrand University Press, 1972), p. 902.

4. On gender and nationalism, see Elleke Boehmer, "Stories of Women and Mothers: Gender and Nationalism in the Early Fiction of Flora Nwapa" in *Motherlands: Black Women's Writing from Africa, the Caribbean and South Asia*, ed. Susheila Nasta (London: Women's Press, 1991); Deniz Kandiyoti, "Identity and Its Discontents: Women and the Nation," *Millenium Journal of International Studies* 20, no. 3 (1991): 429–43; Anne McClintock, "Family Feuds: Gender, Nationalism and the Family," *Feminist Review* 44 (1993): 61–80; Andrew Parker, Mary Russo, Doris Sommer, and Patricia Yaeger, eds., *Nationalisms and Sexualities* (New York: Routledge, 1992); Nira Yuval-Davis and Flora Anthias, eds., *Women—Nation—State* (London: Macmillan, 1992).

5. Elsa Joubert, *The Long Journey of Poppie Nongena* (Johannesburg: Jonathan Ball, 1980). The work was first published in Afrikaans as *Die Swerfjare van Poppie Nongena* (Cape Town: Tafelberg, 1978). The paperback version was published simply as *Poppie Nongena* (London: Coronet, 1981).

6. Margaret McCord, *The Calling of Katie Makanya* (Cape Town: David Philip and New York: John Wiley, 1995); H. Filter, compiler, and S. Bourquin, translator and editor, *Paulina Dlamini. Servant of Two Kings* (Durban: Killie Campbell Library and Pietermaritzburg: University of Natal Press, 1986). For another mediated text with a carefully problematized discussion of collaborative tellings, see Mpho 'M'atsepo Nthunya, *Singing Away the Hunger: Stories of a Life in Lesotho*, ed. K. Limakotso Kendall (Pietermaritzburg: University of Natal Press, 1996 and Indianapolis: University of Indiana Press, 1997). See also the special issue on South African autobiography, *Current Writing* 1, no. 3 (1991).

7. King Cetshwayo, son of King Mpande, was the grandfather of Solomon kaDinuzulu.

8. David Schalkwyk, "Women and Domestic Struggle in *Poppie Nongena*" in *Women and Writing in South Africa: A Critical Anthology*, ed. Cherry Clayton (Johannesburg: Heinemann, 1989), pp. 271-72. See also Anne McClintock, "The Scandal of Hybridity: Black Women's Resistance and Narrative Ambiguity," in *Imperial Leather: Race, Gender and Sexuality in the Colonial Conquest* (New York: Routledge, 1995), pp. 299–328. McClintock draws attention to the unequal

power relations between speaker and author and points out some of the consequences of "the inequity inherent in Joubert's virtuoso orchestration of Nongena's
story" (p. 328).

9. *The Argus*, 16 January 1979, as quoted in Schalkwyk, "Women and Domestic
Struggle," p. 255.

10. Schalkwyk, "Women and Domestic Struggle," p. 262; see also McClintock, "The
Scandal," pp. 323–26.

11. Personal Narratives Group, ed., *Interpreting Women's Lives: Feminist Theory
and Personal Narratives* (Bloomington: Indiana University Press, 1989), p. 6.

12. Nicholas Cope, *To Bind the Nation: Solomon kaDinuzulu and Zulu
Nationalism, 1913–1933* (Pietermaritzburg: University of Natal Press, 1993), p. 130.

13. Rebecca Hourwich Reyher, *Zulu Woman: The Life Story of Christina Sibiya*,
this edition, p. 77. Subsequent page references to the text of *Zulu Woman* are cited
in the body of this afterword. This edition, which has been reset in order to correct
the handling and spelling of certain Zulu phrases, is slightly different from the prior
two editions. See *Zulu Woman* (New York: Columbia University Press, 1948), and
Zulu Woman, 2d ed., (New York: Signet, New American Library, 1970).

14. See appendix 1 C for the record of the original interview between Christina Sibiya
and Rebecca Reyher in which Christina describes her impressions of Mahashini.

15. Elizabeth Gunner, "Songs of Innocence and Experience: Zulu Women as
Composers and Performers of Izibongo, Zulu Praise Poems" in Clayton, *Women and
Writing*, p. 28.

16. Gunner, "Songs," p. 33.

17. Stein, "Reconfiguring the Past." The quote from Walter Benjamin is from
Illuminations (New York: Schocken Books, 1969), p. 257. See also R. L. Simon,
Teaching Against the Grain (New York: Bergin and Garvey), pp.137–53.

18. Helen Bradford, "Women, Gender and Colonialism: Rethinking the History of the
British Cape Colony and its Frontier Zones, c. 1806–70," *Journal of African History*
37 (1996), p. 352.

19. The important royal mother okaSonkehana was probably the daughter of
Sonkeshana Buthelezi, the sister of Mnyamana Buthelezi, Cetshwayo's prime minister.

20. See the 1945 Enquiry Concerning the Zulu Succession, excerpts of which are
included as appendix 2; KCM 2761, Marwick Papers, File 50, Killie Campbell Africana
Library, University of Natal, Durban, pp. 83–87.

21. See Marwick Papers, p. 94.

22. Colin Webb and John B. Wright, eds. and translators, *The James Stuart Archive
of Recorded Oral Evidence Relating to the History of the Zulu and Neighbouring
Peoples*, vol. 3 (referred to subsequently as *The Stuart Archive*) (Pietermaritzburg:
University of Natal Press, 1982), p. 85. The evidence was from Mtshapi.

23. Webb and Wright, *The Stuart Archive*, vol. 4, pp. 132–34. The testimony was
from Mshayankomo.

24. *Ibid.*, pp. 272–73.

25. Cecil Cowley, *Kwa Zulu. Queen Mkabi's Story* (Cape Town: Struik, 1966), p. 28.

26. Cowley, *Kwa Zulu*, p. 75. See also Noleen Turner, "A Detailed Analysis of the
Izibongo of Six Zulu Royal Women with Special Reference to Elements of Satirical
Poetry" (B.A. Hons diss., University of Durban, Westville, 1986).

27. Webb and Wright, *The Stuart Archive*, vol. 4, p. 97.

28. *Ibid.*

29. *Ibid.*, p. 310.

30. Webb and Wright, *The Stuart Archive*, vol. 5, p. 90.

31. *Ibid.*, p. 91.

32. Eileen Krige, "Girls' Puberty Songs and their Relation to Fertility, Health, Morality and Religion Among the Zulu," *Africa* 38 (1968): 173–98.

33. Shula Marks, *The Ambiguities of Dependence in South Africa: Class, Nationalism and the State in Twentieth-Century Natal* (Johannesburg: Ravan, 1986), p. 31.

34. See Cope, *To Bind the Nation*, pp. 123–24.

35. Roy Porter, "History of the Body," in *New Perspectives on Historical Writing*, ed. Peter Burke (Cambridge: Polity Press, 1991), p. 206.

36. The letter is quoted in full in a lengthy and zestful account of the drama at the hearing written by A. W. G. Champion. See *Ilanga laseNatal* (the Natal sun), 7 April 1945, p. 6. A typewritten copy of the original letter, marked "True Copy," and a hand-written English translation, also marked "True Copy," are in the uncataloged A. W. G. Champion Collection Papers in the Kille Campbell Library. My thanks to Janet Twine for pointing me to them. See Killie Campbell Library, Photo Album No. C, pp. 92 and 94, for "2000 Zulus Roar 'Bayete' to their New King," *Sunday Times*, 16 September 1945; and "Minister Proclaims Zulu Chief's Heir" and "How Dispute was Settled," *Daily News*, 15 September 1945.

37. Recent work suggests that patriarchy in Zulu society was increasingly under pressure toward the end of the nineteenth century and in the decades following. Older men were fighting a desperate battle to keep some control over younger men. See Ben Carton, "'Blood from your sons': African Generational Conflict in Natal and Zululand, South Africa, 1880–1910" (Ph.D. diss., Yale University, 1996). Also see Ben Carton, "Men Before Their Time: Youth Power, Competing Patriarchy, and African Generational Conflict in South Africa, 1880–1906," paper presentation, "Colloquium on Masculinities in Southern Africa," University of Natal, Durban, 2–4 July 1997; *Blood from Your Children: African Generational Conflict in South Africa* (Charlottesville: University Press of Virginia, forthcoming); "The New Generation . . . Jeer at Me, Saying We Are all Equal Now": Impotent African Patriarchs, Unruly African Sons in Colonial South Africa," in *Politics of Age and Gerontocracy*, ed. M. Aguilar (Lawrenceville, N.J.: The Red Sea Press, 1998).

38. R. R. R. Dhlomo, *An African Tragedy: A Novel in English by a Zulu Writer* (Tyume: Lovedale Press, n.d. [c. 1928]). My thanks to David Attwell for discussions on this text.

39. R. R. R. Dhlomo, *Indlela yaBabi* (The way of the wicked) (Pietermaritzburg: Shuter and Shooter, 1946).

40. Webb and Wright, *The Stuart Archive*, vol. 4, p. 275; Ndukwana's testimony. And see notes 22 and 23.

appendix 1

Selections from Rebecca Hourwich Reyher's Notebooks (1934)

Six notebooks, labeled Zululand 1934, contain the original record of the interviews with Christina Sibiya, as well as other observations made and interviews conducted between August and October 1934. The following excerpts from the notebooks have been selected so that readers may compare the original transcript and notations with the published text, including what may have been elaborated or omitted. We have endeavored to preserve here the "raw" quality of the notebooks, as well as their historical flavor. The spellings and shorthand used in the notebooks have been faithfully preserved. The few minor editorial alterations that have been made are enclosed in square brackets. Brief orienting statements are supplied as are related page references to this edition of *Zulu Woman*. The archival reference to this material is Reyher Papers, Schlesinger Library, Radcliffe College, acc. 87-M75, Carton 38. These selections have been reprinted with the kind permission of Rebecca Hourwich Reyher's heir, Faith Reyher Jackson, and the Schlesinger Library, Radcliffe College.

Appendix 1 A: Reyher Papers, Zululand 1934, Notebook I

On 24 August 1934, the third day of her narration, Christina Sibiya described how after Solomon kaDinuzulu had claimed her before her missionary patron, they went together to the Zibindini homestead where she was introduced to the widows of Dinuzulu and to Solomon's sisters. It was shortly before the cleansing ceremony to mark the end of the period of mourning. Compare Zulu Woman, *pp. 42–43.*

I was given a chair to sit down & Solomon went out to tell his sisters and his mothers to come and see me. His sisters came in to see me, his mothers didn't because while they are still dressed in black clothes, mourning for Dinizulu, they are not allowed to come into the chief's hut.

[Later, following a description of the introductions and feasting in her honor]

The following morning early all his mothers sent for me and I was taken into their big hut. They asked me if I knew I had come there to marry Solomon

& if he had told me that & if he had brought me there never to return. I replied in the affirmative. They told me I was to show respect to them & to listen to what they told me, not to listen to just what he whom I loved or who loved me told me. This was by way of warning. At that point the Chief came in & took me to his hut. His mothers exclaimed, "We've only just seen her. We are still talking to her." He replied, "You will all see her on other days."

"That time the preparations were being made for the cleansing ceremony. A lot of work was going on."

We were in his hut & he told me to go out & we went out & he told an induna to call up the regiments in order that I might see them. When we were outside I saw multitudes, a thing I had never seen in my life before. I saw them dancing & rushing. He was sitting on a chair & next to him I sat on a mat beside him in front of the regiments (as they reviewed them). He asked me if I had ever seen this before & I said "No".

At that point I was no longer afraid of him. I was talking quite freely with him.

The dancing & rushing about ceased & we returned to his hut. When we went in & he gave instructions food for me was to be prepared & put on the table. He went out & sat by the stockade when my food was brought, & his sister & I had our food. He realized I was a little self-conscious & did not like to eat in his presence. After we had finished, his food was prepared & put on the table. We did not go outside. We moved away from the table & sat on chairs.

He told me if his fathers entered I was to get off the chair and sit on the floor, as this denoted respect, a form of etiquette amongst them (meaning the royal kraal). He told me he was tired & that he would soon be going to sleep. (She laughed embarrassedly) And of a truth he very soon went to bed and I turned in as well. I was not afraid as I had been at the _____ kraal, since I had been told by his mothers & was no longer afraid. He told me he was sending men to my father & asked me if I were agreeable. And I asked him whether I was not going home to my people, for I thought I had only just come on a visit. He said he was going to send me home for a short while during the period in which preparations were being made for the cleansing ceremony. I then thanked him.

Appendix 1 B: Reyher Papers, Zululand 1934, Notebook I

The following day, 25 August, Rebecca asked Christina to give details about the birth of her first child. Compare Zulu Woman, *pp. 49–50.*

I was kneeling on a mat. The child was born onto the mat & was immediately taken by one of the 3 mothers. Another mother had entered making 4 altogether and there was great rejoicing among the mothers.

MTWANA (Baby)—always refers to it that way—

At this point they said to me, "Now you are grown up. Now that you have seen a child which has come from you. Previously you thought of yourself as only a child, but now you are a grown women." They said this very very kindly & with rejoicing.

(Did anyone help her, give her suggestions, wipe her face, during the birth?)

There was one who had been instructed by Solomon. She was the daughter of SONKESHANA, she was the one who had been instructed by Solomon to assist me & advise me. It was she who took the baby & the one who had been bathing my stomach with hot water & anointing me with fat.

They first, before I lay down to go to sleep, they laid the child on the mattress near me & it went off to sleep. Then I lay down to sleep beside the child. The mothers then went out to notify the induna. I remained with the daughter of MTYEKULA and she of MTUNZWA, both Solomon's mothers.

(What do they do with the mat on which the baby is born? Is it a special mat? Do they wash it, or destroy it?)

It was a mat that had been specially prepared for the birth of a child, by SONKESHANA, a smaller size than the ordinary mat used for sleeping on.

Appendix 1 C: Reyher Papers, Zululand 1934, Notebook II
On 26 August, Christina spoke of how Solomon insisted in 1918 that she leave her daughter, then a toddler, behind in Zibindini and accompany him to the new homestead he was just establishing at Mahashini. It was a short distance from this homestead that, in the middle 1920s, he built his modern house and compound, Dlamahlahla. Compare Zulu Woman, *pp. 72–74.*

When we eventually came into first sight of the kraal it was quite close to us. The chief went on ahead with some of the other horsemen & got to the kraal first. It was a habit of his that when he was approaching any of his kraals he never approached at a slow pace. He approached at a fast pace, even a gallop.

I got there & dismounted outside the kraal. The stable was outside the stockade of the kraal & I got out outside the stable. I found a very beautiful kraal with a lovely hedge stockade and nice gates, but just composed of just ordinary huts.

I saw a very nice kraal, and very cool & not hot. At Mahashini at that time there was no girls' hut. I went into the Chief hut of the head wife of Dinizulu, the daughter of MTYEGULA. I went into her hut. This woman was my Aunty, being of the SIBIYA people. She was one of those who had tended to me at the childbirth. She was at that time down at the other kraal. She

:

was *very* pleased to see me. She asked after my child & how big it was. I told her how big it was.

She was the one who was the most important in that kraal. My baggage was also taken into her hut. At that kraal there were only two girls who had married him. He just had a small hut there, not like his huts at the other two kraals. He came to the door & called me together with this girl who had come with us. We then went to the hut & found there was a very large pot of beer there. He then said that beer was to be poured from the big pot into a small pot for us. We were then four of us, including the two girls who were there at the hut. Then came his mothers of that kraal. There were three of them & told him that the influenza was very bad at that place. He replied that even at the Usutu he had arrived to find some who were sick there. There were others who had become sick & he named them to his mothers.

His mothers then told him that Christina's (Zulu's) mother, his grandmother, was sick. He said, "What's going to be done about me? (meaning himself) I can't take medicine." (What did he mean by that?) He was frightened of taking medicine.

At that time the sun was setting. (What did they answer him?)

They said they didn't know what would be done about it, seeing he couldn't take medicine.

He then gave orders to his servants to cook this buck meat & the beef for his mothers. He then told his mothers concerning me saying, "This Christina here, I brought her for the purposes of housekeeping & cooking as she did at Zibindini. I will fix her up with a place to live in." And he added that those that were there would be taught by me what to do & how to do it. He said, I want them to listen to her and respect her. He said, I have already separated her while young from her mother and again separated her from her child which is young and so if she is badly treated her heart will be sore.

(At this point for the first time she had to go into her purse, get a handkerchief, & blow her nose)

He added, "Also I trust her. I have never found her do anything of fault or evil to this day. He turned to me & called to me, Christina, and I answered him & he then said, You have been parted from your nest at the Zibindini. I am not meaning that because you have left your nest at Zibindini that you are to change your common sense. Stand forever in your sense. If there is anything worrying you, whether good or evil, you are to tell me. You have never spoken lies, you have always spoken the truth. I know that here you have arrived at the college (they have adopted this word) of lies." I didn't answer him anything.

And those mothers of his who were in the hut answered him naught. He then asked them why they had nothing to say to him. One of his mothers then replied to him & said, She will never tell you lies having learned to tell the truth. It is meet for her to listen to you always and fear you. That closed the matter.

Then he called a boy, saying that he was to give us food. He said he would build us a hut.

(I asked, "you & the other girl?")

No. All of us girls. And he told them, his mothers, that they had better give one of the mattresses already there for me to sleep on. He said that I would sleep in my Aunty's hut. The other girls slept in the hut of one of his other mothers.

Later in the same session, also concerning the circumstances of her first appearance in Mahashini, Christina told an anecdote about her introduction to one of Solomon's grandmothers and her daughter, Christina (Siyela) Zulu.

Solomon then told me to go and dose his grandmother. I said, O, I am afraid to go & dose your grandmother because I have never seen her, she has never seen me, we have never seen each other. The first thing she would know would be me bringing the medicine, an unknown person, because I had arrived the day before & she was already sick.

(She laughed aloud one of her rare laughs.) Solomon then laughed & said that of a truth I was right that she would think I would kill her. He said we would go together. We then went having already mixed the Epsom salts in a cup, he carrying some sweets in a paper packet. We then proceeded to the hut of his grandmother.

On entering we found her asleep. The MTWANA, Christina, (daughter of a chief, royalty) was sitting at one side. The King said, Wake up granny, KOKO. His granny said, Who is that? And he replied, It is I. His granny then sat up, greeted him, & he returned her greeting. It was Solomon who greeted his grandmother and she returned the greeting. He then asked her how she was and where she was sick. What was the matter with her? She said she had a headache & her stomach was sore. She told him it kept purging her. He said, I have brought you this medicine to rid you of bile. She then said, asking, Is the medicine not bitter? He said, No, it is not bitter because it is white man's medicine. (WA BE LUNGU of the white man)

She then asked, who the girl was who was with him. He replied, She, it is, who is the first wife I took. She then asked if I had brought the child. Has she brought her child with her? He replied. No, she has left it. The King then said, Here is your medicine. It will get cold because it was mixed with water that was hot a little bit. She said, the grandmother, Far better had I seen what you had taken it out of or from where you had taken it. He said, No granny. Just drink it and after you have drunk it, I will give you these sweets. She said, Give it to this woman, SIYELA ([her daughter] Christina's Zulu name). I then gave it to Siyela.

Siyela then said, Drink it now mother! (She laughed aloud again.) She said, Give me the sweets first & let me hold the sweets this side and the medicine this side. Siyela then gave her the sweets. The Chief then said, Drink then! The granny then looked inside & smelled the medicine.

(Christina here fairly roared with laughter.)

She then asked Did Cetywayo ever drink this medicine? (He had been her husband) child of my child? This was asking Solomon. Solomon said I don't know. I was not there at that time. She then asked, Do you ever drink this medicine, child of my child? And he replied, Yes.

(She laughed aloud, again)

That made us all in the hut laugh. It had made me laugh so much I couldn't stop, more so, because it was the first time I had seen one of Cetywayo's wives. She just sat there with the medicine for some time and just before drinking it, said, *now, the Belunga are going to kill us! I am now, also going to die.* (She is still alive today. R. H.) (Christina added, she looks the same, only that time she was not blind.)

Even today they are just the same as they were in the old days. They talk just the same. They act just the same.

She then drank the medicine. When she had finished, the Chief said Eat then the sweets & she ate them. He then said The bile will pass out a lot from you, granny & you will get better. The King then went out. Christina asked me to remain behind, saying she wanted to talk with me. The King said no she will return again when she has time. She has now got work to do. As we came out, his mothers all asked, shouting, Did she drink the medicine? Solomon replied, She wouldn't have drunk it if I had not been there. He then told them what the Ingosigaza had said. It made them all laugh.

Her introduction to the homestead was finalized by the formal presentation of a cow as a welcome.

As soon as the cattle arrived, he called me, I being in his hut. He went with me to the outside of the cattle kraal, then called my Aunt. He then pointed out a beast saying he was giving it to me in honor of my arrival at the kraal. Aunt thanked him & I also then thanked him. He asked me if I would like it killed right away & I said, Yes.

Appendix 1 D: Reyher Papers, Zululand 1934, Notebook IV
Placed at a subordinate and neglected homestead, Christina in 1926 became alienated, although not yet bent upon desertion. On 5

September she spoke of the death of her elder son and suspicions of witchcraft. Compare Zulu Woman, *pp. 144–151.*

I stayed that year out [1926–27], all the time afraid that if I slept with him I would probably get another child, and that would tie me there. In my heart I was saying, no, if God is willing that these my children be healthy, and spared, then they are enough for they are all that I can clothe, now that he no longer clothes them. They are all that I can feed for he no longer feeds them.

These other wives of his with whom I lived, they were beginning to say that they were going to say good-bye and go. I would say to this, no, don't go yet. Let's wait until next year when the children have grown a bit before we go.

(Where did she get clothes and food if the children [sic] didn't give it?)

I just struggled through the best way I could, even hoeing my garden. I didn't know how to. I had never done it before. I was helped by my sister. She plowed a garden for me with oxen and I kept it weeded. These girls were able to do their own hoeing for they were accustomed to it.

With regard to clothing, the thing that helped me was the fact that mother planted tobacco and sold it and I would unexpectedly get a pound or one pound ten shillings from her with the word that I was to look after myself with it, buy what I needed. And I used to also sell goats. The collection of my goats which I had bought and left at home. Whenever I saw that I was short of anything, I would send word home, and ask them to sell 1 or 2 goats and send me the money.

(Why didn't she write to the King?)

I didn't want to trouble him at that time. I just wanted him to realize it for himself, to come to it himself, for it was up to him to look after all of us in every way.

Then my son died. The eldest, in 1927. The King was sick here at Mahashini at the time, and when word was sent to us of his illness we all came to Mahashini and it was while I was there that my child died at Usendeni.

(What was the matter with him?)

He was then a big boy, for he was now able to herd cattle.

Somebody put medicine at the gate of the cattle kraal and when he crossed over it he inhaled it through his nose and his head started to ache. That afternoon his head was terrible. The following morning, early, he died.

Word of that was brought to the King. I started out on foot and slept 3 nights on the road. All the cars belonging to the King were broken down. I arrived when they had already buried him and I had no chance to see him. (It was the first time she looked away, so I could not see the look on her face at all.)

This distressed my heart terribly. (She looked in the distance, tears in her eye, but she held her head up so they couldn't fall) for I had left him perfectly well, without anything the matter with him.

(She swallowed, kept her face and mouth tense and recovered her composure.)

The King also sent 2 men to bear me his sympathies, sending me by them money with which to buy clothes for mourning. He had also written a letter deploring such an awful thing, that the child should die without having been sick. He said also that he would consult native medicine men and find out from them what it was that had caused it.

I replied to him. I lived very unhappily from then on and I was always dreaming about my child.

(What did she reply to the King?)

I, as he did, said that this surprised me.

(Did they ever find out?)

He heard it and he afterwards told me.

(What did he tell her?)

He went to three medicine men. The fourth one he went to was an Indian in Durban. All three medicine men pointed to one thing, and that fact satisfied him that it was the truth. The King said that it was one of his mothers there at the Usendeni kraal, that the medicine men had said that it was one of his mothers, a daughter of NTSHANGASE, who disliked me, and disliked the King, saying that the King loved the child and me.

(*I'SANGOMA*—a person who throws the bones—smells out evil . . . native medicine man?

INYANGA—a native doctor—who gives out medicines.

MT'AKATI—The person who casts spells, poisons—an evildoer—the witch doctor)

This woman had heard from those who had returned from Eshowe that the King had pointed to this boy as being his successor[;] for the Prince had asked the King if he had an oldish boy and the King had indicated this boy.

(Had the boy been with the King?)

No

Appendix 1 E: Reyher Papers, Zululand 1934, Notebook IV

On 8 September, after recounting how she had been fetched back from Durban as a virtual prisoner (accompanied by her sister Beauty), Christina describes arriving at Dlamahlaha amidst the wedding celebrations for yet another of Solomon's marriages. This marriage was to an Ndandwe woman, and Christina could find no place to sleep. She sought refuge with her "Aunt," next door. Compare Zulu Woman, *pp. 173–74.*

I said it would be best for us to go to the Mahashini kraal after the gates opened, to my Aunt, the daughter of Mteygula and of a truth we took our belongings & went to the Mahashini kraal when the gates were opened after daybreak.

When we got to my Aunty she cried a lot. She woke a girl up & told her to boil tea for us and told her girls to bring beer & give it to us. She asked us where we had slept and we told her that we had come very late at night & that we had not slept. We had found everybody drunk & she said, Here even at this kraal, everybody went to bed drunk because there was a lot of beer. I asked her then whether she had heard if my children were still well. She said that she had heard they were all well & that she had long ago asked to have brought to her [Sishoniswapi, the younger daughter, also referred to as Karina Corinna and Sekulenlewane] to be looked after but that the King had refused. She asked me if Beauty & I had been staying together in Durban & I said, No, that I worked at one place & Beauty worked at another and while we were still talking in came a lot of others, brothers of the daughter of Mtyegula, mothers of the King & they exclaimed a lot, saying, Where does the wandering woman come from? (Meaning a loose woman.) They said—She being an old wife sees others leaving & then follows herself, hey? I kept quiet. I did not answer them.

They said, But of how good you were and all the time you were concealing an assegai. So you creep along slowly, do you? You are like a chameleon. When there was discontent among the wives you never said anything & we believed that you would be the one who would stay. I kept quiet & just laughed & did not reply to them. They said, Your upheaval was tremendous caused by you leaving. When it was heard that you had gone the King was struck by great fear. I said, Even now, I have not returned. I am going back. I have come only to speak to him mouth to mouth so that I won't feel the fear of being like one who has run away or escaped.

Christina thereafter demanded that Solomon's secretary Bhengu remind the King that the Durban authorities had ordered that she be well treated and that she awaited a hearing.

We stayed there 2 days eating our own food and on the third day the daughter of Mteygula went to him & said, What do you think those prisoners who are in my hut are eating? He said that he had forgotten what Bhengu had told him. He said that he would send meat & jugo beans. He asked the daughter of Mteygula, saying, Is Christina just the same as ever? And the d. of m. [daughter of Mtshegula] replied, She is as big as this house now and is white as white can be. And he said, Just let me go & see her. Is she in your hut? The d. of m. returned & told us that the King said he was going to send us food & that he was coming himself. In a short while the car arrives at Mahashini (about 200 to 300 yards). The King got out of the car & came to the door of the hut of the daughter of M. where we were. He came & crouched at the door. He said, In the hut here there is a smell of white people from Durban. (She laughed.) He didn't greet us, he just looked at us & then went into the car & left. He went away very angry indeed. He was accompanied by Zazeni.

I heard that he was very very upset & his heart was bitter and even when he got to his room he did not alter. Then a leg of beef and jugo beans were sent by the King & salt & sugar & a tin of coffee and tea leaves. We ate of it & later that afternoon the daughter of Mteygula went to thank him for it.

appendix 2

Selections from Proceedings of the Enquiry Concerning the Zulu Succession (1945)

The extract from the transcript of the Enquiry Concerning the Zulu Succession (1945) reproduces Christina's major statement. Christina's son Cyprian precipitated the Enquiry by contesting the choice of his half-brother, the son of okaMbulawa of the Buthelezi, to be Solomon's heir. The regent and the core of the royal family preferred this youth, Tandayipi, but Cyprian's backers had much greater popular support. The Commission of Enquiry ruled in Cyprian's favor after pubic hearings and testimony that spread over several months. The letter from Solomon to Christina declaring Cyprian to be his chosen heir was never fully authenticated, but was accepted as valid. The record contains the testimony given, without stating the exact question. The questioner is identified, e.g. *BY CHAIRMAN,* and the question can be inferred from the response.

The archival reference is KCM 2761, File 50, Marwick Papers, Killie Campbell Africana Library, University of Natal, Durban. This extract has been reprinted with the kind permission of the Killie Campbell Africana Library.

ENQUIRY RESUMED 9.10 A.M. SATURDAY
24.3.45.

My name is Christina oka Matatela. I am a widow of the late Chief Solomon. I was his first wife. There was no marriage-ceremonial when I married him. I do not know why. Solomon would know.

I admit that it is customary for a woman marrying a Chief to go through certain ceremonials at their weddings. I was, however, satisfied with my informal entry into his household, because he paid lobolo for me, and slaughtered a *qolisa* beast. I considered that sufficient to constitute a lawful and binding marriage. He paid eleven head of cattle for me. My father was a member of the Christian Faith.

I swear that I was not an *isigodhlo* girl (a girl of the harem.) Solomon said I was his wife. I do not know what a harem is. I never saw one *isigodhlo* girl in household. I thought that all the women there were his wives. I bore four children to Solomon.

In order of birth they were:—

1) Velangokuhona—a girl
2) Ezron—a boy
3) Sikukulelwane—a girl
4) Nyangayezizwe, the present claimant, who is sitting there (Bhekuzulu). That was all.

When I was first taken as wife, I was placed at eSibindini where Solomon also lived. When I was about to give birth to Velangokuhona, a hut was built for me.

Prior to that, I had been living in the Chief's own hut.

BY CHAIRMAN: Solomon took several other wives after me. Not all were taken without ceremony (as I was). Some had simple weddings, some ceremonious. Some of them were married in traditional Zulu fashion. Oka Mbulawa was one of them.

I do not admit that those more formally wedded were of better status than I, in my husband's kraal.

I cannot say whether, ordinarily, the ceremonials would imply better standing.

I would not admit it. Others might say so.

I do not know that Solomon ever showed favouritism in his household. I do not know whether he indicated it in any way to us women or to the public: it is for others to say.

You ask whether certain courtesies are not always paid to the principal woman in a kraal. It would not be for me to explain that.

I saw nothing, in my husband's kraal, of the custom of reserving for the chief woman the choicest bits of meat, when beasts were slaughtered. I should have to be told of such a custom. I myself know nothing of it. I can explain regarding Solomon's heir—

It was I who told Cyprian he should find out who had taken away his position (as heir) because when I came to the commemoration ceremony at Mahashini (i.e. on 4.3.40). I heard the nect [sic] day that Tandayipi had been appointed heir at Sokasimbona and that a meeting would be held (i.e. the meeting for the public announcement by Mr. Lugg.) We went to the meeting and heard the announcement that Tandayipi was my late husband's heir.

That was in March, 1940.

That was the first time I had heard anything about Tandayipi's being the heir.

I do not know who made the announcement. I was at the back. I heard a voice but could not see the speaker.

I do not know whether there had been a meeting prior to the announcement—I was not called to attend it.

I heard no response *to* the announcement. I heard talking and grumbling around me. I do not know of a shout of "Bayeti", round where I was sitting.

The people were remonstrating, saying that they had come to a commemoration service, not to the announcing of an heir.

The first time I heard of Tandayipi's nomination was when it was announced in front of the gathering. I was not present at the (preliminary) meeting of the family circle: I was only at the public gathering, where the officials were in attendance. I cannot be quite certain that, in the presence of the officials, there was acclamation. I do know there was an outburst of grumbling comment around me where I sat.

I was sitting amongst the other women,—commoners. I had no place of honour because I had committed an offence.

I had left the chief's kraal. I was no longer living in it at that time. I was living in Vryheid. I had been away for the last two years.

I left my husband's kraal because I felt I was in disgrace, because I had committed a wrong. I was not expelled. I left on my own accord. My husband had brought me back in 1929, on the occasion of my previous desertion—which had been in that same year, shortly before I returned to Solomon and stayed a year that was 1930. In 1931 I left the chief's kraal to go to my own people. I remained there till my husband's death.

I was still living at my father's kraal when Solomon died. Solomon did not divorce me.

I went to Vryheid in 1936. I am at present resident there, living at a commoner's kraal. I have not remarried. The person at whose kraal I am living is not a relative of mine.

I am afraid to live at my husband's kraal because I have transgressed. Ever since my departure Cyprian lived at the Usutu kraal, until, for the purpose of attending school, he was moved to Dhlahlahla.

BY MR. ADDISON: I was not married to Solomon by Christian rites.
(At this stage, Chairman asks witness whether she has any other evidence to substantiate her claim to have been Solomon's wife, and her son the intended heir. Witness produced the document (Exhibit No. 5)

BY CHAIRMAN: I produce a typewritten letter with a signature at the foot. It is the signature of the late Chief. It came into my possession as follows: Solomon called Mapopama Sibiya, a brother of my father, to the Mahashini kraal. I myself was then living at Mapopama's kraal. Mapopama returned with this document. I think this was during the year in which I left Mahashini.

I admit that the letter is dated 1930—the year in which, according to my earlier evidence, I was supposed to be back at Solomon's kraal.

I kept the letter.

I have no objection to it being read aloud to this gathering.

(Letter read to assembly and greeted with tremendous acclamation).

BY CHAIRMAN: I have not brought this letter forward before, because Cyprian was still young. I was afraid he might die: his elder brother died from a cause unknown to me. Ezron was not alive when this letter was written. I was afraid to bring it forward.

I did not confide in anyone that I had this letter. I do not know who prepared the document I do not know whether Solomon had a typewriter: I know he had a Secretary.

I tore up the envelope containing this document. I cannot explain why I did so.

I have nothing else to say concerning the document.

WOMEN WRITING AFRICA

A Project of The Feminist Press at The City University of New York
Funded by the Ford Foundation

Women Writing Africa is a project of cultural reconstruction that aims to restore African women's voices to the public sphere. Through the collection of written and oral narratives to be published in six regional anthologies, the project will document the history of self-conscious literary expression by African women throughout the continent. In bringing together women's voices, Women Writing Africa will illuminate for a broad public the neglected history and culture of African women, who have shaped and been shaped by their families, societies, and nations.

The Women Writing Africa Series, which supports the publication of individual books, is part of the Women Writing Africa project.

The Women Writing Africa Series

ACROSS BOUNDARIES
The Journey of a South African Woman Leader
A Memoir by Mamphela Ramphele

CHANGES
A Love Story
A Novel by Ama Ata Aidoo

HAREM YEARS
The Memoirs of an Egyptian Feminist, 1879–1924
by Huda Shaarawi
Translated and introduced by Margot Badran

NO SWEETNESS HERE
And Other Stories
by Ama Ata Aidoo

TEACHING AFRICAN LITERATURES IN
A GLOBAL LITERARY ECONOMY
Women's Studies Quarterly 25, nos. 3 & 4 (fall/winter 1998)
Edited by Tuzyline Jita Allan